Investment Strategies

Reviews in alphabetical order of surname

"Dr Jiang provides a comprehensive and practical introduction to factor strategies. The book explains the guiding principles behind factor investing with clarity and intuition. Its foundational overview of general and factor investing principles is a good compendium of the literature and a helpful resource to investors and practitioners."

—Jennifer Bender, PhD, *Senior Managing Director, Head of Research (Global Equity Beta), State Street Global Advisors*

"Written by an expert in the field, this book provides an excellent overview of investment strategies that are backed by extensive evidence. Bill Jiang explains key articles written by leading academics in understandable terms, and describes how professional systematic investors apply these concepts in practice. The various topics are discussed in a concise manner, focusing on the main takeaways, with plenty of references for further reading. I particularly recommend this book to readers unfamiliar with factor investing who are looking for a crash course on the subject."

—David Blitz, PhD, *Chief Researcher, Robeco*

"Dr Jiang's book represents a major and much needed advancement in the practitioner literature by properly including systematic factor premia and sustainable investing in the spectrum of investment choices. In this era of big data and high-powered computing, our ability to distinguish between compensated and uncompensated risks has not only made portfolio construction more risk-efficient but has opened up a world of possibilities in using factors as building blocks for precision, outcome-oriented strategies. Dr Jiang's culminating chapter on multi-factor investing represents state-of-the-art thinking in this space."

—Michael R. Hunstad, PhD, *Chief Investment Officer, Global Equities, Northern Trust Asset Management*

"Factor-based investment strategies are important building blocks in modern portfolio management. This book provides a practical overview of popular factor-based strategies employed by institutional investors. It can serve as a useful introduction to factor investing for both university students and investment practitioners."

—Dimitris Melas, PhD, CFA, *Managing Director, Global Head of Index Research and Product Development, MSCI*

"Bill Jiang has written an informative guide to the 'middle ground' between active managers and the creators of index-based investment products: factor-based investment strategies. These strategies, in increasingly common use over the last few years, are essential knowledge for both the involved private investor and the young investment professional. By explaining what these strategies are, why they exist, and how they can be implemented, Bill provides the private investor with useful, practical knowledge of how their money is being invested, and the investment professional with a grounding on which to build their skills."

—Gareth Parker, *Chief Indexing Officer, Morningstar*

Bill Jiang

Investment Strategies

A Practical Approach to Enhancing Investor Returns

Bill Jiang
Legal & General Investment Management
London, UK

ISBN 978-3-030-82710-6   ISBN 978-3-030-82711-3 (eBook)
https://doi.org/10.1007/978-3-030-82711-3

© The Editor(s) (if applicable) and The Author(s), under exclusive license to Springer Nature Switzerland AG 2022
This work is subject to copyright. All rights are solely and exclusively licensed by the Publisher, whether the whole or part of the material is concerned, specifically the rights of translation, reprinting, reuse of illustrations, recitation, broadcasting, reproduction on microfilms or in any other physical way, and transmission or information storage and retrieval, electronic adaptation, computer software, or by similar or dissimilar methodology now known or hereafter developed.
The use of general descriptive names, registered names, trademarks, service marks, etc. in this publication does not imply, even in the absence of a specific statement, that such names are exempt from the relevant protective laws and regulations and therefore free for general use.
The publisher, the authors, and the editors are safe to assume that the advice and information in this book are believed to be true and accurate at the date of publication. Neither the publisher nor the authors or the editors give a warranty, expressed or implied, with respect to the material contained herein or for any errors or omissions that may have been made. The publisher remains neutral with regard to jurisdictional claims in published maps and institutional affiliations.

Cover credit: RRice/shutterstock.com

This Palgrave Macmillan imprint is published by the registered company Springer Nature Switzerland AG
The registered company address is: Gewerbestrasse 11, 6330 Cham, Switzerland

This book is dedicated to my family:

Jessica Jiang
Alice Jiang
Emily Jiang

and the memory of my mother:

Xiuping Shi

Preface

The investment landscape in the modern world continues to evolve in response to technological advances, regulatory requirements and changing market dynamics. Investment models and processes must continually adapt to changes in the increasingly complex and competitive investment environment. Successful investing relies heavily on effective and resilient investment strategies implemented against the backdrop of dynamic market conditions. Investment strategies play a central role in helping investors achieve defined financial objectives. They directly affect investment outcomes and become even more important in times of economic uncertainty and low return expectations across major asset classes.

Factor investing has attracted significant investor interest in recent years. This investment approach is positioned between active management and passive investing to combine their advantages. Factor investing seeks to outperform the market with lower investment costs than active strategies. It is designed to capture the return premiums of risk factors in a systematic and efficient way. Factor returns are cyclical in nature and susceptible to market conditions. To harvest factor premiums, some investors adopt factor rotation to actively change factor positions across different economic phases. However, it is practically difficult to detect turning points in the business cycle and reliably predict factor performance. The failure to capture strong factor returns can only result in disappointing investment performance. The emergence of multifactor strategies is a natural development in the evolution of factor investing. The multifactor approach essentially allows investors to gain balanced and consistent exposure to a combination of factors over time. It provides an effective solution to capture factor premiums and reduce portfolio volatility without the challenging task of factor timing.

Factors are systematic drivers of return and the foundation of investment portfolios. Academic and investment studies have identified a range of risk factors in equity investing. Common style factors include size, quality, momentum, value, yield, volatility and liquidity. These factors have proved the ability to generate excess returns over time. The size factor is related to the smallcap effect that smaller companies tend to outperform their larger peers in the long term. It is firmly established in the three-factor model developed by the Nobel Prize winner Eugene Fama and his research partner Professor Kenneth French. The quality factor captures excess returns delivered by companies with superior quality characteristics. Quality has been widely adopted in the investment sector either as a factor strategy or an element integrated into the investment process. Momentum reflects the observation that share price often continues to move in the direction of a price trend. The momentum strategy aims to produce excess returns by capitalising on established price trends in the market. The value effect refers to the tendency of stocks with attractive valuations to outperform the market over a long period of time. The value factor outperformed other common style factors during the 40 years to 2017. The yield factor captures excess returns provided by companies with high dividend yields. Dividend yield serves as a style factor and source of investment return. The sustained low interest-rate environment since the 2008 financial crisis has prompted investors to actively chase yields. The volatility effect is the phenomenon that stocks with low price volatility tend to generate long-term outperformance. It is a market anomaly in finance that seriously challenges the prevailing theory stating higher returns require more risk. The liquidity premium compensates investors for holding assets with low liquidity.

Investors are encouraged to understand current investment themes and long-term trends in the market for the purpose of strategic asset allocation. Sustainable investing has gained strong market acceptance and continues to rise in prominence. It integrates environmental, social and governance (ESG) standards into investment decisions. ESG issues are increasingly recognised as critical factors that determine the long-term success of companies. The ESG approach provides a framework for the analysis of companies regarding sustainability issues and opportunities. Sustainable investing also allows investors to align personal values with financial objectives. It has become increasingly common for investors to consider ESG criteria in the investment process. MSCI and other leading index providers have launched a series of ESG indices to track the performance of companies with high ESG scores.

Successful investing requires a clear understanding of fundamental investment principles, such as diversification and loss control. Diversification is a simple and effective strategy to mitigate investment risk. It controls exposure to any single asset to protect investment portfolios against disastrous losses in the uncertain market. Diversification reduces portfolio volatility and potentially improves risk-adjusted returns. Investors can construct diversified portfolios by allocating capital across different asset classes and risk factors. Investments should be managed as a portfolio rather than individual assets. A disciplined approach is essential to manage losing positions given the prevalence of unprofitable investments in the market. The failure to cut losses quickly can result in severe damage to investment capital. Investors are advised to regularly review portfolios and take decisive actions against companies with deteriorating fundamentals.

This book presents a range of investment strategies to help investors enhance return potential. It is primarily written for private investors and investment practitioners such as equity analysts and investment advisors. It is also suitable for university students who are interested in learning practical investment strategies and traditional asset classes. The book is structured into 16 chapters to discuss investment approaches. Chapter 1 provides an overview of investment basics, such as risk tolerance and investment constraints. Chapter 2 discusses asset allocation, investment vehicles, investment risks and performance attribution. Chapter 3 examines the asset class of equities with a specific focus on its risk and return characteristics. Chapter 4 covers bonds and cash as two major asset classes frequently used to form the core of defensive investment portfolios. Chapter 5 shows the historical performance and investment benefits of precious metals. Chapter 6 illustrates the importance of diversification in investing to reduce downside risk and capture upside returns. Chapter 7 discusses loss control as a key investment principle to protect portfolios against extreme losses. Chapter 8 provides an introduction to sustainable investing regarding its investment objectives, approaches and benefits. Chapter 9 introduces the size effect that smaller companies tend to outperform their larger peers in the long term. Chapter 10 presents quality investing as a widely accepted investment strategy to outperform the market. Chapter 11 examines the momentum effect that excess returns can be earned by following price trends. Chapter 12 describes the value effect that stocks with attractive valuations tend to generate excess returns. Chapter 13 focuses on the discussion of dividend yield as a common style factor and return component. Chapter 14 covers the volatility effect serving as a market anomaly to challenge the conventional view that higher returns require more risk. Chapter 15 discusses the liquidity premium and the investment risk of holding excessive illiquid assets. Chapter 16 concludes the book with a detailed description of the multifactor investing approach.

London, UK   Bill Jiang

Disclaimer

The MSCI data contained herein is the property of MSCI Inc. (MSCI). MSCI, its affiliates and its information providers make no warranties with respect to any such data. The MSCI data contained herein is used under license and may not be further used, distributed or disseminated without the express written consent of MSCI.

S&P® and S&P 500® are registered trademarks of Standard & Poor's Financial Services LLC, and Dow Jones® is a registered trademark of Dow Jones Trademark Holdings LLC. © 2020 S&P Dow Jones Indices LLC, its affiliates and/or its licensors. All rights reserved.

Contents

1	**Investment Basics**	1
	1.1 Introduction	1
	1.2 Time Value of Money	3
	1.3 Investment Objectives	5
	1.4 Risk Tolerance	7
	1.5 Investment Constraints	9
	Reference	11
2	**Asset Allocation**	13
	2.1 Asset Allocation	13
	2.2 Investment Vehicles	16
	2.3 Investment Risk	17
	2.4 Performance Attribution	20
	References	27
3	**Common Stock**	29
	3.1 Equity Investments	29
	3.2 Equity Indices	32
	3.3 Long-Term Performance	34
	3.4 Equity Risk	35
	3.5 Distribution of Stock Returns	38
	References	39
4	**Bonds and Cash**	41
	4.1 Bonds	41
	4.2 Investment Benefits	43

	4.3	Bond Risk	44
	4.4	Credit Rating	45
	4.5	Yield Curve	47
	4.6	Bond Return	49
	4.7	Cash	50
	References		52
5	**Precious Metals**		**53**
	5.1	Precious Metals	53
	5.2	Historical Performance	55
	5.3	Characteristics of Gold	58
	5.4	Diversification Effect	60
	5.5	Drivers of Gold Price	62
	5.6	Investment Methods	65
	References		66
6	**Portfolio Diversification**		**67**
	6.1	Portfolio Diversification	67
	6.2	Efficient Frontier	69
	6.3	Downside Protection	72
	6.4	Upside Capture	73
	6.5	Risk-Adjusted Return	74
	References		77
7	**Loss Control**		**79**
	7.1	Disposition Effect	79
	7.2	Breakeven Return	81
	7.3	Profit Warning	83
	7.4	Broker Research	85
	7.5	Short Selling	86
	References		87
8	**Sustainable Investing**		**89**
	8.1	Sustainable Investing	89
	8.2	ESG Factors	93
	8.3	ESG Integration	96
	8.4	Investment Benefits	98
	References		100
9	**Size Effect**		**103**
	9.1	Size Effect	103
	9.2	Definition of Smallcap	108
	9.3	Characteristics of Smaller Companies	109

	9.4	Fama–French 3-Factor Model	112
	9.5	Return Premium	114
	References		116
10	**Quality Investing**		119
	10.1	Quality Investing	119
	10.2	Characteristics of Quality Companies	123
	10.3	Quality Measures	125
	10.4	Return Premium	127
	References		130
11	**Momentum Investing**		133
	11.1	Momentum Investing	133
	11.2	Momentum Measures	136
	11.3	Momentum Quality	139
	11.4	Return Premium	142
	References		145
12	**Value Effect**		147
	12.1	Value Investing	147
	12.2	Valuation Metrics	149
	12.3	Return Premium	151
	12.4	Return Decomposition	155
	12.5	Return Forecasting	157
	References		159
13	**Dividend Yield**		161
	13.1	Dividend Investing	161
	13.2	Dividend Yield	164
	13.3	Return Premium	167
	13.4	Dividend Safety	168
	References		171
14	**Volatility Effect**		173
	14.1	Volatility Effect	173
	14.2	Capital Asset Pricing Model	177
	14.3	Return Premium	178
	14.4	Construction Methods	180
	References		182
15	**Liquidity Premium**		185
	15.1	Asset Liquidity	185
	15.2	Liquidity Measures	188

15.3	Return Premium	189
References		190

16 Multifactor Investing — 193
- 16.1 Multifactor Investing — 193
- 16.2 Cyclical Performance — 196
- 16.3 Investment Merits — 198
- 16.4 Construction Methods — 201
- 16.5 Factor Combinations — 204
- References — 205

Index — 207

About the Author

Bill Jiang started his career as an Assistant Professor at the University of Birmingham before entering the industry. He has written 25 research papers in the areas of business management and software engineering. His research work has been published in *International Marketing Review*, *Psychology & Marketing*, *Construction Management and Economics*, *Journal of Software: Evolution and Process*, *Journal of the Operational Research Society* and other academic journals. Dr Jiang won the Best Paper award at the 2009 Annual Conference of Society for Marketing Advances in New Orleans. His research article in the *Journal of Business & Industrial Marketing* achieved the recognition as the most downloaded paper of the journal in 2012. Dr Jiang completed his doctoral research at Manchester Business School and received an MSc in Applied Statistics from the University of Oxford. He is a CFA charterholder and holds the Financial Risk Manager designation.

List of Figures

Fig. 1.1	The effect of inflation on real money value	4
Fig. 1.2	The growth of portfolio value with compound return	5
Fig. 2.1	The performance of portfolios with different risk levels	14
Fig. 3.1	Historical performance and risk of five asset classes (1980–2019)	34
Fig. 3.2	The dramatic rise and collapse of Wirecard shares	36
Fig. 3.3	Historical price of the S&P 500 Index (January 2006–June 2020)	37
Fig. 4.1	Normal, flat and inverted yield curves	48
Fig. 4.2	Historical yield spread between 10-year and 1-year US Treasury securities	49
Fig. 4.3	Historical 10-year US Treasury yield and the S&P 500 Index	50
Fig. 4.4	Historical yield on 3-month US Treasury bills and the inflation rate	51
Fig. 5.1	Historical prices of gold and silver (rebased)	56
Fig. 5.2	The performance of gold during extreme negative market events	59
Fig. 5.3	Portfolio construction with gold and the S&P 500 Index	61
Fig. 5.4	Performance of a balanced portfolio and the S&P 500 Index	62
Fig. 5.5	Gold price and the trade-weighted US dollar index (2007–2011)	64
Fig. 6.1	The effect of diversification on reducing portfolio risk	68
Fig. 6.2	Efficient frontier constructed with two risky assets	70
Fig. 6.3	Maximum drawdowns of a balanced portfolio and the S&P 500 Index	73

Fig. 6.4	Performance of a balanced portfolio and the S&P 500 Index (rebased)	76
Fig. 7.1	The relationship between investment loss and breakeven return	82
Fig. 7.2	Historical share prices of Capita and Ted Baker (2011–2020)	83
Fig. 8.1	The growth in the number of signatories to the Principles for Responsible Investment	90
Fig. 8.2	The distribution of global sustainable investment assets by ESG approach	93
Fig. 9.1	Historical performance of smallcap and the S&P 500 Index	105
Fig. 9.2	Cumulative relative performance of smallcap against largecap	106
Fig. 11.1	An illustration of upward and downward price momentums	134
Fig. 11.2	Annual performance of the momentum factor	136
Fig. 11.3	Four patterns of share price movements	139
Fig. 11.4	An illustration of momentum quality with real share prices	142
Fig. 11.5	Annualised returns of portfolios formed on momentum (1927–2019)	144
Fig. 12.1	Historical performance of value relative to growth	154
Fig. 12.2	10-year rolling relative performance of value	155
Fig. 12.3	The return decomposition of the S&P 500 Index	156
Fig. 12.4	Market return forecasting with a four-factor model	158
Fig. 13.1	The contribution of dividend yield to cumulative return	165
Fig. 13.2	Incremental dividend payouts of Walmart and Nestlé	169
Fig. 14.1	Annual performance of the volatility factor	174
Fig. 16.1	Historical performance of style factor indices	194

List of Tables

Table 1.1	Performance of portfolios with different risk profiles	8
Table 2.1	Performance attribution with the Brinson model	23
Table 2.2	Return decomposition with a fundamental risk factor model	26
Table 3.1	Global sector weights	31
Table 3.2	Country weights in the global equity market	32
Table 3.3	Holding period and the frequency of outperformance by equities	38
Table 4.1	The inverse relationship between bond price and yield	42
Table 4.2	Major global credit rating systems	46
Table 4.3	Credit rating transition rates over a 1-year period (%)	47
Table 5.1	Correlations of four precious metals	54
Table 5.2	Performance of precious metals (1996–2020)	55
Table 5.3	Annual price changes of precious metals (2011–2020)	57
Table 6.1	Annual returns of eight asset classes (2011–2020)	75
Table 7.1	The impact of the disposition effect on investment results	80
Table 7.2	A sample of stocks with downward price trends	81
Table 9.1	Constituent sizes of four European smallcap indices (31 March 2020)	109
Table 9.2	The performance of 25 portfolios formed on size and quality	116
Table 10.1	Annual performance of the quality factor	121
Table 10.2	A sample of quality measures used in the investment sector	126
Table 10.3	Performance of portfolios formed on profitability and size	128
Table 10.4	Global evidence of the quality factor premium	129

List of Tables

Table 11.1	The relevance of time window in momentum investing (1931–2019)	137
Table 11.2	The strength of momentum quality in enhancing returns	141
Table 11.3	Performance of portfolios formed on past 6-month return	143
Table 12.1	Average annual returns of portfolios formed on valuation metrics and past sales growth	152
Table 13.1	The level of dividend yield by sector	166
Table 14.1	The performance of the volatility factor during bear markets	175
Table 14.2	Performance of portfolios with different volatility levels	179
Table 14.3	Sample indices formed with different volatility methods	182
Table 15.1	Optimal allocation to illiquid assets	187
Table 15.2	Size and liquidity premium	189
Table 16.1	Annual relative returns of style factor indices	197
Table 16.2	Performance comparison of single and multiple factor strategies	199
Table 16.3	Investment horizon and the frequency of factor outperformance	200
Table 16.4	Factor combinations in multifactor investing	205

1

Investment Basics

1.1 Introduction

Investment is the process of allocating capital to assets that are expected to provide a financial return. It is an important way to earn income and accumulate wealth in the modern world. Investors seek to achieve different goals through the practice of investing. Investment decisions can be driven by the motivation to increase wealth, support family planning or simply realise personal financial goals. In general, investors aim to achieve positive returns through the investment in assets that provide either or both of capital growth and income. Growth investors focus on capital appreciation and frequently direct their financial resources to equity investments. Income investors typically pursue stable and sustainable income streams and are often willing to compromise on capital gains. Income can be harvested from various sources, such as stock dividends, rental income and interest on savings accounts. Many investment assets have the potential to deliver good capital growth while offering reliable income.

Many people choose saving as a primary means of increasing wealth. Saving into a deposit account allows individuals to have financial security and resources for short-term planning. Money in savings accounts is easily accessible and particularly valuable in times of economic downturn. However, saving is essentially not investing and typically offers a much lower rate of return than common financial instruments in the market. A potential risk is that the interest earned on a savings account fails to keep pace with inflation, thus reducing the purchasing power of money. Investing, however, provides the opportunity to earn attractive returns with an appropriate level of risk. All investments involve the element of risk, including the permanent loss of capital. By following certain rules to carefully manage investment risk, investors can pursue their financial goals with great confidence. Given the increasing diversity of investment options, it is beneficial for investors to understand fundamental investment principles and techniques. Knowledgeable investors are more likely to make rational decisions that are consistent with their investment plans.

Investors can be broadly classified into two categories: individual and institutional. Individual investors are market participants who invest for their personal accounts. Individual investors are large in number but typically have limited investable resources and trade in relatively small amounts. They often make investment decisions without extensive and in-depth analysis. This is mainly due to the limitations in investment knowledge and skills as well as the restricted access to resources. Individual investors often do not follow a disciplined investment approach and are subject to behavioural biases. Given the large retail investment space, individual investors can have a significant influence on market sentiment. For example, it is estimated that 80% of trading volume in the China A-shares market is contributed by individual investors [1]. The dominance of individual investors in market trading has a profound impact on market movements. For the 12 months to 12 June 2015, the Shanghai Stock Exchange (SSE) Composite Index experienced a dramatic rise of 151.8% in price return. Subsequently, the index suffered a period of significant decline until 28 January 2016, recording a cumulative loss of 48.6% in under 8 months. This illustrates the power of individual investors in increasing market volatility and inefficiency. Institutional investors are entities that pool money to invest in different asset classes. This broad investor category covers many different types of market participants, such as investment companies, pension funds, endowments and foundations, insurance companies and sovereign wealth funds. Institutional investors generally have good expertise and resources to identify investment opportunities and perform thorough analysis. They usually follow a rigorous and disciplined investment process shaped by specific investment objectives and constraints. Institutional investors with strong resources and capabilities often manage their investments internally. They also frequently allocate capital to asset managers for professional investment services.

The success in investing depends on many factors, including rigorous analysis and disciplined execution. This book provides a range of investment strategies to help investors improve performance and avoid common mistakes. Meanwhile, it is essential for investors to develop a clear investment plan to guide investment decisions. Many investments are volatile in the short term and can fall significantly in difficult market conditions. This often results in emotional responses of individual investors as they watch their investments decline in value. A systematic investment plan can help investors effectively navigate market volatility and meet defined investment goals. It serves as a roadmap to guide investors towards their investment destination. The creation of an investment plan starts with a formal assessment of the current financial situation. This is followed by a clear definition of realistic and measurable investment goals and objectives. Risk tolerance is a critical factor to consider before a suitable investment portfolio is designed. It is also required to properly identify specific investment constraints, such as liquidity needs, time horizon and ethical issues. Subsequently, the investment plan determines the investment approach and asset classes used for portfolio construction. Based on the defined asset allocation framework, individual investments are selected to form a portfolio that aligns closely with investment objectives and constraints. The investment portfolio will be reviewed and updated regularly to ensure that it is on track to deliver expected financial results.

1.2 Time Value of Money

A fundamental principle in finance is that money has a time value attached to it. The time value of money holds that money available now is worth more than the identical amount in the future. This principle explains the reason to compensate depositors with interest, because money loses value over time. The gradual loss of money value is primarily caused by the combined forces of inflation and opportunity cost. Inflation constantly erodes the real value of money through the rise in prices. Investors can easily understand the effect of inflation by comparing food prices in the past. Otherwise, a consumer price index can be used to objectively measure the reduction in the purchasing power of money caused by inflation. The time value of money is also related to the concept of opportunity cost. Money available today can be invested to earn additional income and accumulate a larger amount of capital in the future. The inability to receive money now and invest means the loss of opportunity to earn financial returns. The time value of money recognises the importance of investing to protect against inflation and produce future cash flows. This principle is widely applied in financial management to specifically incorporate cash flows from different time periods into investment decisions.

Inflation erodes the purchasing power of money due to a rise in general prices. Figure 1.1 illustrates the gradual decline of money value over time caused by price inflation. For the purpose of simplicity, the inflation rate is assumed to be constant over the entire period of 50 years. To maintain price stability in the economy, many central banks in the world target the inflation rate of 2%. Based on this inflation rate, the capital of $10,000 will see its real value decline steadily over time to about $3,715 after 50 years. If the inflation rate increases to 5%, then the real value will be worth only $872 at the end of the period. Without any investment return, the real value of capital will invariably fall because of inflation. Many people prefer to keep their money in a savings account rather than investing in financial assets like equities and bonds. The fact is that if the interest earned is lower than the inflation rate, then the real value of savings still declines over time. For example, the 1% interest rate earned from a savings account will produce a negative real return of −2%, if the inflation rate is actually higher at 3%.

The negative effect of inflation underlines the importance of investing to preserve money value and build long-term wealth. Investors should really capitalise on the power of compounding in investing. The compounding effect is the ability of an investment to produce exponential returns by reinvesting income over time. It allows investors with a long-term horizon to reap huge rewards from a series of seemingly insignificant investments. Assume an investor allocates $1,000 to an investment portfolio that is expected to generate an average compound return of 8% per year (net of all costs). The value of this investment will increase to $46,902 after 50 years, representing

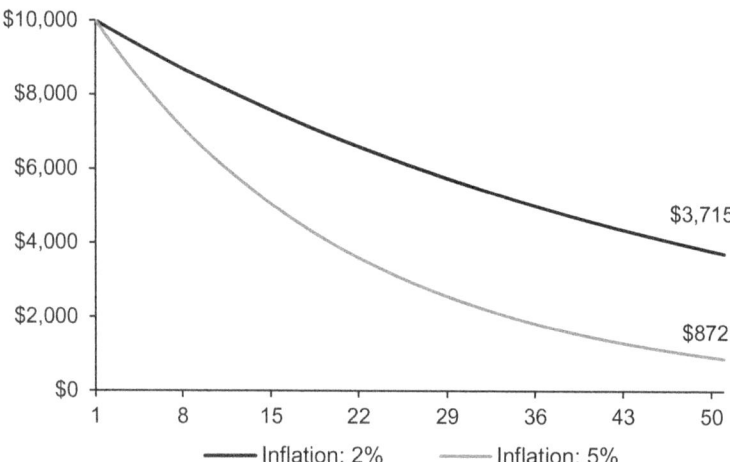

Fig. 1.1 The effect of inflation on real money value

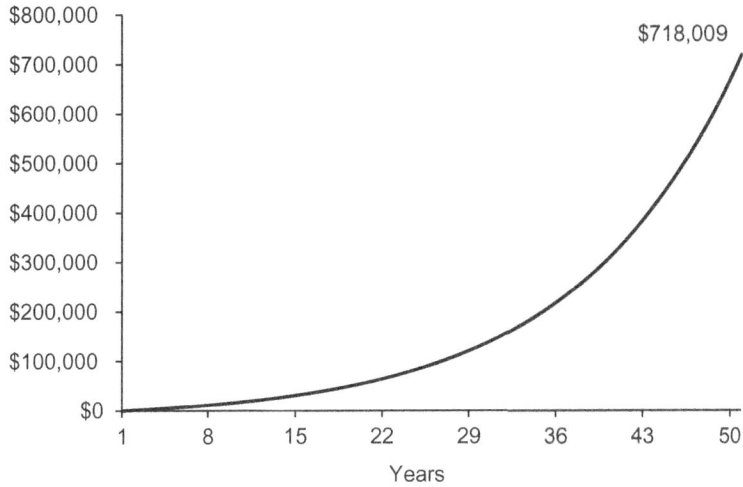

Fig. 1.2 The growth of portfolio value with compound return

a cumulative return of 4590%. Based on the annual inflation rate of 2%, the real value will be $17,425 when the 50-year period ends. The investment significantly enhances the real value of the original capital by delivering a good inflation-adjusted return. Alternatively, the investor can save regularly and allocate a small amount of $100 to the same investment portfolio at the start of each month. Based on the assumption of 8% annual return, the total value accumulated over 50 years will be substantial. As exhibited in Fig. 1.2, the portfolio value is expected to grow strongly to $718,009 at the end of the period. This results from the combined forces of the compounding effect and investment return. Note that the total amount of capital contributed by this investor is only $60,000 over the entire period.

1.3 Investment Objectives

A standard investment plan for individual investors starts with a formal assessment of the current financial situation. With a clear understanding of current status, financial goals and investment objectives can be determined to form the basis of an investment framework. A proper definition of financial goals is essential, because it will guide the formulation of an investment strategy tailored to meet the goals. Financial goals provide direction for investment efforts and help individuals stay disciplined in the investment process. They are defined according to a range of factors, such as age, income, employment status and family circumstances. A properly defined financial goal must contain the element of time horizon. For example, a short-term financial goal may be to pay off credit cards and personal loans within 2 years. Medium-term financial goals typically take 3–10 years to realise, such as financing a property purchase, business venture or college education. For long-term goals like retirement planning, a significant time commitment of more than 10 years is usually required to achieve expected results.

Investment objectives of individual investors are developed to fulfil their specific financial goals. The definition of investment objectives can follow the SMART criteria: specific, measurable, actionable, realistic and timely. Clearly defined investment objectives that are measurable and realistic in a definitive time frame can help investors stay focused on their financial goals and avoid common investment mistakes. Objectives in an investment plan usually contain two interdependent components: risk and return. The risk objective limits the return potential of a portfolio by determining the suitability of investment assets. As a key factor in investment, risk can be measured in absolute or relative terms. The most common measure of absolute risk is price volatility, which is often calculated as the annualised standard deviation of price returns. Absolute risk can also be measured by downside risk metrics, such as maximum drawdown and value at risk (VaR). The maximum drawdown of an investment is the largest peak-to-trough decline in its value during a specific time period. For example, the S&P 500 Index experienced a maximum drawdown of 56.8% over the 2008 financial crisis, falling from the peak value of 1,565.2 (9 October 2007) to the lowest point of 676.5 (9 March 2009). VaR estimates the maximum possible loss that can occur over a period based on a given confidence level. Suppose an investment portfolio is estimated to have a weekly VaR of 10% with a 95% confidence interval. This means there is only a 5% probability that the portfolio will lose more than 10% of its value over a weekly period. Relative risk measures are used to evaluate the risk of an investment relative to a specific benchmark, such as tracking error and beta. Tracking error provides an indication of how closely a portfolio tracks the performance of its benchmark. It is frequently calculated as the standard deviation of relative returns. The risk objective is primarily determined by risk tolerance, time horizon and specific investment constraints. A risk objective may be stated as: minimise downside risk with a maximum daily volatility of 5%. Return is the second component of investment objectives and must be consistent with the defined risk objective. Investment performance can be measured on an absolute or relative basis. Absolute performance is usually represented by total return consisting of capital growth and investment income. Relative return measures the performance of an investment relative to a specific benchmark. A relative-return objective may be expressed as: annual outperformance of 2% against the S&P 500 Index. The return objective can also be stated in nominal or real terms, subject to the adjustment for inflation. A real-return objective of 5% per year seeks to achieve an annual return of 5% above the inflation rate. Besides, investment performance can be explicitly defined as gross or net return. Compared to gross return, net return excludes all investment costs (e.g. fees and taxes).

The investment objectives of institutional investors are shaped by the nature of their business. For endowments and foundations, the primary objective is to generate sufficient income to cover spending needs, while preserving the real value of investment assets. For defined benefit pension plans, a typical investment objective is to ensure that assets are sufficient to meet pension liabilities. Insurance companies also typically follow a liability-driven investment approach to fulfil obligations stated in insurance policies. Investment companies, however, usually do not have specific liabilities to meet. For most investment funds, the primary objective is to maximise investment returns at an appropriate level of risk. Actively managed funds generally seek to outperform a defined benchmark, generate stable income streams or target an absolute return.

1.4 Risk Tolerance

Risk tolerance is the degree of variability in investment returns that an investor is willing to accept. Along with investment objectives, risk tolerance is a fundamental factor in determining asset allocation to form optimal investment portfolios. Investors with high risk appetite tend to be comfortable with market volatility in the pursuit of superior returns. They are usually more willing to risk capital in an attempt to achieve better returns than conservative investors. In general, the risk tolerance of an individual investor is a function of two factors: ability and willingness. The ability to take risk is affected by a number of factors, such as financial circumstances, liquidity needs and time horizon. The willingness to take risk (i.e. risk attitude) is related to the psychological profile of an investor. Some investors find it stressful to watch their investments fall in value. Investment education can help them overcome psychological biases and improve knowledge in the practice of investing. Note that the two components of risk tolerance must be compatible with each other. Sometimes there is a conflict between the ability and willingness to take risk. A prudent approach is to choose the lower level of the two components as the measure of risk tolerance.

Financial advisors often use questionnaires to objectively assess risk tolerance for their clients. The risk profiling process can help determine the optimal level of investment risk to achieve defined financial goals. Based on the risk tolerance level, investors can be classified into five categories: very conservative, conservative, moderate, aggressive and very aggressive. Conservative investors emphasise the importance of investment stability, with a primary objective of protecting capital. They are willing to accept relatively low returns in order to reduce investment risk. Conservative investors usually allocate a significant portion of their investments to cash and fixed-income securities. Moderate investors are characterised by modest risk appetite, seeking to achieve a balance between capital preservation and growth. They are willing to assume a moderate level of risk to earn reasonable returns by gaining balanced exposure to different asset classes. Aggressive investors primarily pursue capital growth and are willing to accept substantial investment volatility and losses. Their investments are mainly directed to equities and other risky assets.

Portfolios with different risk and return characteristics can be constructed to meet specific investment goals. Table 1.1 compares the performance of portfolios with different risk profiles. These portfolios are formed by four assets with different weightings: US stocks, global (excluding US) stocks, bonds and cash. Stocks are represented by the S&P 500 and MSCI World ex USA indices, while bonds and cash are respectively based on 10-year and 3-month US Treasury yields. The portfolios are rebalanced annually and their returns are tracked over the 50 years to 2019. The conservative portfolio is

Table 1.1 Performance of portfolios with different risk profiles

	Conservative	Balanced	Growth	Aggressive
Composition:				
US stocks	20%	30%	40%	50%
World ex US	0%	20%	30%	40%
Bonds	50%	30%	20%	10%
Cash	30%	20%	10%	0%
Annual Return:				
Average	6.9%	8.4%	9.3%	10.0%
Volatility	4.3%	8.7%	12.0%	15.4%
Best year	15.8%	24.5%	31.0%	37.5%
Worst year	-5.1%	-18.4%	-26.9%	-35.4%
Best 10-year	11.7%	15.0%	16.9%	18.8%
Worst 10-year	3.2%	2.7%	1.8%	0.7%

suitable for investors with low risk tolerance, while the aggressive portfolio is designed for investors seeking strong capital growth. With good diversification across the four assets, the balanced portfolio is created for investors with medium risk appetite. The growth portfolio is biased towards stocks to provide good capital growth with relatively high risk. The results confirm the conventional view that higher returns require more risk. Across the four portfolios, annual volatility increases dramatically from only 4.3% to 15.4%. However, portfolio return increases steadily as the risk level rises. The aggressive portfolio achieved the highest average return of 10.0% per annum, significantly better than 6.9% produced by the conservative portfolio. In the short term, portfolios with higher weightings to stocks are associated with greater downside risk. During the 50-year period, the aggressive portfolio suffered the worst annual return of −35.4%, compared to only −5.1% for the conservative portfolio. Downside risk can possibly be mitigated by extending the investment horizon. For all the four portfolios, they never produced a negative return when the holding period increases to 10 years. Even the aggressive portfolio still managed to deliver an annualised return of 0.7% as the worst 10-year performance. This suggests that investors with a long time horizon can potentially raise the risk tolerance level and earn higher returns by increasing exposure to risky assets. The aggressive portfolio recorded the best annual return of 37.5%, easily eclipsing 15.8% provided by the conservative portfolio. For the best 10-year return, the aggressive portfolio generated a substantial outperformance of 7.1% per annum relative to the conservative portfolio. This example shows that risk tolerance is a key factor that determines portfolio composition and return potential.

1.5 Investment Constraints

Investment constraints are factors that restrict or limit investment options available to an investor. It is necessary to consider constraints in investing because they affect the ability of an investor to take full or partial advantage of certain investments. The definition of investment objectives and risk tolerance must properly consider the impact of investment constraints. Investors can be subject to many different constraints, such as liquidity needs, time horizon, tax considerations, regulatory restrictions and ethical issues. Individual investors concerned about liquidity risk may decide to hold sizeable cash positions at the cost of investment return. Liquidity risk is usually a major concern for institutional investors, including insurance companies and investment managers. Insurance companies need to ensure that they have sufficient liquid assets to cover cash flow requirements resulting from unpredictable insurance claims. To meet redemption requests, investment funds usually maintain reasonable liquidity so that cash can be easily raised by selling assets.

In financial planning, a principal objective is to ensure that sufficient assets are available to cover financial obligations. Time horizon is a primary factor to consider when determining asset allocation to fulfil investment goals. Conservative investments are suitable for portfolios created to meet short-term financial needs. Risk tolerance may increase with the extension of investment horizon. Investment portfolios designed for long-term goals (e.g. retirement planning) usually gain heavy exposure to risky assets like stocks. Time horizon can make a significant impact on investment returns. This can be illustrated by the historical performance of the S&P 500 Index. This broad market index has a reasonable chance of producing a negative return within a very short time frame. However, the probability of negative return often falls as the time period is extended. During the period from 1988 to 2018, the frequency of negative weekly return is 42% for the S&P 500 Index. The calculation is based on all rolling 1-week returns over the entire period. If the time horizon is extended to one year, then the frequency of loss falls significantly to 17%. If the holding period increases to 10 years, the frequency of negative return drops to only 9%. For any point over the 31-year period, this index never made a loss if the holding period is more than 12 years.

Tax concerns can become an investment constraint because taxes reduce investment returns. Investors are encouraged to optimise their portfolios to reduce tax burden. In general, most equity investments are liable for taxes on capital gains and dividend income. Investors can delay the realisation of capital gains by selecting investments that are expected to be held for a long time period. This strategy can help mitigate the tax effect and preserve investment capital. To reduce dividend tax liabilities, investors can focus on stocks and investment funds with low dividend yields. Dividends paid by foreign stocks may be subject to withholding tax imposed by a foreign government. Due to this additional tax layer, effective dividend yield for foreign stocks is often lower than that quoted on financial platforms.

Legal and regulatory requirements can also impose constraints on investing. They are mainly applicable to institutional investors who must meet compliance standards. For example, investment funds registered under the European UCITS framework must follow its rules regarding eligible investments, liquidity, disclosure and many others. They may also be prohibited from making certain investments due to ethical reasons. In response to the growing concern about ethical issues, many investment funds aim to avoid companies with controversial business activities (e.g. gambling, alcohol). Individual investors may have special investment constraints arising from unique circumstances, such as personal values and financial resources. Unique constraints should be properly considered when formulating an investment plan.

Reference

1. *China A-Shares: Tap into Broader Investment Opportunities as Chinese Markets Open Up.* 2019, BNP Paribas Asset Management.

2

Asset Allocation

2.1 Asset Allocation

Asset allocation is the process of determining optimal portfolio exposure to different asset classes. It aims to achieve an optimal balance of risk and return in an investment portfolio. This investment process is expected to address key considerations in investing, such as capital protection, return potential and income generation. It relies on the fundamental principle that asset classes in the market have different risk and return characteristics. Common asset classes, such as equities and bonds, often perform differently in changing economic and market conditions. Investors usually allocate substantial capital to equities in bull markets characterised by rising investor optimism and willingness to increase risk exposure. Capital frequently flows into the safer bond market during times of market volatility. Asset allocation is an essential part of the investment process that directly affects portfolio performance. Many institutional investors have achieved excellent returns primarily due to their exceptional performance in asset allocation. For instance, the Yale endowment fund maintains a diversified exposure to different asset classes. According to its 2019 annual report [1], the Yale endowment portfolio was positioned with the target weightings as: absolute return (23.0%), venture capital (21.5%), leveraged buyouts (16.5%), foreign equity (13.75%), real estate (10.0%), cash and fixed income (7.0%), natural resources (5.5%) and domestic equity (2.75%). Successful asset allocation helped the Yale Endowment deliver an annualised return of 11.4% over the 20 years to June 2019. This performance significantly exceeds the average annual return of 6.4% produced by the broad US equity market during the same period.

Asset allocation essentially seeks to find the optimal weightings to defensive and growth assets in a portfolio. Growth assets like equities generally have higher return potential but carry greater risk than defensive assets such as bonds and cash. Conservative portfolios are mainly formed of defensive assets, while aggressive portfolios assign heavy weightings to growth assets. Figure 2.1 compares the performance of three portfolios constructed by equities, bonds and cash. Equities are represented by the S&P 500 Total Return Index, bonds are based on the ICE BofA 3–5 Year US Corporate Total Return Index, and cash is the 3-month US Treasury bill. The aggressive portfolio is formed of 70% equities, 20% bonds and 10% cash. The moderate portfolio maintains a balanced exposure to equities (50%), bonds (30%) and cash (20%). The conservative portfolio allocates heavier weightings to defensive assets (bonds: 50%, cash: 30%), with equities only accounting for 20% of portfolio value. All the three portfolios are rebalanced on a monthly basis to restore target weightings. During the 30 years to 2019, the aggressive portfolio produced the highest average return of 8.7% per year, resulting from its high exposure to equities. This performance was delivered at the cost of highest volatility (10.1%) among the three portfolios. In comparison, the conservative portfolio produced a materially lower annualised return

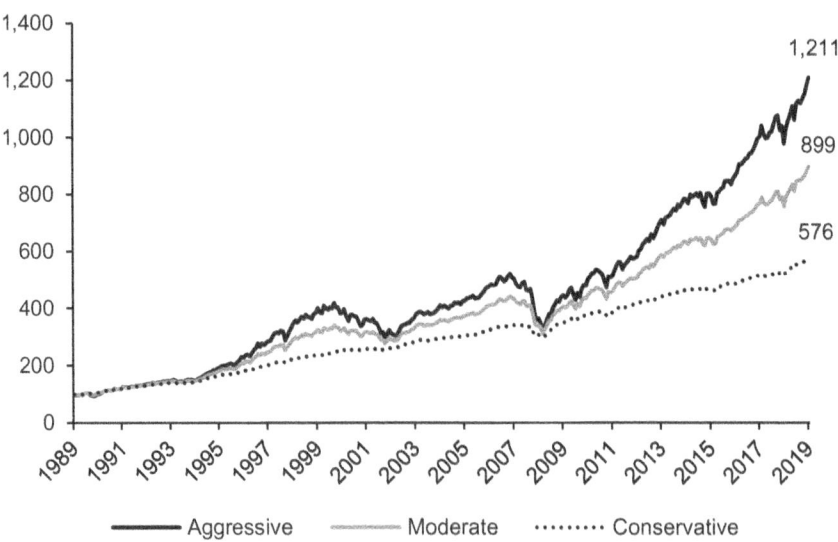

Fig. 2.1 The performance of portfolios with different risk levels

of 6.0% over the same period. This significant underperformance is not surprising, since it allocated 80% of portfolio value to defensive investments. However, the conservative portfolio had the lowest volatility of only 3.6%. On a risk-adjusted basis, the efficiency ratios are 0.86, 1.03 and 1.66 respectively for the aggressive, moderate and conservative portfolios. This suggests that the conservative portfolio actually provided the highest risk-adjusted return over the entire period. Investors with low risk tolerance may prefer the conservative portfolio to control volatility risk.

Individual investors can employ advanced models to determine optimal portfolio weightings to defensive and growth assets. Alternatively, they can simply use the formula 100 − age to estimate a suitable level of equity exposure. If the age is 20, this rule suggests 80% of portfolio value should be invested in equities. If the age is 70, then allocation to equities is recommended to be only 30%. This simple rule recognises that the exposure to equities should decrease as time horizon shortens. Another approach for asset allocation is the core-satellite portfolio structure. The idea behind this approach is that the core of a portfolio is formed of long-term and diversified investments, while a small portion is allocated to special investments. The separation of a portfolio into two distinct segments prevents investors from being unduly exposed to worrying levels of risk.

An asset allocation decision can be considered strategic or tactical in nature. Strategic asset allocation seeks to determine the target weightings of different asset classes. Portfolios are rebalanced periodically to restore target asset exposures. Strategic asset allocation is often the primary determinant of investment outcomes. Tactical asset allocation actively adjusts portfolio weightings to meet changing market conditions or exploit investment opportunities [2]. It attempts to enhance returns by adopting a dynamic approach to portfolio management. Despite its intuitive appeal, tactical allocation overall has failed to consistently deliver encouraging results. According to a Morningstar study, investment funds in the tactical allocation category on average underperformed the Vanguard Balanced Index Fund by 3.2% per year during the 15 years to 2018 [3]. Besides, only 9% of tactical funds survived and outperformed this benchmark over the 10-year period to 2018. The results demonstrate the difficulty of improving returns through tactical allocation strategies.

2.2 Investment Vehicles

Investment vehicles in the market can be broadly categorised into direct and indirect investments. Direct investments allow investors to exercise control over specific assets to purchase and transaction time. Indirect investments are made primarily through collective investment schemes managed by professional asset managers. The fund industry offers numerous investment products designed to meet different investor needs. Investing through indirect vehicles has become increasingly common for individual investors. This is partially due to the rise of passive strategies providing cost-effective investment solutions. Investors can earn market returns through index funds created to replicate the performance of market indices. Besides, factor investing has gained significant interest among institutional investors. Factor strategies target specific factors in a systematic and transparent way. They offer the potential for outperformance, while retaining the many benefits of passive investing.

A wide range of asset classes are available for investors to build diversified portfolios. Asset classes have different investment characteristics in terms of risk and return. They can be broadly divided into two categories: traditional and alternative investments. Traditional investments mainly refer to the three asset classes of stocks, bonds and cash. Stocks are generally classified as largecap, midcap, smallcap and microcap according to their market value. They are also commonly defined by their investment characteristics as value, growth or blend stocks. The interaction of size and style provides a set of investment choices for equity investors (e.g. largecap value, smallcap growth). These two variables are employed by the popular Morningstar Style Box to determine the positioning strategy of an investment fund. Besides, stocks can be fundamentally categorised by industry type according to their principal business activity. The GICS and ICB systems are widely used to classify companies into different industries. Stocks can also be defined by geographical location based on country or region, or simply classified as domestic or foreign investments. Bonds as a traditional asset class can be issued in many different forms. They are broadly represented by government and corporate bonds. Government bonds are debt securities issued by governments to finance public spending. Corporate bonds are issued by companies to raise capital for business purposes. Bonds can be segmented by credit quality into investment and speculative grades or grouped by term to maturity. Cash is known as a defensive asset class that plays a central role in the construction of conservative portfolios. It comprises savings accounts, certificates of deposit, commercial paper, money market funds and other short-term debt instruments.

The broad category of alternative investments covers all assets that are beyond the scope of traditional asset classes. The CAIA Association classifies alternative investments into four categories: hedge funds, private equity, real assets and structured products [4]. Hedge funds pool money from investors and employ various strategies to pursue abnormal returns. Private equity is a pooled investment vehicle that provides capital to private companies with the objective to finance their restructuring or expansion. Venture capital and leveraged buyouts are the two primary forms of private equity investment. The real assets category covers physical assets with intrinsic value, such as commodities, real estate and infrastructure. Structured products are financial instruments that provide returns linked to the performance of an underlying asset or market index.

2.3 Investment Risk

Investment risk is the probability of an investment losing its value or failing to produce expected returns. Risk is an integral part of investment that cannot be completely avoided. It is an important factor to consider when making decisions on asset allocation and investment selection. Asset classes in the market have different investment characteristics regarding the risk level and return potential. A fundamental principle in finance is that greater risk requires higher expected return to compensate investors for taking on additional risk. The risk-return tradeoff means that investment assets with low perceived risk normally have limited return potential. For example, money market instruments are considered relatively safe investments and generally provide lower returns than equities. Successful investment requires a good understanding of different risks that can potentially affect investment results. This section presents a range of general investment risks that are frequently considered in investment analysis.

- **Market Risk**

Market risk can be defined as the potential risk of loss due to adverse movements in market prices. It affects the entire market and cannot be eliminated through diversification. Sources of market risk include economic recessions, political instability, trade wars, terrorist attacks and natural disasters. The coronavirus pandemic that ravaged the world in 2020 provides a good example of market risk. All major stock market indices across the globe fell sharply during the coronavirus outbreak.

- **Inflation Risk**

Inflation risk is the loss of purchasing power as a result of general increase in prices. Inflation risk is particularly acute for fixed-income instruments. An investment providing a nominal return of 3% will actually produce a negative real return of −2% in an environment of 5% inflation rate. Investment returns must exceed inflation to increase the real value of capital.

- **Currency Risk**

Currency risk is the potential risk of loss caused by the exposure to unfavourable currency movements. When investing in foreign markets, currency exposure is an important source of risk that must be carefully managed. Currency crises that happened in emerging markets over the last three decades resulted in substantial capital losses for foreign investors. A typical example is the severe devaluation of the Turkish lira in 2018 caused by the financial and economic crisis in Turkey.

- **Interest Rate Risk**

Interest rate risk is defined as the probability that the value of an investment will decline because of adverse movements in interest rates. Interest rate is used by central banks as a monetary policy to achieve price stability and manage economic fluctuations. Compared to equity investments, fixed-income assets are more susceptible to interest rate risk. Bond prices and market interest rates usually move in opposite directions.

- **Country Risk**

Country risk is the general level of uncertainty associated with investing in a specific country. It reflects the overall business environment of a country shaped by its economic, financial, political and social conditions. Countries with high risk (e.g. political instability) may find it difficult to attract foreign investment. Country risk is a critical factor to consider when investing in foreign countries.

- **Industry Risk**

Industry risk is the likelihood that a set of factors specific to an industry negatively affect its overall performance. Industry analysis forms an essential part of security analysis in equity investment. It can help investors understand the attractiveness of an industry by assessing growth prospects, industry structure, competitive forces and external factors.

- **Credit Risk**

Credit risk is the potential financial loss that arises from the failure of a borrower to make required payments to fulfil contractual obligations. Credit risk is a major concern for debt investors. Companies that experience financial difficulties may struggle to honour debt obligations. Credit rating agencies issue opinions to help investors understand the level of credit risk associated with a specific issuer or debt instrument.

- **Liquidity Risk**

Liquidity risk is defined as the risk that an asset cannot be traded quickly in the market without adversely affecting its price. The liquidation of the Woodford Equity Income Fund in 2019 was primarily caused by its excessive exposure to illiquid assets. Investors should balance the return potential of illiquid assets with their liquidity risk. Stocks with low liquidity generally have wide bid-ask spread and low trading volume in the market.

- **Volatility Risk**

Volatility risk is the potential loss caused by fluctuations in the price of an asset. High volatility means large dispersion of returns and great investment risk. While price volatility presents opportunities to buy assets at attractive valuations, it also indicates a high probability of investment loss. The most common measure of price volatility is the standard deviation of price changes.

- **Downside Risk**

Downside risk is the potential size of loss in the value of an investment. Downside protection is an essential aspect of risk management in investing that seeks to reduce the probability and magnitude of capital loss. Common measures of downside risk include: value at risk (VaR), expected shortfall (ES) and maximum drawdown (MDD). VaR is the maximum loss expected on an investment based on a given time horizon and probability. ES measures the expected size of a loss that exceeds the VaR level. MDD is the largest peak-to-trough decline in an investment over a specific time period.

2.4 Performance Attribution

Performance evaluation is an integral part of the investment process. It seeks to understand and assess investment results against defined investment objectives. Performance evaluation mainly involves the tasks of performance measurement, attribution and appraisal. Investors may be particularly interested in performance attribution to gain valuable insight into portfolio returns. Performance attribution is a quantitative method used to explain the excess return of a portfolio relative to its benchmark. It seeks to identify the sources of return by decomposing the excess return into different components. This analysis can help portfolio managers understand performance drivers and improve investment decisions. Historically, a number of quantitative models have been developed for the purpose of performance attribution. The Brinson model is one of the major developments in attribution analysis. This model was introduced in two short papers published respectively in 1985 and 1986 [5, 6]. Despite its simplicity and intuitive appeal, the Brinson method is widely considered a foundation for portfolio performance attribution.

The Brinson model decomposes the excess return into three attribution terms: asset allocation, investment selection and interaction between the two terms. For a portfolio composed of N asset classes, the portfolio return r is calculated as:

$$r = \sum_{i=1}^{N} w_i \times r_i$$

where w_i and r_i are respectively the weight and return of asset class i in the portfolio. Similarly, the return of the benchmark b is:

$$b = \sum_{i=1}^{N} W_i \times R_i$$

where W_i and R_i are the weight and return of asset class i in the benchmark. The sum of weights should be equal to 1:

$$\sum_{i=1}^{N} w_i = 1 \text{ and } \sum_{i=1}^{N} W_i = 1$$

The excess return $r - b$ is calculated as:

$$r - b = \sum_{i=1}^{N} w_i \times r_i - \sum_{i=1}^{N} W_i \times R_i$$

The Brinson model decomposes the above excess return into three components:

$$\text{Allocation effect: } \sum_{i=1}^{N} (w_i - W_i) \times R_i$$

$$\text{Selection effect: } \sum_{i=1}^{N} W_i \times (r_i - R_i)$$

$$\text{Interaction effect: } \sum_{i=1}^{N} (w_i - W_i) \times (r_i - R_i)$$

For the allocation term, the contribution by asset class i is: $(w_i - W_i) \times R_i$. This implies that the contribution is positive if an overweight asset class (i.e. $w_i > W_i$) successfully delivers a positive return (i.e. $R_i > 0$). In fact, the contribution should also be considered positive if a negative return produced by an overweight asset class still exceeds the overall benchmark return. For this reason, the allocation effect is amended to be:

$$\text{Allocation effect: } \sum_{i=1}^{N} (w_i - W_i) \times (R_i - b)$$

The contribution by asset class i now becomes $(w_i - W_i) \times (R_i - b)$. Note that the modified formula provides exactly the same allocation effect as that from the original formula:

$$\sum_{i=1}^{N} (w_i - W_i) \times (R_i - b) = \sum_{i=1}^{N} (w_i - W_i) \times R_i - \sum_{i=1}^{N} (w_i - W_i) \times b$$

$$= \sum_{i=1}^{N} (w_i - W_i) \times R_i - b \times \left(\sum_{i=1}^{N} w_i - \sum_{i=1}^{N} W_i \right) = \sum_{i=1}^{N} (w_i - W_i) \times R_i - b \times (1 - 1)$$

$$= \sum_{i=1}^{N} (w_i - W_i) \times R_i$$

The interaction effect is included as an independent term in the model to ensure that the excess return is perfectly decomposed. In practice, the interaction effect is not very meaningful, because portfolio managers rarely seek to add value through this variable. It is intuitive to understand asset allocation and investment selection, but the interaction effect is a rather controversial concept. For this reason, the interaction term is often absorbed into the selection effect:

$$\text{Selection effect: } \sum_{i=1}^{N} W_i \times (r_i - R_i) + \sum_{i=1}^{N} (w_i - W_i) \times (r_i - R_i)$$

$$= \sum_{i=1}^{N} w_i \times (r_i - R_i)$$

Table 2.1 provides a simple example to illustrate performance attribution with the Brinson model. The portfolio outperformed its benchmark by 6.0% during the period. The excess return is primarily explained by the selection effect (5.0%). The health care sector made the largest contribution of 2.0% to the allocation effect. It had a 10% overweight position in the portfolio and produced a positive return of 20% in the benchmark. In contrast, the underweight position in the financials sector resulted in the most negative contribution of −1.5% to the allocation effect. Compared to the benchmark, the portfolio maintained a neutral position of 10% in the energy sector. This means that this sector had no effect on the performance of asset allocation. However, the energy sector was actually the best contributor (4.0%) to the selection effect, resulting primarily from the significant relative return (40%). The portfolio failed to show good selection skill in the utilities sector. Its underperformance (−25%) in this sector caused the worst contribution of −2.5% to the selection effect.

The Brinson model explains the arithmetic difference of return between a portfolio and its benchmark. If the portfolio and benchmark returns are 10% and 8% respectively, then the arithmetic excess return is simply 2%. The problem with arithmetic attribution is that it cannot be directly applied for multi-period performance attribution. This is because arithmetic excess return cannot be compounded over multiple periods. To overcome this problem, a feasible solution is to use geometric attribution models that calculate relative performance based on geometric excess return. Alternative solutions include the use of smoothing and linking algorithms to combine single-period performance attributions. Another weakness of the Brinson model is that attribution results are subject to the grouping variables used

Table 2.1 Performance attribution with the Brinson model

Sector	Portfolio		Benchmark		Allocation	Selection	Interaction
	Weight	Return	Weight	Return			
Energy	10%	20%	10%	-20%	0.0%	4.0%	0.0%
Materials	5%	10%	5%	0%	0.0%	0.5%	0.0%
Industrials	5%	-20%	10%	-10%	0.5%	-1.0%	0.5%
Consumer Discretionary	10%	-10%	5%	-20%	-1.0%	0.5%	0.5%
Consumer Staples	5%	10%	10%	0%	0.0%	1.0%	-0.5%
Health Care	20%	20%	10%	20%	2.0%	0.0%	0.0%
Financials	5%	10%	20%	10%	-1.5%	0.0%	0.0%
Information Technology	20%	5%	10%	10%	1.0%	-0.5%	-0.5%
Communication Services	5%	-10%	5%	-20%	0.0%	0.5%	0.0%
Utilities	10%	-5%	10%	20%	0.0%	-2.5%	0.0%
Real Estate	5%	10%	5%	-40%	0.0%	2.5%	0.0%
Total:	100%	6.0%	100%	0.0%	1.0%	5.0%	0.0%

in the analysis. For example, a Brinson attribution may select country as the single factor to perform attribution analysis. The attribution results are expected to change if sector is selected instead as the grouping variable. Due to the limitations of the Brinson framework, advanced performance attribution often relies on risk factor models. The following section briefly introduces the principle of multifactor models.

Multifactor models are constructed under the general framework of the arbitrage pricing theory (APT) proposed by the economist Stephen Ross in 1976 [7]. This theory holds that the expected return of an asset can be expressed as a linear combination of multiple risk factors. The sensitivity to changes in a factor is represented by a beta coefficient (i.e. factor exposure). Factor models can be broadly classified into three categories: macroeconomic, fundamental and statistical models. Macroeconomic factor models use observable economic variables (e.g. interest rate, inflation) to explain the behaviour of asset returns. Fundamental factor models employ security attributes (e.g. earnings growth, profit margin) to define factors and estimate their returns. Statistical factor models utilise statistical methods to examine patterns in return data and derive underlying factors. According to a research paper in the Financial Analysts Journal [8], fundamental factor models have better performance in explaining security returns than the other two types. To model the returns of N securities, fundamental factor models can be expressed in the general matrix form as:

$$R = BF + E$$

Here, R is the $N \times 1$ matrix of absolute returns (or relative returns against the risk-free rate). R is usually measured in local currency to control the currency effect on security returns. B is the $N \times M$ matrix of beta coefficients representing factor exposures (i.e. sensitivity to changes in a factor). F is the $M \times 1$ matrix of factor returns. E is the $N \times 1$ matrix of specific returns (i.e. residual returns unexplained by the model). The above expression shows that a security return can be decomposed into the return due to the exposure to common factors and the residual portion unique to the security. Factor returns are usually estimated by using regression analysis on observed security returns. Return contribution to a security by a specific factor is simply the product of the estimated factor return and the security exposure to the factor.

Different fundamental factor models are available from leading risk model providers, such as Axioma, Barra and Northfield. These commercial models can help portfolio analysts easily perform attribution analysis. Under the general APT framework, investment managers have great flexibility in developing their own factor models. A multifactor fundamental equity risk model consisting of the market factor, style factors, industries and countries can be defined as:

$$R_i = F_m + \sum_j \beta_{i,j}^S F_j^S + \sum_k \beta_{i,k}^I F_k^I + \sum_l \beta_{i,l}^C F_l^C + \varepsilon_i$$

R_i is the local return of stock i, F_m is the market return, F_j^S is the return of style factor j, F_k^I is the return of industry k, F_l^C is the return of country l, $\beta_{i,j}^S$ is the exposure of stock i to style factor j, $\beta_{i,k}^I$ is the exposure of stock i to industry k, $\beta_{i,l}^C$ is the exposure of stock i to country l, and ε_i is the return specific to stock i that is unexplained by the model. This model specifies that the observed stock return can be expressed as a linear function of fundamental risk factors. Whereas the categories for industry and country can be easily determined, there is no market consensus regarding the composition of style factors. Commercial factor model vendors have their own methodology in the definition and measurement of style factors. Common style factors used in fundamental models include size, quality, growth, value, momentum, volatility and liquidity. These factors are usually measured by a combination of individual risk metrics. For example, the quality factor is often represented by the metrics of return on equity, earnings volatility and financial leverage.

The market return F_m is captured by the market factor and often represents the main source of risk and return for equities. All stocks in the factor model have a unit exposure to the market factor. For industries and countries, individual factor exposures can only be 1 or 0. If stock i belongs to industry k and country l, then its factor exposures $\beta_{i,k}^I$ and $\beta_{i,l}^C$ are equal to 1 (0 otherwise). This means that a Japanese stock in the financial industry will have an exposure of 1 to both Japan and Financials, while its exposures to all other industries and countries are invariably 0. To calculate exposures for style factors, raw scores of factor components are first standardised to z-scores and combined with weighted average. The resulting composite scores are further standardised to obtain factor exposures. After the calculation of factor exposures, regression analysis is performed to estimate factor returns. The factor model can be used to decompose the absolute return of a portfolio. The contribution to portfolio return by a factor is the product of the factor return and the portfolio exposure to this factor. The portfolio exposure is calculated as the weighted average of stock exposures. Besides, the factor model can be applied for performance attribution. The absolute returns of a portfolio and its benchmark are first decomposed independently. The results of the two decompositions are then combined to identify the sources of excess return.

Table 2.2 provides an example to explain return decomposition with the above fundamental factor model. This simplified model only contains 11 factors: the market factor, 3 style factors, 4 industries and 3 countries. Factor returns are estimated by linear regression on observed stock returns. The portfolio only held four stocks with equal weighting. Stock exposures to different factors are shown in the table. In this example, stock 1 is a German company in the materials sector. Its exposures to the three style factors were -0.5 (size), 0.5 (quality) and -0.5 (value) respectively. The exposure to the market factor is invariably equal to 1 for all stocks. Factor exposure at the portfolio level is simply the average of stock exposures according to equal weighting. The contribution to portfolio return by a specific factor is calculated as the product of portfolio exposure and factor return. For example, the return contribution by the size factor was 0.75%, resulting from the positive portfolio exposure (0.50) and factor return (1.5%). Although the value factor produced a negative return of -1.0% during the period, its contribution to portfolio performance was still positive at 0.50%. This is because the portfolio had a negative exposure to the value factor (-0.50). Health care was the best performance contributor (1.0%) among the four industries, primarily due to its strong return of 4.0% over the period. The total return contribution by all factors is equal to 14.0%. If the actual portfolio return is 20%, then 6% is unexplained by the model and can be attributed to stock selection skill.

Table 2.2 Return decomposition with a fundamental risk factor model

Factor	Factor Return	Factor Exposure					Return Contr.
		Stock 1	Stock 2	Stock 3	Stock 4	Portfolio	
Market	10.0%	1	1	1	1	1	10.00%
Size	1.5%	-0.5	1.5	-1.0	2.0	0.50	0.75%
Quality	2.0%	0.5	1.0	1.5	0.0	0.75	1.50%
Value	-1.0%	-0.5	-1.0	-1.5	1.0	-0.50	0.50%
Materials	2.0%	1	0	0	0	0.25	0.50%
Financials	-1.0%	0	0	0	1	0.25	-0.25%
Health Care	4.0%	0	1	0	0	0.25	1.00%
Utilities	0.0%	0	0	1	0	0.25	0.00%
Germany	-1.0%	1	0	0	0	0.25	-0.25%
France	-0.5%	0	1	0	1	0.50	-0.25%
Italy	2.0%	0	0	1	0	0.25	0.50%
						Total:	14.00%

References

1. *The Yale Endowment 2019*. 2019, Yale Investments Office.
2. *Investor Guide: Asset Allocation*. 2015, Columbia Threadneedle Investments.
3. McCullough, A., *Do Tactical-Allocation Funds Deliver?* 2019, Morningstar ETF Specialist.
4. Chambers, D.R., Black, K.H. and Lacey, N.J., *Alternative Investments: A Primer for Investment Professionals*. 2018, CAIA Association.
5. Brinson, G.P. and Fachler, N., *Measuring Non-US Equity Portfolio Performance*. Journal of Portfolio Management, 1985. **11**(3): p. 73–76.
6. Brinson, G.P., Hood, L.R. and Beebower, G.L., *Determinants of Portfolio Performance*. Financial Analysts Journal, 1986. **42**(4): p. 39–44.
7. Ross, S.A., *The Arbitrage Theory of Capital Asset Pricing*. Journal of Economic Theory, 1976. **13**(3): p. 341–360.
8. Connor, G., *The Three Types of Factor Models: A Comparison of Their Explanatory Power*. Financial Analysts Journal, 1995. **51**(3): p. 42–46.

3

Common Stock

3.1 Equity Investments

Equity securities represent a partial ownership interest in a company. Equity investors are entitled to share company profits and exercise certain control over company management. Both companies and investors can potentially benefit from the form of equity investment. Companies raise equity capital from investors primarily to fund business growth or improve financial position. Equity investors purchase company shares in the expectation that the invested capital will provide returns in the form of capital growth and dividend income. Equities represent a major asset class that has the potential to generate superior returns in the long term. At the end of June 2020, Apple, Microsoft, Amazon and Alphabet were ranked as the four largest companies in the United States by market value ($1.6, $1.5, $1.4 and $1.0 trillion respectively). On 2 August 2018, Apple passed the $1 trillion mark to become the first American company that ever reached this valuation level in history. Only after two years, Apple achieved a new milestone of $2 trillion in its market value on 19 August 2020. Its share price increased by over 625 times (i.e. 34.0% per annum) from January 1998 to December 2019. As a leading technology company, Microsoft delivered an annualised price return of 23.1% to its investors between 1987 and 2019. In comparison, the S&P 500 Index produced an average price return of 8.2% per year during the same period. Founded by Jeff Bezos in 1994, Amazon experienced phenomenal growth and reshaped the entire retail landscape in the subsequent 25 years.

© The Author(s), under exclusive license to Springer Nature
Switzerland AG 2022
B. Jiang, *Investment Strategies*,
https://doi.org/10.1007/978-3-030-82711-3_3

Amazon witnessed its share price rise from $1.54 to $2,758.82 through the 23 years to June 2020, posting an annualised return of 38.5%. Alphabet, the parent company of Google, joined the $1 trillion club on 16 January 2020. It generated an annualised return of 19.2% over the 15 years to December 2019. This represents an excess return of more than 10.0% per year relative to the S&P 500 Index during the 15-year period.

Equity securities can be issued and traded in private or public markets. Private equity securities are highly illiquid and primarily offered to institutional investors through private placements. It is more common for companies to raise capital through public offerings. Public equities are listed on a stock exchange and easily accessible to investors. They generally provide reasonable liquidity and often form a core component of a diversified investment portfolio. Common stock (i.e. ordinary shares) is the main type of public equities issued by companies. It allows investors to have an ownership stake in a company and participate in major corporate decisions (e.g. board elections, executive compensation) through voting rights. Whereas common stock provides no guarantee of dividend payments, its most attractive feature is that the upside return potential is almost unlimited. The value of a company with favourable growth and earnings prospects can rise substantially over time. The primary risk of common stock is that its value can fall to zero. In the event of bankruptcy, common shareholders are generally the last to have a residual claim on company assets. Companies may also issue preferred stock (i.e. preference shares) to give its owners certain advantages over common shareholders. Although preferred stock usually carries no voting rights, it has priority over common stock in terms of dividend payments and claim on company assets upon liquidation. Preferred stock is generally considered a hybrid financial instrument, because it combines features of both debt and equity securities. Preference shares typically provide regular and fixed dividend payments which are higher than that on common shares. However, companies are not contractually obliged to pay dividends on preference shares. Preferred stock can be issued with conversion and call features. The conversion option allows investors to convert preference shares to common shares under certain conditions. The call provision gives the issuer the right to redeem preference shares at a specific call price before the maturity date.

Sector and country are among the fundamental risk factors used to classify stocks. MSCI and S&P Dow Jones Indices developed the GICS industry classification system in 1999. The GICS (Global Industry Classification Standard) structure consists of 11 sectors and 4 hierarchical tiers. Based on the

Table 3.1 Global sector weights

Sector	Weight
Information Technology	20.0%
Financials	13.3%
Health Care	12.9%
Consumer Discretionary	11.9%
Industrials	10.3%
Communication Services	8.6%
Consumer Staples	7.7%
Materials	5.0%
Real Estate	3.7%
Energy	3.4%
Utilities	3.2%

Source: MSCI

principal business activity, each company is assigned a single GICS classification at the sub-industry level. Table 3.1 shows the sector weights of the MSCI ACWI All Cap Index as of 30 June 2020 (source: index factsheet). This index captures approximately 99% of global equities across developed and emerging markets. The comprehensive coverage provided by this index offers valuable insight into the relative sizes of different sectors in the world. Information technology represents the largest sector by market value, followed by financials, health care, consumer discretionary and industrials. Due to the impact of falling oil prices, the energy sector has seen its weight in global equities shrink significantly to only 3.4%. Note that sector weights may change materially over different stages of a business cycle. This is because cyclical and defensive sectors respond differently in performance to changing economic conditions.

Table 3.2 displays country weights in the global equity market according to the S&P Global Broad Market Index as of 30 June 2020 (source: index factsheet). This market index comprises more than 11,000 stocks across 50 developed and emerging countries. It can provide a general idea of relative equity market size around the world. The United States has a dominant position in the index, accounting for 55.3% of global equities by market value. The next four positions are occupied by Japan (8.2%), China (4.7%), the United Kingdom (4.0%) and Canada (2.8%). These five countries represent about 75.0% of total equity market value in the world.

Table 3.2 Country weights in the global equity market

Rank	Country	Weight	Rank	Country	Weight
1	United States	55.3%	11	South Korea	1.6%
2	Japan	8.2%	12	India	1.4%
3	China	4.7%	13	Netherlands	1.1%
4	United Kingdom	4.0%	14	Sweden	1.0%
5	Canada	2.8%	15	Hong Kong	0.9%
6	Switzerland	2.7%	16	Italy	0.7%
7	France	2.7%	17	Spain	0.7%
8	Germany	2.5%	18	Brazil	0.7%
9	Australia	2.0%	19	Denmark	0.6%
10	Taiwan	1.6%	20	South Africa	0.4%

Source: S&P Dow Jones Indices

3.2 Equity Indices

An equity index is a portfolio of stocks constructed to measure the performance of an equity market or investment strategy. The market is saturated with numerous equity indices developed to meet different investor needs. Dow Jones Industrial Average (DJIA), Nasdaq Composite and S&P 500 are among the most widely followed market indices around the world. The DJIA index measures the performance of 30 large public companies in the United States. It adopts the simple price-weighting scheme to combine the returns of index constituents. Although DJIA is a closely watched market index, it is generally considered an inadequate representation of the overall US stock market due to the small sample size and weighting method. In comparison, the S&P 500 and Russell 3000 indices serve as a more comprehensive barometer of the broad US market. Stocks in both indices are weighted based on their float-adjusted market capitalisation. The free-float adjustment excludes the proportion of shares that are not available to the public. Indices constructed with this weighting method provide a more accurate reflection of market movements and the investable opportunity set. In Europe, the overall stock market is often represented by the STOXX Europe 600 Index. This index tracks the performance of 600 largest companies in Europe measured by float-adjusted market cap.

Leading global index providers include MSCI, S&P Dow Jones Indices, FTSE Russell and STOXX. They strictly maintain objective, transparent and investable rules in the construction of equity indices. Equity indices were originally developed to measure the performance of a broad equity market. They provide a valuable synthesis of overall market activity to help investors understand market sentiment and make informed investment decisions. It is often the case that the market factor is the primary source of risk and return in investment portfolios. Today equity indices are widely used by both active and passive funds in the investment management industry. Active funds seek to outperform a defined benchmark by exploiting pricing anomalies in the market. Equity indices are frequently used by investors to evaluate the performance of active funds in generating excess returns. They are also used as model portfolios for the development of passive investment products. Index funds follow the strategy of passive investing to track the performance of an underlying market index. For example, the iShares UK Equity Index Fund seeks to replicate the performance of the FTSE All Share Index designed to represent UK equities.

Equity indices can be largely classified into four main categories: broad market, multi-market, sector and style. A broad equity market index represents the performance of an entire stock market. For example, the Russell 3000 Index is composed of the largest 3,000 US companies capturing about 98% of the investable US equity market. The Nikkei 225 Index measures the performance of 225 large companies traded on the Tokyo Stock Exchange. A multi-market equity index consists of stocks from different countries to provide a broader representation of market performance. For instance, the MSCI ACWI Index covers about 85% of the global investable equity universe across developed and emerging markets. The S&P Global 1200 Index is constructed as a composite of multiple regional market indices to provide an efficient coverage to the global equity market. Sector indices track the returns of different economic sectors classified by GICS, ICB or other systems. MSCI and S&P Dow Jones Indices have created a wide range of sector indices from their flagship market indices (e.g. MSCI World Consumer Staples, S&P 500 Financials). Style indices are designed to measure the performance of securities classified according to one or more characteristics, such as market capitalisation and valuation. A simple example is the FTSE 250 Index representing the midcap segment of stocks listed on the London Stock Exchange. As a leading provider of factor indices, MSCI has created a series of style indices to support the development of factor strategies (e.g. MSCI World Quality Index). Factor indices seek to capture the performance of factors that are expected to generate excess returns in the long term. Style factors are often combined to form multifactor strategies for the purpose of reducing portfolio volatility and enhancing return potential. For example, the MSCI World Diversified Multiple-Factor Index is constructed to maximise exposure to four factors: value, momentum, quality and low size.

3.3 Long-Term Performance

Equities have proved their ability to generate superior returns in the long term. This can be illustrated by the historical performance of the S&P 500 Index. From 1926 to 2019, this broad US equity market index delivered an annualised total return of 9.8%. Based on this performance, an investment of $100 made at the beginning of 1926 would grow to about $655,571 in 2019. Assume the average annual inflation rate was 3.0% during the entire period. After 94 years, the initial investment would see its inflation-adjusted value increase by about 406 times, resulting from the strong performance of the S&P 500 Index. Historically, equities have delivered higher long-term returns than most asset classes. Figure 3.1 examines the risk and return profiles of five asset classes based on their performance over the 40 years to 2019. Equities, bonds, cash, real estate and gold are represented respectively by the S&P 500 Index, ICE BofA 3–5 Year US Corporate Index, 3-month Treasury bill, NCREIF Property Index and gold spot price. Equities produced an annualised return of 11.8% during the 40 years, outperforming real estate (8.7%), bonds (7.6%), cash (4.3%) and gold (2.8%). The outperformance of equities was delivered with the highest volatility. The results support the observation that equities are generally positioned at the higher end of the risk and return spectrum among common asset classes.

Long-term real returns on equities, bonds and bills in different countries are available in the Global Investment Returns Yearbook published annually by Credit Suisse. This report is co-authored by Professor Elroy Dimson,

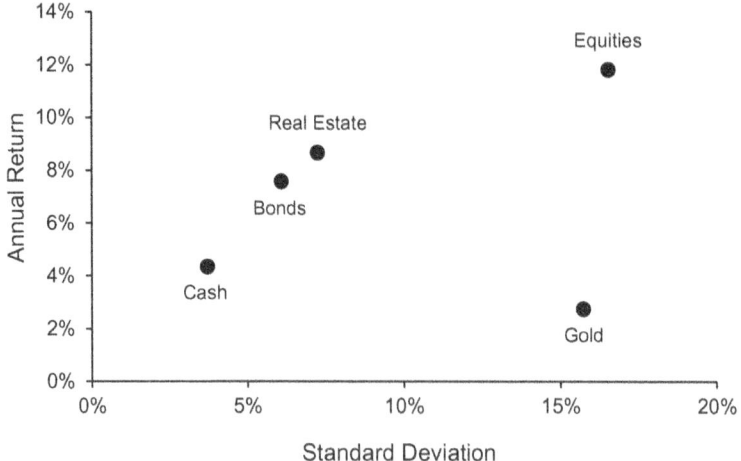

Fig. 3.1 Historical performance and risk of five asset classes (1980–2019)

Professor Paul Marsh and Dr. Mike Staunton at London Business School. The long-term returns of major asset classes around the world are first produced in their book *Triumph of the Optimists: 101 Years of Global Investment Returns* (Princeton University Press, 2002) [1]. According to the 2020 Yearbook [2], the average annual inflation rate in the US is estimated to be 2.9% between 1900 and 2019. During the 120-year period, US equities generated an annualised return of 6.5% in real terms. This performance completely dominates the average annual real returns provided by US Treasury bonds (2.0%) and bills (0.8%). Developed markets outside the US also produced strong real equity returns over the same period, such as the UK (5.5%), Switzerland (4.6%) and Japan (4.2%). Over the 120 years, the global equity market achieved an annualised real return of 5.2% with a standard deviation of 17.4%. This represents a return premium of 3.1% per year relative to government bonds. The equity premium against bonds is consistently significant across the 21 countries analysed in the report. The results demonstrate the strength of equities in delivering attractive excess returns over the long term.

3.4 Equity Risk

Equities have the potential to deliver significant long-term returns comprising a combination of capital appreciation and dividend income. However, they are essentially risky assets that can result in substantial losses. Share prices may decline significantly at any time and potentially fall to zero. In the event of liquidation, common shareholders will likely lose all capital invested. This is because they rank behind debtholders and preference shareholders when exercising claims on company assets. The residual claim will have no value until all company liabilities have been satisfied. Investors should be mindful of the great risk inherent in stock investment. Figure 3.2 shows the historical share prices of Wirecard from January 2016 to June 2020. Wirecard is a German technology company that provides payment processing and risk management services. For many years, Wirecard continually reported fast revenue growth and increased earnings guidance. Its share price experienced a dramatic increase of more than 300% in under two years, reaching an all-time high of €199 on 4 September 2018. Wirecard replaced Commerzbank in 2018 to join the prestigious DAX Index composed of the 30 largest companies listed on the Frankfurt Stock Exchange. However, the Financial Times wrote a series of articles that questioned the success story and accounting practices of Wirecard. On 18 June 2020, Wirecard shares crashed 61.8% as its auditor EY warned that €1.9 billion in cash was missing from

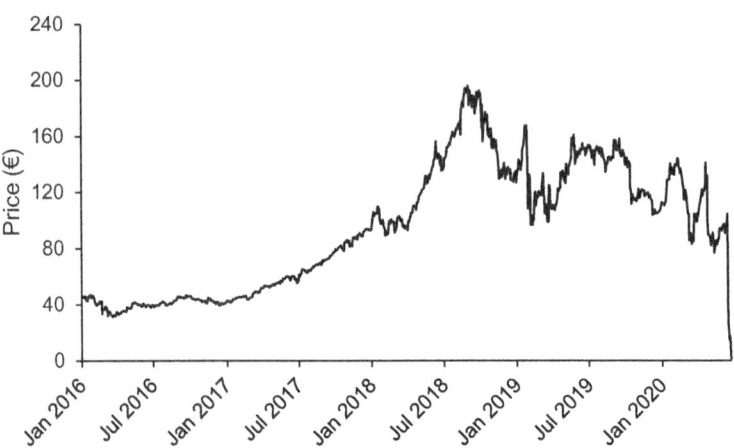

Fig. 3.2 The dramatic rise and collapse of Wirecard shares

the balance sheet. Subsequently, it was revealed that Wirecard committed a series of accounting frauds involving multiple parties around the world. As the accounting scandal exploded, the share price of Wirecard plunged from €104.50 to only €1.28 after 7 trading days. On 25 June 2020, Wirecard filed for insolvency proceedings on the grounds of impending insolvency and over-indebtedness. Its dramatic fall from grace highlights the importance of corporate governance in protecting the interests of investors.

The Wirecard case shows the value of diversification in mitigating company-specific risk. A diversified portfolio limits exposure to any single asset to control the impact of extreme losses. However, diversification cannot reduce systematic market risk. Share prices can move sharply in reaction to economic and market events. On 15 September 2008, Lehman Brothers as the fourth largest investment bank in the US declared bankruptcy. The dramatic collapse triggered the plunge of stock markets around the world. The Dow Jones and S&P 500 indices tumbled by 4.4% and 4.7% respectively on that day. During the financial crisis in 2008, the S&P 500 Index suffered a maximum drawdown of 56.8% from the peak value of 1,565.15 on 9 October 2007. In 2020, global stock markets fell sharply in response to the outbreak of the coronavirus pandemic. The FTSE 100 Index plunged by 7.7% on 9 March 2020 and crashed another 10.9% on 12 March 2020. The S&P 500 Index plummeted into bear market territory, falling 7.6% and 9.5% respectively on these two trading days. It suffered another historic decline of 12.0% on 16 March 2020, recording a cumulative loss of 29.2% within a month. Figure 3.3 displays the historical price movements of the S&P 500 Index over the period covering the 2008 financial crisis and 2020 coronavirus

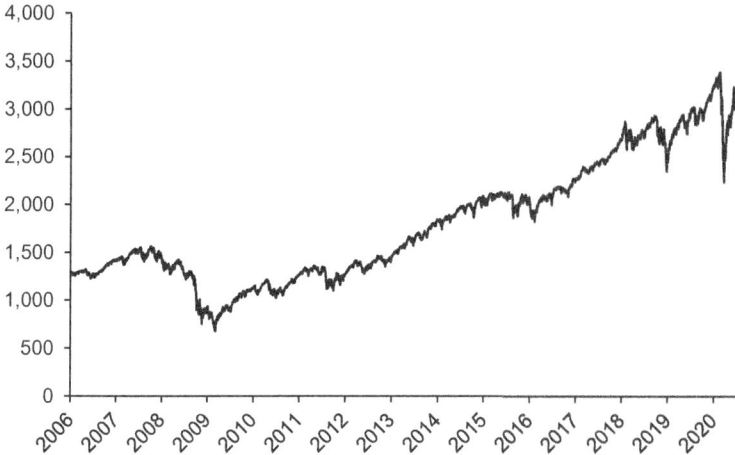

Fig. 3.3 Historical price of the S&P 500 Index (January 2006–June 2020)

outbreak. It is interesting to see how quickly this broad market index recovered from deep losses. After reaching the trough on 9 March 2009, the S&P 500 Index delivered a phenomenal return of 68.6% in the next 12 months. The recovery speed during the coronavirus crisis is even more impressive. The S&P 500 Index was sent into freefall by the eruption of the coronavirus disease. Subsequently, it rebounded sharply following a month of unprecedented chaos. From the lowest point of 2,237 on 23 March 2020, the S&P 500 Index climbed to 3,232 on 8 June 2020. This represents a price return of 44.5% in under 3 months. The strong rally helped this broad market benchmark recoup nearly all losses caused by the coronavirus crisis.

The volatile nature of the stock market indicates that investing in equities requires a long-term view. The performance of equities relative to bonds and cash is very uncertain in the short term. However, historical evidence shows that the chance of outperformance by equities often increases as the investment horizon lengthens. This is illustrated by the results in Table 3.3 where equities are based on the S&P 500 Index. Bonds and cash are represented by the 10-year US Treasury note and 3-month US Treasury bill respectively. For each holding period, monthly rolling returns of the three asset classes are calculated over the time period between 1990 and 2019. The resulting sample of rolling returns is used to determine the frequency of outperformance by equities. As shown in the table, the frequency largely increases with the holding period. For the 3-month holding period, equities outperformed cash with a moderate frequency of 68.4%. For the 1-year holding

Table 3.3 Holding period and the frequency of outperformance by equities

Holding Period (in months)	vs Bonds	vs Cash
1	62.2%	64.2%
3	66.8%	68.4%
6	70.1%	74.1%
12	76.5%	80.8%
24	78.3%	80.1%
120	80.1%	87.1%
180	99.4%	100.0%

period, the frequency of outperformance improved to 80.8%. Equities never underperformed cash when the holding period is extended to 15 years.

3.5 Distribution of Stock Returns

Empirical studies show that the distribution of cumulative stock returns is very skewed. The overall market return is primarily determined by a small proportion of stocks. The research paper *The Capitalism Distribution* provides empirical evidence on the skewed distribution of stock returns [3]. The research analyses the performance of the Russell 3000 Index members between 1983 and 2006. According to the research findings, the return of the US stock market over the entire period could be fully explained by the 25% best-performing stocks. Investors would earn a total return of 0% if their portfolios unfortunately held the bottom 75% of stocks during the period. Besides, 64% of stocks underperformed the Russell 3000 Index in their lifetime. These results indicate the difficulty of finding superior stocks to outperform the market. The skewness of the return distribution can also be confirmed by the absolute returns of individual stocks. The top 14% of stocks achieved an annualised return of more than 20%, compared to the bottom 65% with an annualised return below 10%. Over the 24-year period, 39% of stocks were unprofitable investments with a negative lifetime return.

A J.P. Morgan study analyses the returns of about 13,000 stocks that were members of the Russell 3000 Index from 1980 to 2014 [4]. The results show that 40% of all stocks provided negative absolute returns and about two thirds underperformed the index during their lifetime. Besides, roughly 40% of stocks in the sample suffered a permanent decline of over 70% from their peak value. A research conducted by S&P Dow Jones Indices provides further evidence that the distribution of stock returns is skewed [5]. The research examines the pattern of cumulative returns for the constituents of the S&P 500 Index over the 20 years to May 2016. For all stocks in the sample, the median cumulative return was 141%, noticeably lower than the average return of 377%. This is because 70% of stocks produced a cumulative return below the sample average. The conclusion is that the performance of the S&P 500 Index is driven by its best-performing constituents.

A paper in the Journal of Financial Economics also reveals that strong returns in the equity market are concentrated in a small percentage of stocks [6]. The paper analyses the returns of about 25,000 US stocks in the CRSP database from July 1926 to December 2016. The CRSP database covers all common stocks listed on the NYSE, Amex and Nasdaq exchanges. The research found the top-performing 4% of stocks were disproportionately responsible for the entire outperformance of the US stock market against the 1-month US Treasury bills over the 90-year period. Remarkably, the aggregate performance provided by the other 96% of stocks only matched the return on 1-month Treasury bills during the period. In addition, more than 50% of the stocks in the database produced a negative lifetime return (including reinvested dividends) and only about 43% managed to outperform 1-month Treasury bills. The results underline the importance of diversification in portfolio management. Concentration increases the probability of missing the relatively few stellar stocks in the market. The skewed distribution of stock returns really presents a serious challenge for investors to beat the market through stock selection. Individual investors even have a lower chance of identifying superior stocks than institutional investors due to limited investment expertise and resources. Therefore, investing through professionally managed funds is probably an ideal option for most individual investors to earn reasonable returns.

References

1. Dimson, E., Marsh, P. and Staunton, M., *Triumph of the Optimists: 101 Years of Global Investment Returns*. 2002, Princeton University Press.
2. Dimson, E., Marsh, P. and Staunton, M., *Credit Suisse Global Investment Returns Yearbook 2020 (Summary Edition)*. 2020, Credit Suisse.
3. Wilcox, C. and Crittenden, E., *The Capitalism Distribution*. 2008, Longboard Asset Management.
4. Cembalest, M., *The Agony and the Ecstasy: The Risks and Rewards of a Concentrated Stock Position*. 2014, J.P. Morgan Asset Management.

5. Edwards, T. and Lazzara, C.J., *Fooled by Conviction*. 2016, S&P Dow Jones Indices.
6. Bessembinder, H., *Do Stocks Outperform Treasury Bills?* Journal of Financial Economics, 2018. **129**(3): p. 440–457.

4

Bonds and Cash

4.1 Bonds

Asset allocation is one of the most critical decisions in the investment process. Equities and bonds are fundamental asset classes frequently used to construct investment portfolios. While equities provide an ownership interest in a company, bonds represent a financial obligation that the issuer is required to make periodic interest payments to investors until the maturity date. Bond issuers are typically companies and governments seeking to raise capital in primary bond markets. Corporate bonds are issued by companies to raise money for business purposes, such as to fund product development or strengthen financial position. Government bonds are offered by governments primarily to support public spending. Securities issued by the US Department of the Treasury have the lowest level of default risk among all debt instruments. This is because they are backed by the full faith and credit of the US government. Since US Treasury securities are liquid and almost free of credit risk, their yields can help investors determine minimum interest rates required on different debt instruments in the market. Bonds can be classified into a number of categories, including fixed-rate bonds, floating-rate notes, zero-coupon and inflation-linked bonds. Since the 1980s, the bond market has changed dramatically in terms of market structure and product diversity. Today, many complex bond products with advanced features are available in the market to meet different investor needs.

The obligations of the issuer and the rights of bondholders are specified in the bond indenture. A bond indenture is a legal agreement that specifies the basic features and conditions relating to a bond issue, such as maturity date, face value and coupon rate. The maturity date is the time when the bond issuer must redeem the bond by paying the principal value. Bond maturities typically range from 1 to 30 years. The face value is the amount that the issuer is obligated to pay bondholders at the maturity date. The coupon rate is the nominal interest rate that the issuer promises to pay until the bond matures. For example, if a bond has a face value of $1,000 and a coupon rate of 5%, then the total amount of annual coupon payments is $50. The yield required by the market may deviate significantly from the nominal yield indicated by the coupon rate. For a standard fixed-rate bond, the relationship between the coupon rate and the required yield directly affects its market price relative to the face value. If the yield exactly matches the coupon rate, the bond trades at the face value in the market. If the yield is higher (lower) than the coupon rate, then the bond trades at a discount (premium) to the face value. For the above example, assume the maturity is 10 years and the coupon is paid annually. If the required yield is 5%, the bond price will be equal to the face value of $1,000. When the required yield increases to 6%, the market price of the bond falls to about $926. Conversely, if the yield declines to 4%, the bond is expected to trade at a premium price of $1,081. As a basic principle in bond investing, bond prices move in the opposite direction of yields. Table 4.1 illustrates the inverse relationship based on the present value of future bond payments under different yields. The results show that the bond price falls steadily as the required yield increases from 3% to 7%.

Table 4.1 The inverse relationship between bond price and yield

Year	Payment	Present Value				
		3%	4%	5%	6%	7%
1	50	48.5	48.1	47.6	47.2	46.7
2	50	47.1	46.2	45.4	44.5	43.7
3	50	45.8	44.4	43.2	42.0	40.8
4	50	44.4	42.7	41.1	39.6	38.1
5	50	43.1	41.1	39.2	37.4	35.6
6	50	41.9	39.5	37.3	35.2	33.3
7	50	40.7	38.0	35.5	33.3	31.1
8	50	39.5	36.5	33.8	31.4	29.1
9	50	38.3	35.1	32.2	29.6	27.2
10	50	37.2	33.8	30.7	27.9	25.4
10	1,000	744.1	675.6	613.9	558.4	508.3
	Price:	1,171	1,081	1,000	926	860

4.2 Investment Benefits

Bonds represent a major asset class that plays a fundamental role in the construction of investment portfolios. They are mainly traded by financial institutions, such as pension funds, insurance companies and investment managers. Pension funds and insurance companies typically buy bonds to match their liabilities. Individual investors can easily gain exposure to bond assets by allocating capital to bond funds in the market. Bonds are essentially conservative investments used frequently to form the core of defensive portfolios. Compared to equities, bonds are generally considered safer investments with a lower level of volatility risk. Bondholders enjoy certain protections and priority over shareholders. In the event of company liquidation, bondholders are ranked above shareholders in the claim on company assets. Overall, bonds offer investors four primary investment benefits: income stream, capital preservation, capital growth and diversification. While many investments can generate income, bonds are the asset class that provides the most predictable income streams in the form of coupon payments. Even when the prevailing market interest rates are low, many bonds can still offer attractive yields due to the great diversity of the bond market. Bonds with high credit ratings provide an effective solution to preserve capital. The face value of a bond is returned to the bondholder at the maturity date. This can be an attractive feature for investors concerned about losing investment capital. Besides, bonds have the potential to provide capital growth. Bonds with price appreciation may be sold in the secondary markets before they mature.

Diversification is a primary consideration when holding bonds in portfolios. Bonds are generally considered less sensitive to economic conditions than stocks. Historically, the correlation between bonds and equities has been fairly unstable. Graham Capital Management conducted a research to analyse the equity-bond correlation since the 1870s [1]. Equities and bonds are represented by the S&P 500 Index and 10-year US Treasury bond respectively. Their monthly returns are used to calculate rolling 5-year correlations over the period of more than 140 years. The research found the equity-bond correlation was positive about two thirds of the time. The instability of the correlation is the result of dynamic interactions among a set of macroeconomic factors. According to a research paper in the Journal of Fixed Income, economic outlook, market volatility, inflation and monetary policy are the four key factors that can potentially affect the correlation between equities and bonds [2]. For example, economic growth and volatility shocks often cause stock and bond prices to move in opposite directions. Stocks tend to outperform bonds during economic expansions and underperform when the economy contracts. In times of market turmoil, US Treasury bonds usually rise in price as the flight to safety happens.

4.3 Bond Risk

Bonds offer a steady source of income and represent a safer asset class than equities. Despite their defensive characteristics, bonds still expose investors to many different types of investment risk. Liquidity, currency and inflation are among the common risk factors to consider when investing in bonds. Liquidity risk arises when a bond cannot be sold quickly in the market at a fair price. Bonds overall carry higher liquidity risk than equities, because they are primarily traded in over-the-counter markets rather than public exchanges. Currency risk is the loss in the value of a bond resulting from adverse currency movements. This is a common risk when investing in assets denominated in a foreign currency. Inflation risk is the decrease in the real value of a bond caused by inflation. This happens when the inflation rate exceeds the rate of return earned on a bond investment. Bond investors concerned about inflation risk can buy inflation-linked bonds. These special bonds have variable principal and coupon payments linked to an inflation measure (e.g. consumer price index).

Bond investors are also exposed to investment risks that are more specific to fixed-income securities. These include reinvestment risk, credit risk and interest rate risk. Reinvestment risk is the possibility that proceeds received from coupon and principal payments must be reinvested at a lower rate of return. This often happens in an environment of falling interest rates. Credit risk in bond markets primarily includes three types: default, credit spread and downgrade. Default risk is the possibility that a bond issuer fails to fulfil the obligation of making scheduled coupon or principal payments. Credit spread risk is the potential loss in the value of a bond due to an increase in the yield spread. Downgrade risk is the probability that the credit rating of a bond issue or issuer is downgraded by major rating agencies. The deterioration in credit quality will have a negative impact on bond price.

Interest rate risk is a primary source of risk faced by bond investors. This is reflected in the inverse relationship between bond prices and interest rates. Bond prices typically increase when the prevailing interest rates in the market fall. This is because falling interest rates will make existing bonds more attractive to investors. Conversely, bond prices tend to decline in a market of rising interest rates. This allows bond yields to be adjusted upwards so that they align with the current market rates. In general, the price sensitivity of a bond to changes in interest rates increases with the length of maturity and decreases with the coupon rate. The effect of maturity can be illustrated by comparing 5-year and 20-year bonds. For the purpose of simplicity, assume both bonds have a yield of 5%, a face value of $100 and a coupon rate of 5% with annual coupon payments. Because the yield is equal to the coupon rate, the two bonds trade at the face value of $100 in the market. Suppose the rise of market interest rates pushes the required yield to 8%. Under this scenario, the price of the 5-year bond will fall to $88.02. The 20-year bond will experience a steeper price decline to $70.55. Most bond investors understand interest rate risk and the related concept of bond duration. Duration measures the approximate percentage change in the price of a bond resulting from a 1% change in the yield. For example, if interest rates rise by 1%, a bond with a duration of 5 will roughly lose 5% in value. Bonds with longer durations are more sensitive to interest rate movements than those with shorter durations. If interest rates are expected to fall, investors will prefer longer-duration bonds because their prices can increase more than comparable shorter-duration bonds. Duration is often actively managed by bond fund managers according to their views on future interest rates.

4.4 Credit Rating

A credit rating is a formal and independent evaluation of the credit risk associated with an entity or debt issue. It indicates the ability of an entity to meet its financial obligations or the probability of default for a specific debt instrument. Credit ratings are issued by independent rating agencies, such as S&P, Fitch and Moody's. These three rating agencies have a dominant position in the global credit rating market. Their credit opinions are widely followed by investors and other market participants. Table 4.2 shows that S&P, Fitch and Moody's use very similar rating systems to assess credit quality. The simple structure and symbols provide an efficient way to understand and compare credit ratings. The default risk increases as the credit rating becomes worse. Credit ratings can be broadly divided into two grades: investment and speculative. The investment grade indicates a low credit risk, while the speculative grade suggests a high probability of default. In general, bonds rated investment grade offer a lower yield than those rated speculative grade. Credit ratings of the investment grade range from AAA (or Aaa) to BBB− (or Baa3). According to S&P, the AAA rating represents extremely strong capacity to meet financial commitments [3]. The speculative grade covers the credit

Table 4.2 Major global credit rating systems

	S&P	Fitch	Moody's	Credit Quality
Investment Grade	AAA	AAA	Aaa	Highest
	AA+	AA+	Aa1	High
	AA	AA	Aa2	
	AA-	AA-	Aa3	
	A+	A+	A1	Upper Medium
	A	A	A2	
	A-	A-	A3	
	BBB+	BBB+	Baa1	Lower Medium
	BBB	BBB	Baa2	
	BBB-	BBB-	Baa3	
Speculative Grade	BB+	BB+	Ba1	Low
	BB	BB	Ba2	
	BB-	BB-	Ba3	
	B+	B+	B1	Speculative
	B	B	B2	
	B-	B-	B3	
	CCC+	CCC+	Caa1	Very Speculative
	CCC	CCC	Caa2	
	CCC-	CCC-	Caa3	
	CC	CC	Ca	Extremely Speculative
	C	C	C	
	D	D	-	Default

ratings from BB+ (or Ba1) to D. Bonds with a rating of CCC+ (or Caa1) or lower are subject to very high credit risk. The D rating is reserved to represent the default status in the S&P and Fitch rating systems. Default in the Moody's system is covered by the lowest credit rating C. A credit rating is often accompanied by a rating outlook (e.g. negative) to indicate its potential direction in the medium term.

A credit rating system can be based on quantitative models, qualitative analysis or typically a combination of the two. To form an unbiased credit opinion, credit rating agencies examine many factors and ensure that sufficient information is available. For example, the S&P corporate credit rating system evaluates a wide range of factors that may affect the credit quality of a company [3]. These include capital structure, financial policy, industry risk, competitive position and government influence. The S&P credit rating system has performed very well in assessing default risk. S&P publishes an annual report about global corporate default and rating transition. According to the 2019 report [4], global companies with the AAA rating never defaulted over a 1-year time horizon between 1981 and 2019. In contrast, companies

Table 4.3 Credit rating transition rates over a 1-year period (%)

	AAA	AA	A	BBB	BB	B	CCC/C	D	Not Rated
AAA	87.0	9.1	0.5	0.1	0.1	0.0	0.1	0.0	3.1
AA	0.5	87.2	7.7	0.5	0.1	0.1	0.0	0.0	3.9
A	0.0	1.7	88.4	5.0	0.3	0.1	0.0	0.1	4.4
BBB	0.0	0.1	3.4	86.3	3.5	0.4	0.1	0.2	6.0
BB	0.0	0.0	0.1	4.7	77.8	6.6	0.5	0.6	9.6
B	0.0	0.0	0.1	0.2	4.8	74.8	4.5	3.3	12.4
CCC/C	0.0	0.0	0.1	0.2	0.6	13.0	43.6	27.1	15.5

Source: S&P

with the CCC/C rating had an average 1-year default rate of 27.1%. Overall, the actual default rate increases steadily as the credit rating deteriorates. This demonstrates the reliability of the S&P credit rating system in evaluating corporate credit risk. The rating transition matrix can provide additional insights into the S&P credit model. Table 4.3 displays the average 1-year transition rates by credit category during the 39 years to 2019. The results show that corporate credit ratings are fairly stable over a 1-year period. For example, companies rated AAA had an average frequency of 87.0% to retain their credit rating after one year. However, issuers with the low CCC/C rating are rather vulnerable to default risk: 27.1% defaulted against 43.6% retained the rating.

4.5 Yield Curve

The yield curve is a graphical representation of the relationship between bond yield and time to maturity. The US Treasury yield curve is closely watched by market participants. It can help investors understand market expectations of future interest rates and economic outlook. Figure 4.1 shows three common shapes of a yield curve. The yield curve typically slopes upwards under normal economic conditions. The assumption behind a normal yield curve is that interest rates will rise with economic growth in the future. Therefore, investors demand higher yields as the bond maturity increases. A flat yield curve occurs when the yield remains fairly constant across different maturities. It is generally viewed as a transition between normal and inverted curves. A flat yield curve is frequently caused by short-term rates rising faster than long-term rates. This typically happens when central banks increase interest

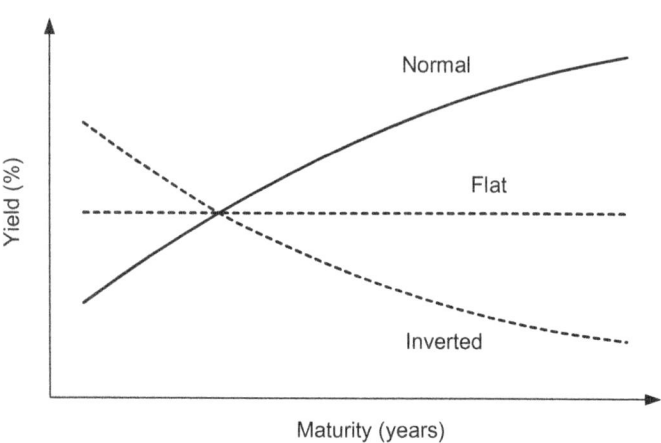

Fig. 4.1 Normal, flat and inverted yield curves

rates to prevent economic overheating and control inflation. An inverted yield curve reflects the situation that bond yield decreases with maturity. This implies that the market expects interest rates to decline in the future, a warning sign that a recession may be impending. Therefore, investors are willing to secure current interest rates before they fall further.

An inverted yield curve serves as a leading indicator to warn market participants that an economic downturn is looming. Historically, the US Treasury yield curve usually inverted about 6–24 months before a recession. According to a study published by the FRBSF Economic Letter, the yield curve has invariably inverted before every economic recession since 1955 [5]. The research calculates yield spread as the difference between 10-year and 1-year Treasury yields from January 1955 to February 2018. It found that all the nine recessions during this period were preceded by a negative yield spread. An inversion of the yield curve was always followed by a recession, except one false signal in 1965 when an economic slowdown ensued. The great predictive power supports the fact that the Treasury yield curve is closely monitored by the market. It provides market participants with insightful information about economic outlook and investor sentiment.

Historical Treasury yield curve rates are available from the official website of the US Treasury. For example, the yields on 3-month, 1-year, 10-year and 30-year Treasury securities were 0.08%, 0.45%, 3.85% and 4.65% respectively on 4 January 2010. These yields changed to 1.54%, 1.56%, 1.88% and 2.33% on 2 January 2020. Figure 4.2 shows the historical yield spread between 10-year and 1-year Treasury securities from January 2000 to August 2020. The yield spread fluctuates over time as a reflection of changing market expectations about economic prospects. It normally stays in positive territory

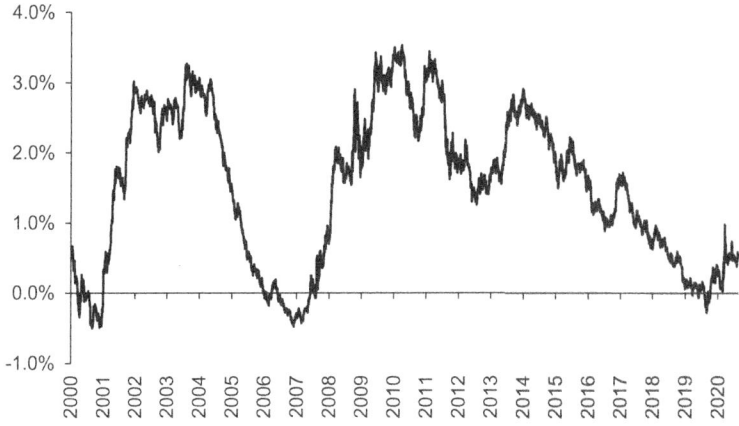

Fig. 4.2 Historical yield spread between 10-year and 1-year US Treasury securities

as the market expects interest rates to rise in the future. The yield spread effectively turned negative before the two recessions triggered by the dot-com bubble (2000) and financial crisis (2008) respectively.

4.6 Bond Return

Bonds are generally considered a defensive asset class with lower volatility than equities. They usually produce lower returns than equities over a long period of time. From 1934 to 2019, 3-month US Treasury bills provided an average return of about 3.4% per annum. Long-term Treasury securities delivered an additional annual return of more than 2.0%. The performance of Treasury securities is measured by many bond indices in the market, such as Bloomberg Barclays US Treasury Total Return Index. Historical Treasury yields can provide an indication of the potential return on US government bonds. For the 10-year US Treasury note, the average yield was 6.3% between 1970 and 2019. In comparison, the S&P 500 Index delivered an annualised total return of 10.6% during the same period. Figure 4.3 shows the historical 10-year Treasury yield and the S&P 500 Index over the 50 years to June 2020. The yield data are sourced from the Federal Reserve Bank of St. Louis. Since 1982, the Treasury yield has largely been on a downward trend. After the 2008 financial crisis, the bond market has been profoundly shaped by the protracted low interest-rate environment. The 10-year Treasury yield reached a relatively high level of 3.24% on 8 November 2018. But it declined significantly to only 0.66% on 30 June 2020.

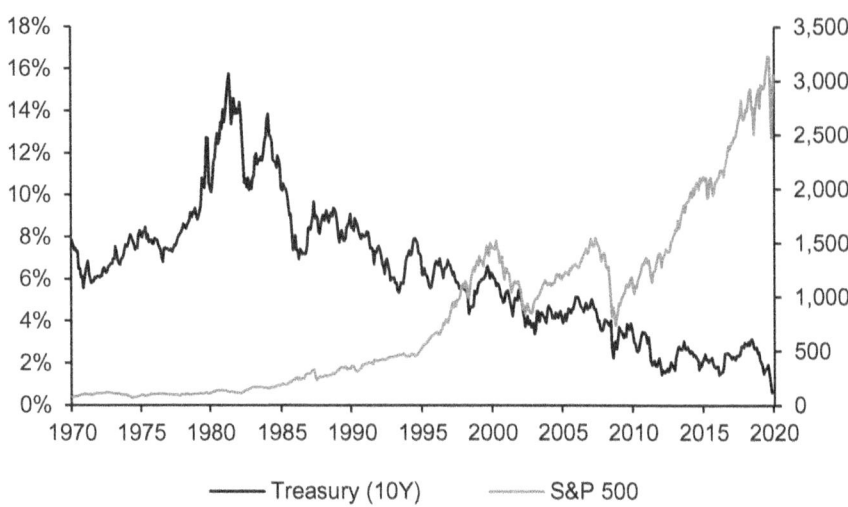

Fig. 4.3 Historical 10-year US Treasury yield and the S&P 500 Index

The ICE BofA Corporate indices can help investors compare historical returns of corporate bonds with different credit and maturity characteristics. A small sample of these indices is available in the data library maintained by the Federal Reserve Bank of St. Louis. According to ICE BofA US Corporate total return indices, US corporate bonds with the AAA credit rating generated an average annual return of 6.3% over the 30 years to 2019. This is slightly lower than 7.2% provided by corporate bonds with the BBB rating. Despite greater default risk, corporate bonds with speculative ratings achieved a higher annualised return of 8.4%. This performance still looks attractive compared to the annualised return of 10.0% delivered by the S&P 500 Index over the same period. Bonds with longer maturities usually have higher yields than comparable bonds with shorter maturities. During the 30-year period, corporate bonds with a maturity of 15 or more years realised an annualised return of 8.1%. This represents an excess return of 3.0% per year compared to corporate bonds with a maturity between 1 and 3 years.

4.7 Cash

Cash can be strictly defined as a physical form of money. It is a broader concept in investing that covers a range of cash investments, such as certificates of deposit, commercial paper and short-term government bonds. These money market securities are generally safe and liquid assets with short maturities. Individual investors can easily access the money markets through investment funds that focus on short-term debt instruments. Cash represents a major asset class that plays a fundamental role in the construction of defensive portfolios. Cash investments have low exposure to market risk and can protect capital in difficult times. Besides, sufficient cash reserves are important for investors to comfortably meet liquidity needs. They also allow investors to take advantage of investment opportunities as they arise.

The benefits of cash investments must be carefully weighed against their potential disadvantages. Cash investments typically provide lower returns than equities and bonds in the long term. They are subject to substantial inflation risk and often provide a negative return when the inflation effect is considered. This means that cash investments may fail to preserve the real value of invested capital. This can be illustrated by comparing historical yields on Treasury bills with the inflation rate in the United States. Figure 4.4 shows the historical yield on 3-month Treasury bills and the inflation rate over the 70 years to 2019. The data are sourced respectively from the Federal Reserve Bank of St. Louis and the US Bureau of Labor Statistics. Annual inflation rates are based on the Consumer Price Index for All Urban Consumers. Since the 2008 financial crisis, the yield on 3-month Treasury bills has largely remained below the inflation rate. The entrenched low-interest environment will continue to pose significant challenges for investors to earn decent returns from cash investments.

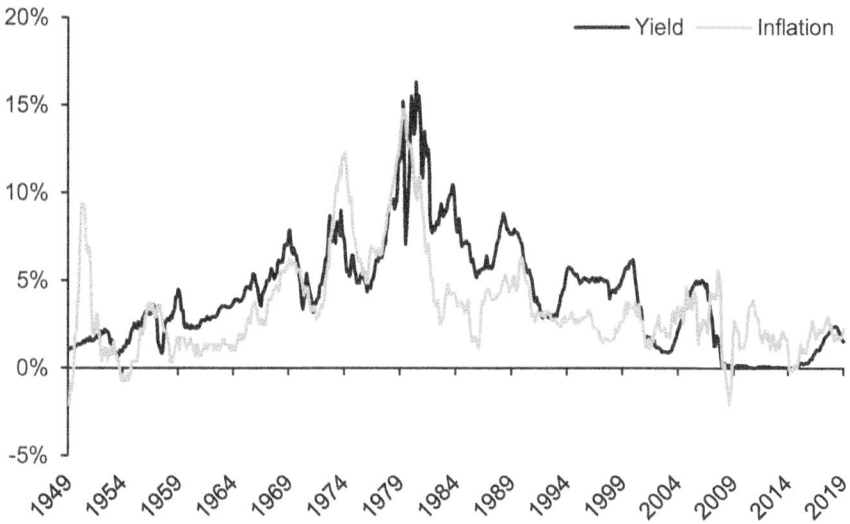

Fig. 4.4 Historical yield on 3-month US Treasury bills and the inflation rate

References

1. Fan, J. and Mitchell, M., *Equity-Bond Correlation: A Historical Perspective*. 2017, Graham Capital Management.
2. Ilmanen, A., *Stock-Bond Correlations*. Journal of Fixed Income, 2003. **13**(2): p. 55–66.
3. *Guide to Credit Rating Essentials*. 2018, Standard & Poor's Financial Services.
4. Kraemer, N.W., et al., *2019 Annual Global Corporate Default and Rating Transition Study*. 2020, Standard & Poor's Financial Services.
5. Bauer, M.D. and Mertens, T.M., *Economic Forecasts with the Yield Curve*. 2018, FRBSF Economic Letter.

5

Precious Metals

5.1 Precious Metals

Precious metals are natural resources with the defining qualities of rarity and high economic value. The asset class of precious metals primarily includes gold, silver, platinum and palladium. Historically, gold and silver served as a standard of value and medium of exchange. Precious metals today are mainly considered investment and industrial commodities as well as for aesthetic purposes. Precious metals can be traded with financial derivatives or in physical form with relatively uniform prices across the globe. Besides physical demand, the investment sector is a primary driving force behind price movements of precious metals. A unique property of precious metals is that they have low or negative correlations with many other assets. This makes precious metals an attractive asset class for portfolio construction and risk management.

Gold and silver are the best known precious metals as a result of their traditional use for decoration and value storage. The investment community often views them as a hedge against inflation and economic downturns. While gold is typically regarded as a safe-haven asset, silver is more widely available and has a much broader base of industrial applications. Silver effectively performs a dual role as an industrial metal and a vehicle to store value. Its price is strongly affected by industrial demand and sensitive to changes in economic conditions. This may explain the fact that silver usually has a higher level of price volatility than gold. Whereas gold and silver remain as the most common precious metals, there has been growing investment

Table 5.1 Correlations of four precious metals

	Gold	Silver	Platinum	Palladium
Gold	1.00	0.73	0.57	0.24
Silver		1.00	0.60	0.34
Platinum			1.00	0.51
Palladium				1.00

interest in platinum and palladium. Platinum and palladium are very rare precious metals with significantly lower global productions than gold. They are used in automotive, electronics, medical and other industries due to many unique physical properties. Like other industrial commodities, the prices of platinum and palladium are heavily influenced by industrial demand and global economic conditions. Therefore, the two precious metals are usually more volatile in price than gold. Table 5.1 shows the correlations of the four precious metals based on monthly price changes over the 25 years to 2020. Gold and silver have the highest correlation of 0.73 among all pairwise correlations. The correlations of platinum with gold and silver are moderate at 0.57 and 0.60 respectively, while palladium has relatively low correlations with the two common precious metals (both below 0.40).

Precious metals have a place in properly diversified investment portfolios. They serve as a hedge against inflation, market volatility and economic uncertainty. Precious metals tend to have lower correlations with equities than many other asset classes. A research of Aberdeen Standard Investments examines the correlations of five alternative investments with equities from 1994 to 2017 [1]. The US and global equities are represented by the S&P 500 and MSCI World indices respectively. The results show that precious metals have the lowest correlations with both equities among the alternative investments, followed by commodities and REITs. The two investment vehicles of hedge funds and private equity were found to be strongly correlated with equities. The research findings suggest that investors should allocate sufficient capital to precious metals to achieve proper portfolio diversification.

Whereas precious metals can help construct diversified portfolios, they tend to have inadequate representation in investment portfolios. The iShares S&P GSCI Commodity-Indexed Trust tracks the results of an index comprising a diversified group of commodity futures. At the end of 2020, the precious metals sector was assigned the lowest portfolio weighting of 6.8%. In contrast, the energy sector occupied a dominant position of 51.5% in the fund. The UBS Bloomberg CMCI Index is a broad commodity index designed to provide enhanced exposure to a range of commodities. It gained balanced exposure to the energy (31.8%), agriculture (30.2%) and industrial metals (25.7%) sectors on 30 September 2020. However, the precious metals sector only received a low weighting of 7.7%.

5.2 Historical Performance

Precious metals do not provide interest or dividend income to investors. The return on the investment in precious metals is attributed to price appreciation. Based on price change, gold produced an annualised return of 8.2% from 1971 to 2020, reasonably higher than 5.7% provided by silver. In comparison, the S&P 500 Index delivered an annualised total return of 10.9% during the same period. For the 30 years to 2020, annual price volatilities of gold and silver were 14.5% and 25.3% respectively, compared to 17.0% for the S&P 500 Index. The higher price volatility of silver reflects the fact that its price is heavily affected by industrial demand. While gold and silver historically failed to outperform the broad equity market, investors are attracted to precious metals due to their distinctive investment characteristics.

Table 5.2 compares the annualised returns and volatility levels of the four precious metals between 1996 and 2020. Gold and silver delivered comparable returns and materially underperformed the S&P 500 Index in this period. Platinum generated a fairly low annualised return of 4.0% with relatively high volatility. In comparison, palladium recorded an attractive average return of 12.5% per annum, eclipsing the performance of the other three precious metals. However, the strong return was accompanied by very high price volatility. Although gold trailed palladium in absolute return, it actually outperformed on a risk-adjusted basis. Based on the Efficiency ratio, the S&P 500 Index realised the highest risk-adjusted return, followed by gold, palladium, silver and platinum.

Figure 5.1 illustrates the price movements of gold and silver over the

Table 5.2 Performance of precious metals (1996–2020)

	Return	Volatility	Efficiency
Gold	6.6%	15.0%	0.44
Silver	6.7%	26.5%	0.25
Platinum	4.0%	22.3%	0.18
Palladium	12.5%	46.6%	0.27
S&P 500	9.6%	17.4%	0.55

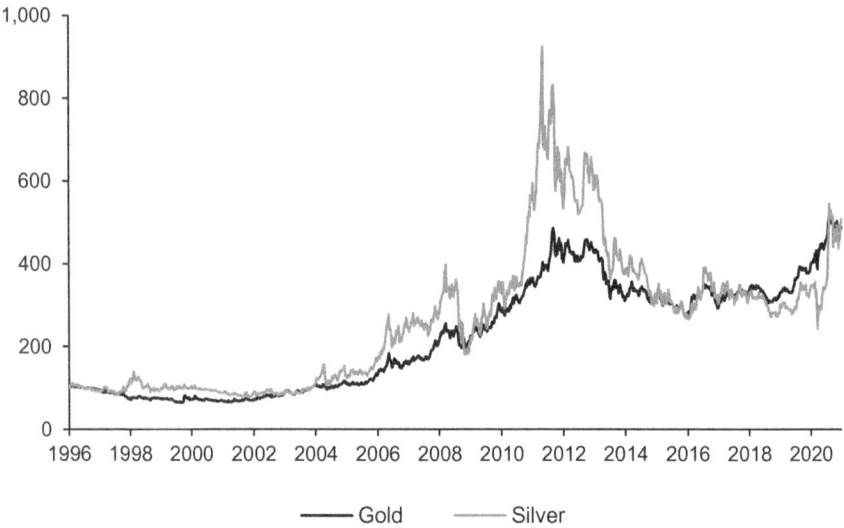

Fig. 5.1 Historical prices of gold and silver (rebased)

25 years to 2020. The prices are rebased with a starting value of 100 to facilitate comparison. Silver experienced significantly higher price volatility than gold during the period. The gold price increased substantially over the 2008 financial crisis and continued to rise until September 2011. Subsequently, it largely followed a downward trend to December 2015 and stabilised across the following three years. From the start of 2019 the gold price recovered steadily and surged in 2020 amid economic uncertainty and a weaker US dollar. The defensive characteristic of gold is reflected in its price movements through the entire period. Gold typically outperforms during times of market turbulence and underperforms when economic conditions improve.

Precious metals do not have perfect correlations with each other. A portfolio with balanced exposure to different precious metals can capture their abnormal returns over time. Table 5.3 shows the annual price changes of the four precious metals between 2011 and 2020. It is clear that no single asset could consistently win the race of outperformance. The exceptional performance of palladium is reflected in its ability to secure the leading position in 6 out of the 10 years. In particular, palladium delivered substantial returns of 56.1% and 53.2% in 2017 and 2019 respectively. It successfully stayed in positive return territory in 2013 and 2014 when the silver price collapsed. Although gold failed to match the performance of palladium, it achieved higher price stability over the period. It was the best performer in 2011 and 2015 when platinum and palladium registered sharp price declines. Silver climbed to the top position in 2020 with a price surge of 47.7%. But the

Table 5.3 Annual price changes of precious metals (2011–2020)

2011	2012	2013	2014	2015	2016	2017	2018	2019	2020
Gold 10.0%	Platinum 10.4%	Palladium 0.9%	Palladium 11.8%	Gold -10.4%	Palladium 21.6%	Palladium 56.1%	Palladium 19.3%	Palladium 53.2%	Silver 47.7%
Silver -10.3%	Silver 9.4%	Platinum -10.9%	Gold -1.8%	Silver -11.8%	Silver 15.1%	Gold 13.1%	Gold -1.5%	Platinum 21.3%	Palladium 25.9%
Palladium -18.5%	Palladium 7.7%	Gold -28.0%	Platinum -12.2%	Platinum -26.0%	Gold 8.5%	Silver 6.3%	Silver -8.6%	Gold 18.3%	Gold 25.0%
Platinum -21.2%	Gold 7.1%	Silver -35.9%	Silver -19.3%	Palladium -29.5%	Platinum 1.4%	Platinum 2.8%	Platinum -14.3%	Silver 15.2%	Platinum 10.5%

strong rise failed to offset its dramatic loss that happened during the 3 years to 2015. Silver posted a negative annualised return of −1.6% over the 10 years. Platinum suffered a difficult 10-year period with five negative annual returns. While frequently remaining at the bottom of the ranking table, platinum marginally outperformed silver in 2012 to claim the top position.

5.3 Characteristics of Gold

Gold is a special precious metal with many unique characteristics. On the negative side, gold has an intrinsic disadvantage of offering no income stream. Because gold does not generate cash flows, there are no earnings that can be regularly distributed to investors. This means that price appreciation is the only source of return on the investment in gold. The lack of income creates a potential performance drag for investment portfolios containing gold. Gold is broadly viewed as an investment asset rather than industrial metal. It has low sensitivity to industrial demand in changing economic conditions. This is because gold has limited industrial applications. Historically, gold exhibited lower price volatility than silver, crude oil and many other commodities. It has negative or low correlations with traditional investments such as equities. Gold typically outperforms during times of market downturn and underperforms in rising markets. As a defensive asset, gold plays a central role in the construction of diversified and resilient investment portfolios.

Gold has generated decent investment returns despite the fact that it produces no income. The gold price increased by an annualised rate of 8.2% over the 50 years to 2020. This performance is very reasonable given the defensive nature of gold. Gold is considered a monetary asset and a vehicle to store value, supported by the fairly transparent pricing mechanism in the world. According to the data of World Gold Council, gold reserves held by central banks and governments represented 17% of global physical gold at the end of 2019 [2]. Jewellery is the largest segment in the gold market with an average weighting of 51% from 2010 to 2019. Physical demand for gold has a diverse regional base across the globe. Emerging markets are the main source of demand for physical gold. For the 10 years to 2019, China and India accounted for 27% and 23% respectively of global gold demand. With the fast economic and income growth in emerging markets, gold demand will continue to be strong in the future. Gold price is determined by the dynamics of supply and demand. Whereas gold has resilient global demand, it is inherently in limited supply. For this reason, many investors hold physical gold in an attempt to profit from its price appreciation in the long term.

Gold is conventionally viewed as a natural inflation hedge due to its intrinsic value. Historically, gold prices soared to high levels when stock markets slumped in the years with very high inflation. During periods of hyperinflation, gold is perceived as an asset of last resort for central banks and governments. Gold as a store of value also offers protection against deflation. This is because the purchasing power of gold becomes stronger in a deflationary environment. Besides, gold is an effective hedge against the decline in the value of the US dollar. After the 2008 financial crisis, investors expected the dollar to depreciate against other currencies because of the massive monetary stimulus and increase in the US government debt. Investors moved capital to gold in an effort to preserve wealth. This prompted the strong rise in gold price over a prolonged period of time.

Gold is widely accepted as a safe-haven asset that offers protection against economic uncertainty and market volatility. In times of market stress, there is often a flight to safe assets as investors seek to protect capital. Gold as an investment asset has no credit risk and provides downside protection. Therefore, the exposure to gold creates a safety net when the market exhibits high volatility. Gold price typically strengthens during market crisis when equities, crude oil and industrial metals broadly endure significant losses. Figure 5.2 displays the annual returns of gold and the S&P 500 Index for the years with extreme negative market events between 1970 and 2012. Gold invariably outperformed the broad market benchmark against the backdrop of these extreme events. For example, the S&P 500 Index lost 22.1% in value during

Fig. 5.2 The performance of gold during extreme negative market events

the market downturn in 2002, while gold price appreciated significantly by 24.4%. The defensive property of gold was very pronounced in the 1970s recession partially caused by the oil crisis. The S&P 500 Index fell by 14.7% and 26.5% respectively in 1973 and 1974. In contrast, gold defied the falling market by posting substantial price returns of 67.0% and 72.3% in the two years. These historic events support the role of gold as a financial insurance against market crashes.

5.4 Diversification Effect

Gold as a defensive asset can be used to construct diversified portfolios that are resilient to unpredictable market events. Historically, gold has proved its ability to provide downside protection during times of market turbulence. It has low or negative correlations with equities and many other asset classes. Based on annual returns from 1971 to 2020, gold has a negative correlation of −21.8% with the S&P 500 Index. This indicates that portfolio volatility can possibly decrease significantly by combining gold with equities. Besides, portfolios with balanced exposure to gold and equities can potentially achieve higher risk-adjusted returns than pure equity portfolios. Suppose an investor constructs a portfolio based on gold and the S&P 500 Index. The portfolio assigns the weights of w_1 and w_2 respectively to the two assets. The expected portfolio return r and variance σ^2 are calculated as:

$$r = w_1 r_1 + w_2 r_2$$

$$\sigma^2 = w_1^2 \sigma_1^2 + w_2^2 \sigma_2^2 + 2\rho_{12} w_1 w_2 \sigma_1 \sigma_2$$

where r_1 and r_2 are the expected returns, σ_1 and σ_2 are the volatilities and ρ_{12} is the correlation of gold and the S&P 500 Index. Historical data can be used to represent the values of these parameters. Gold provided an annualised return of 8.2% from 1971 to 2020, while the S&P 500 Index returned an average of 9.8% per annum over the 95 years to 2020. The two assets have a negative correlation of −21.8%, with the volatilities estimated to be 14.5% and 17.0% respectively based on 30 years of annual returns to 2020.

Figure 5.3 displays the risk and return curve of the possible portfolios constructed with gold and the S&P 500 Index. At point A, the portfolio realises the lowest volatility of 9.8% by assigning a weight of 56.5% to gold. At point B, the portfolio is fully invested in the S&P 500 Index with the highest expected annual return of 9.8% and volatility of 17.0%. The curve between A and B represents the efficient frontier. It comprises the set of

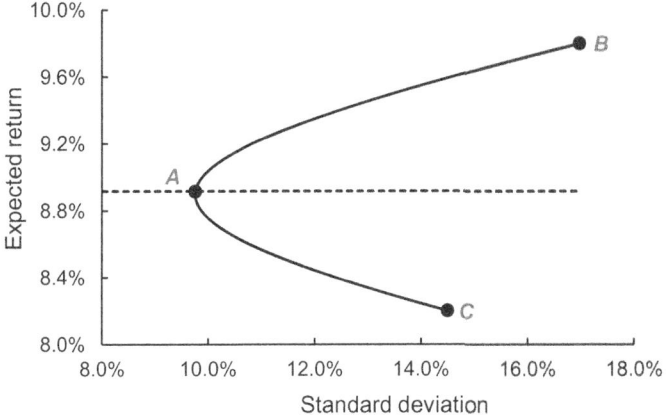

Fig. 5.3 Portfolio construction with gold and the S&P 500 Index

optimal portfolios providing the highest expected return at a defined level of risk. The curve between A and C contains suboptimal portfolios, since they do not provide sufficient return for a given risk. For example, the portfolio entirely invested in gold (point C) is not efficient. This is because a higher return can be achieved from the efficient frontier at the volatility level of gold. The shape of the efficient frontier clearly shows the diversification potential of gold in investment portfolios. From point B to A, the expected annual return only decreases slightly from 9.8% to 8.9%, while volatility declines significantly from 17.0% to 9.8%.

Gold generated attractive returns during the 50 years to 2020, although it is classified as a defensive asset. Investors can potentially enhance returns by allocating a portion of capital to gold. Assume a simple portfolio is constructed with gold and a passive equity fund replicating the results of the S&P 500 Index. The portfolio is rebalanced annually and allocates a fixed weighting of 30% to gold. Portfolio return is tracked over time based on the historical performance of gold and the S&P 500 Index. Figure 5.4 exhibits the movements of portfolio value between 2001 and 2020. The balanced portfolio had an annual volatility of 13.0% over the period, significantly lower than 17.3% for the S&P 500 Index. Besides, the portfolio produced an annualised return of 8.9%, reasonably exceeding 7.5% returned by the broad market index. The results demonstrate the potential benefits of holding gold in investment portfolios. Gold with the defensive property can help portfolios reduce volatility and enhance risk-adjusted returns.

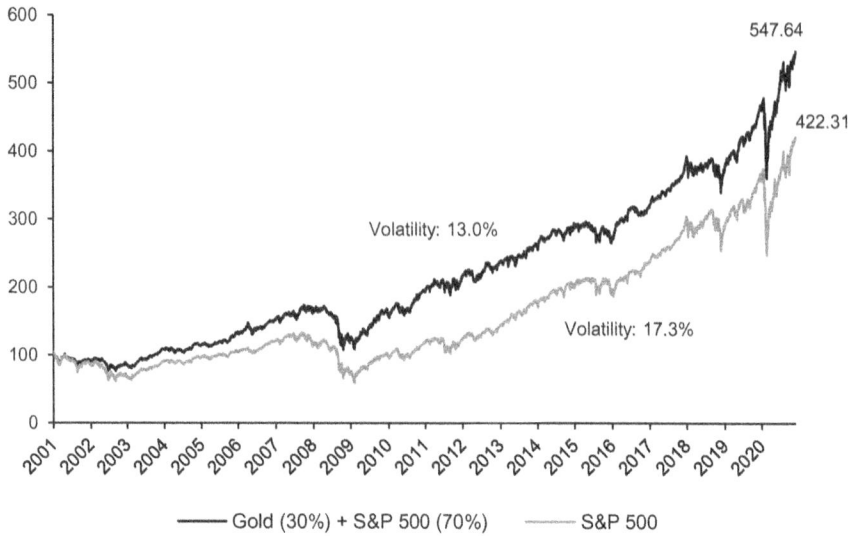

Fig. 5.4 Performance of a balanced portfolio and the S&P 500 Index

5.5 Drivers of Gold Price

The gold price is determined by the interaction of supply and demand in the market. Gold as a precious metal is essentially in limited supply. This positively contributes to the resilience and long-term appreciation of gold prices. The demand for gold is affected by many factors such as inflation and real interest rates. To successfully invest in gold, it is necessary for investors to understand the driving forces behind gold demand. The dynamic interplay of multiple forces shapes the price movements of gold. This section briefly discusses a range of factors that can potentially influence the price of gold.

- **Market Conditions**

Market conditions are an influential factor that drives the price movements of gold. During times of market turbulence, investors actively seek safe-haven assets to protect capital. Gold is widely regarded as a form of financial insurance against extreme market events. The strength in gold prices often reflects the level of market anxiety shaped by various factors, such as geopolitical tensions and trade wars. Gold prices tend to appreciate in falling markets and decline when market conditions improve.

- **Economic Outlook**

Gold prices often move in the opposite direction of the stock market as economic conditions change across the business cycle. Positive economic data encourage investors to increase exposure to risky assets and weaken the defensive appeal of gold. Besides, the optimism about the economic outlook increases the chance that central banks will gradually raise interest rates to control inflation. Rising interest rates are considered negative for gold prices due to the opportunity cost associated with holding gold.

- **Interest Rates**

The negative relationship between the gold price and real interest rates is supported by many investment studies [3, 4]. This is attributed to the fact that gold produces no income stream. When interest rates rise, the opportunity cost of holding gold increases. The expectation of rising interest rates will encourage investors to move capital into interest-bearing assets rather than gold. Conversely, gold becomes a more attractive investment asset when interest rates decline. The opportunity cost is significantly reduced in an environment of low interest rates. Historically, gold produced very strong returns when real interest rates were negative [5].

- **Inflation**

Inflation erodes the purchasing power of money and can cause negative real investment returns. Gold is widely accepted as an effective hedge against inflation. Its price often appreciates to preserve real value in response to rising inflation. For the 48 years to 2018, the gold price increased by an average annual rate of 15.1% during the periods when the US inflation rate was above 3% [5]. It had a moderate positive correlation of 0.41 with the US Consumer Price Index based on monthly data from January 1975 to June 2020 [6]. The correlation is not expected to be stable over time. This is because price movements of gold are influenced by multiple forces.

- **The US Dollar**

Gold and many other commodities in the world are primarily priced in the US dollar. The depreciation of the dollar makes gold appear more attractively priced in other currencies. Besides, investors will seek alternative investments such as gold to store value when the dollar is expected to weaken. Therefore, a falling dollar has a positive effect on the demand for gold. Figure 5.5 shows

Fig. 5.5 Gold price and the trade-weighted US dollar index (2007–2011)

the price movements of gold and the trade-weighted US dollar index between 2007 and 2011. The two data series had a moderate negative correlation of −0.47 based on monthly changes during the 5 years. From March 2009 to July 2011, the US dollar index largely followed a downward trend while the gold price climbed steadily.

- **Consumer Demand**

Consumer demand plays a central role in shaping gold price performance. This is because jewellery is the largest sector in the global gold market. Emerging markets are the leading source of demand for gold jewellery. Jewellery demand will benefit from the rising level of disposable income in emerging markets. This is a positive factor to support the long-term appreciation of the gold price.

- **Central Banks**

The official sector represents an important source of gold demand. Central banks hold gold reserves to protect against economic and financial risk. The significant change in global gold reserves is expected to have a material impact on the gold price. If a central bank decides to unload substantial gold reserves immediately, this will put downward pressure on gold prices. In the wake of the global financial crisis, central banks around the world have been net buyers of gold since 2010 [2].

5.6 Investment Methods

Several investment options are available to gain exposure to precious metals. Physical ownership is a common form of investing in precious metals. Investors can directly purchase and hold physical precious metals, such as jewellery and bullion. Holding precious metals in the physical form allows investors to exercise direct control over the physical assets. However, physical precious metals require storage, safekeeping and other costs. They have lower liquidity than financial instruments and may involve high transaction costs. Exchange-traded commodities (ETCs) provide a more flexible and efficient solution to invest in precious metals. They are investment vehicles designed to passively track the performance of a single commodity or commodity index. ETCs are traded and settled like common shares on a regulated exchange and have transparent pricing. Investors can easily participate in the global precious metals market through ETCs. For example, the iShares Physical Gold ETC seeks to track the return of the gold spot price. Financial derivatives such as futures contracts are also used to trade precious metals. These complex financial instruments support market participants to speculate on the short-term price movements of precious metals.

Mining companies and mutual funds offer alternative approaches to accessing the precious metals market. They provide investors with an opportunity to indirectly invest in precious metals while receiving income in the form of dividends. The performance of mining stocks is closely linked to the strength in the prices of the related commodities. Leading gold-mining companies in the world include Newmont and Barrick Gold. Alternatively, investors can simply gain exposure to precious metals through mutual funds. Many actively managed funds in the market target companies with the principal business activity in precious metals. For example, the Franklin Gold and Precious Metals Fund focuses on companies in the business of precious metals around the world. Launched in 1985, the Fidelity Select Gold Portfolio primarily invests in gold-mining equities and may hold physical bullion.

References

1. *Portfolio Strategy: Potential Benefits of a Precious Metals Allocation.* 2018, Aberdeen Standard Investments.
2. *The Relevance of Gold as a Strategic Asset.* 2020, World Gold Council.
3. Gisimundo, V., Portelli, L. and Tazé-Bernard, E., *Gold in Central Banks' Asset Allocation.* 2019, Amundi Asset Management.
4. *The Investment Case for Gold.* 2019, WisdomTree.
5. *Debunking 5 Common Gold Misconceptions.* 2019, State Street.
6. McDonald, J.D., Phillips, D.J. and De Juan, M., *The Role of Gold: A Less Than Perfect Inflation Hedge.* 2020, Northern Trust.

6

Portfolio Diversification

6.1 Portfolio Diversification

Diversification is a fundamental principle in investment and risk management. It is an effective approach to reducing investment risk by spreading capital across many different assets. Diversification controls exposure to any single asset to protect a portfolio against extreme losses. It helps portfolios reduce downside risk and improve resilience to market volatility. This simple strategy allows portfolios to capture diverse sources of return and potentially enhance investment performance. Subject to investment objectives and risk tolerance, portfolios can be diversified across equities, bonds, real estate and other asset classes. Equity portfolios can be diversified based on multiple risk factors, such as sector, country and investment style.

The concept of diversification is formalised by the modern portfolio theory introduced in 1952 [1]. The theoretical framework shows that portfolio risk can be reduced by holding a diversified portfolio of assets. The total risk of a portfolio can be decomposed into the systematic and specific components. Systematic risk is the overall market risk that affects all investments, such as economic recession and oil price shock. Investors are compensated for bearing systematic risk because it cannot be avoided. Specific risk is related to individual investments and can be mitigated or eliminated through diversification. Figure 6.1 illustrates the principle of diversification in reducing portfolio risk. Specific risk declines gradually as more stocks are added to the portfolio. Since systematic risk remains constant in the portfolio, the reduction in specific risk decreases the overall portfolio risk.

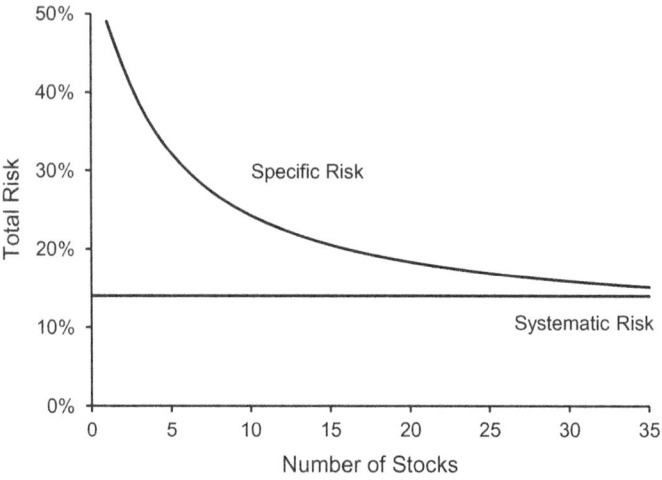

Fig. 6.1 The effect of diversification on reducing portfolio risk

The investment community has no consensus on the number of stocks required to reduce specific risk in equity portfolios. Investors often apply the simple rule of 25 stocks to judge if an equity portfolio is diversified. This is based on the fact that specific risk has been significantly removed when a portfolio contains 25 or more stocks. Academic studies provide valuable insights into the portfolio size required to eliminate diversifiable risk. A research in the Journal of Business found 90% of specific risk can be removed by just holding 16 stocks [2]. A paper published by the Omega Journal shows that 20 stocks can eliminate 95% of the diversifiable risk in a portfolio [3]. But the portfolio requires additional 80 stocks to remove another 4% of specific risk. The results indicate that a portfolio can efficiently harvest the diversification benefits by gaining balanced exposure to 20–30 stocks.

The Herfindahl–Hirschman Index (HHI) is a common measure of market concentration. It can also be applied to evaluate the level of portfolio concentration. For a portfolio of N stocks, the HHI is simply calculated as:

$$HHI = 10000 \times \sum_i w_i^2$$

where w_i is the weight of stock i in the portfolio. The HHI considers stock weights and penalises portfolios with concentrated positions in a number of names. If a portfolio assigns a large weighting of 20% to a stock, the HHI score will be at least 400, regardless of the positions in other stocks. In comparison, an equal-weighted portfolio of 30 stocks only has an HHI of 333. The HHI can be used to compare the concentration levels of different portfolios. In general, low HHI values indicate a high level of diversification. Investors can define boundaries of the HHI to classify portfolios into concentration categories. For example, if the HHI is above 600, the portfolio can be considered highly concentrated. If the HHI is below 400, it indicates low concentration. The portfolio can be classified as moderately concentrated if the HHI is between the two values.

6.2 Efficient Frontier

The economist Harry Markowitz introduced the modern portfolio theory (MPT) in 1952 [1]. This pioneering work guided the investment community to move beyond the traditional practice of stock selection and consider portfolio characteristics in investing. The MPT provides a mathematical framework of portfolio management to demonstrate the possibility of constructing efficient portfolios through diversification. It assumes that investors are risk averse and willing to accept more risk if compensated by higher expected returns. Risky assets can be combined in numerous ways to form portfolios with different risk and return characteristics. The efficient frontier comprises the set of optimal portfolios that provide the highest expected return at a given level of risk. It can be easily constructed by computer programs based on mean–variance optimisation.

Investment portfolios can be created with various combinations of assets. Assume a portfolio is formed of two assets with the expected returns of r_1 and r_2, standard deviations of σ_1 and σ_2, and a correlation of ρ. The portfolio assigns the weightings of w_1 and w_2 to the two assets. The expected portfolio return r and variance σ^2 are expressed as:

$$r = w_1 r_1 + w_2 r_2$$

$$\sigma^2 = w_1^2 \sigma_1^2 + w_2^2 \sigma_2^2 + 2\rho w_1 w_2 \sigma_1 \sigma_2$$

If the correlation between the two assets is equal to 1, the standard deviation of the portfolio becomes:

$$\sigma = \left(w_1^2 \sigma_1^2 + w_2^2 \sigma_2^2 + 2 w_1 w_2 \sigma_1 \sigma_2 \right)^{1/2} = w_1 \sigma_1 + w_2 \sigma_2$$

Note that $w_1 + w_2 = 1$. The above formulas can be rearranged to display a linear relationship between the expected return r and standard deviation σ of the portfolio:

$$r = \frac{r_2\sigma_1 - r_1\sigma_2}{\sigma_1 - \sigma_2} + \left(\frac{r_1 - r_2}{\sigma_1 - \sigma_2}\right)\sigma$$

The linear relationship is represented by the straight line AB in Fig. 6.2. Asset 1 has a lower expected return and standard deviation than asset 2. The portfolio can be entirely invested in asset 1 (point A), asset 2 (point B) or a combination of the two assets. The expected portfolio return increases linearly with the standard deviation as the portfolio allocates more weighting to asset 2. Because the two assets have a perfect positive correlation, their combinations do not result in efficient portfolios. In practice, portfolios can be constructed more efficiently by combining assets with low or negative correlations. If the correlation ρ is lower than 1, the portfolio standard deviation σ^* is:

$$\sigma^* = \left(w_1^2\sigma_1^2 + w_2^2\sigma_2^2 + 2\rho w_1 w_2 \sigma_1 \sigma_2\right)^{1/2} < w_1\sigma_1 + w_2\sigma_2 = \sigma$$

The expected portfolio return r^* is:

$$r^* = w_1 r_1 + w_2 r_2 = r$$

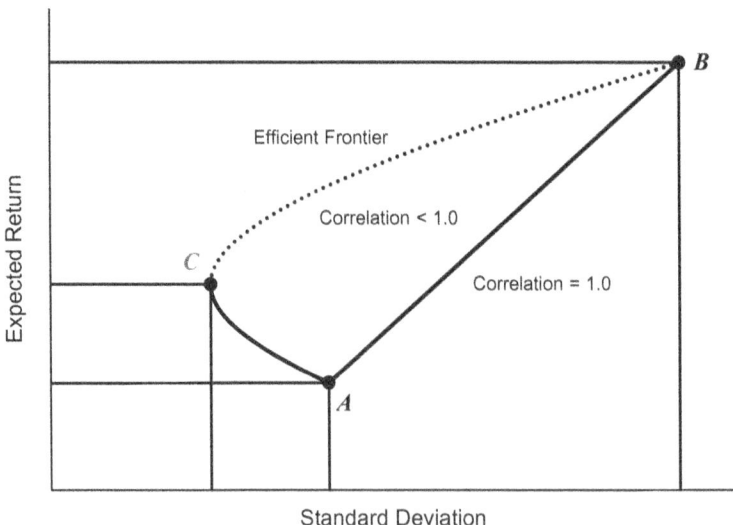

Fig. 6.2 Efficient frontier constructed with two risky assets

The results indicate that it is possible to reduce portfolio risk without compromise on the expected return. Portfolios on the curve ACB in Fig. 6.2 can achieve the same expected return with a lower standard deviation compared to those on the line AB. The portfolio at point C features the lowest variance, while the portfolio at point B has the highest expected return. The curve between C and B represents the efficient frontier containing the set of optimal portfolios. These portfolios provide the highest expected return at a given level of risk.

Investment portfolios are usually diversified across many different assets. For a portfolio of N assets, the variance of portfolio return is calculated as:

$$\sigma^2 = \sum_i w_i^2 \sigma_i^2 + \sum_i \sum_{j \neq i} w_i w_j \sigma_{ij}$$

where w_i and σ_i^2 are the weight and variance of asset i, and σ_{ij} is the covariance between the returns of assets i and j. Define the average variance and average covariance as:

$$\bar{\sigma}^2 = \frac{\sum_i \sigma_i^2}{N}$$

$$\Delta = \frac{\sum_i \sum_{j \neq i} \sigma_{ij}}{(N-1) \times N}$$

If equal weighting is applied to all assets in the portfolio, the portfolio variance can be simplified as:

$$\sigma^2 = \sum_i \frac{1}{N^2} \times \sigma_i^2 + \sum_i \sum_{j \neq i} \frac{1}{N^2} \times \sigma_{ij} = \frac{\bar{\sigma}^2}{N} + \frac{N-1}{N} \Delta$$

The formula indicates that portfolio variance can be significantly reduced by combining many assets with low correlations. When the portfolio size N becomes very large, the component $\bar{\sigma}^2/N$ is negligible and $(N-1)/N$ is close to 1. Therefore, portfolio variance is largely determined by the average covariance of the assets in the portfolio. Practically, portfolios can have very low volatility if they are constructed with assets that have weak or negative correlations.

6.3 Downside Protection

Downside risk is a key consideration in the construction of investment portfolios. Portfolios with concentrated positions are vulnerable to unpredictable market events and investment-specific risk. Diversification controls exposure to single assets to mitigate the impact of extreme events on portfolio performance. This basic principle helps investors avoid disastrous investment outcomes and preserve capital to generate future returns. Individual investors are encouraged to strictly follow the diversification approach. They generally have limited knowledge and experience to perform thorough investment analysis. Besides, individual investors have resource and time constraints to closely monitor investments and market conditions. It is practically difficult for them to quickly capture market information to make informed investment decisions. Institutional investors commonly maintain diversification as a fundamental strategy to reduce investment risk. Historically, a series of corporate frauds and accounting scandals happened in heavily regulated markets. These unexpected corporate failures highlight the importance of diversification in investing. A case in point is the collapse of the Spanish company Gowex in 2014. The telecom services provider deceived the market by massively falsifying its financial accounts since 2005. In July 2014, the US firm Gotham City Research issued a research report warning that over 90% of the revenues stated by Gowex never exist and the company value is zero. Subsequently, Gowex declared bankruptcy and its disgraced chief executive faced criminal investigations. Its dramatic collapse stunned the market and caused huge capital losses to investors. This case shows that even institutional investors with strong research capabilities and due diligence standards are still subject to significant investment risk. Diversification is a sensible approach to protecting capital against the damaging effects of extreme events.

Portfolios can be diversified across multiple asset classes to mitigate downside risk. Equities are risky assets that often experience material losses in poor market conditions. During the 2008 financial crisis, the US equity market represented by the S&P 500 Index (total return) suffered a maximum drawdown of 55.3%, compared to only 16.7% for the ICE BofA US Corporate Index. Maximum drawdown (peak-to-trough decline) measures the maximum loss in the value of an asset or portfolio over a specific period. Portfolios can potentially reduce downside risk by gaining balanced exposure to diverse asset classes. Common asset classes are located in different positions of the risk-return spectrum and usually behave differently in changing market conditions. Figure 6.3 exhibits the largest intra-year declines of a balanced portfolio and the S&P 500 Index over the 20 years to 2020. The balanced

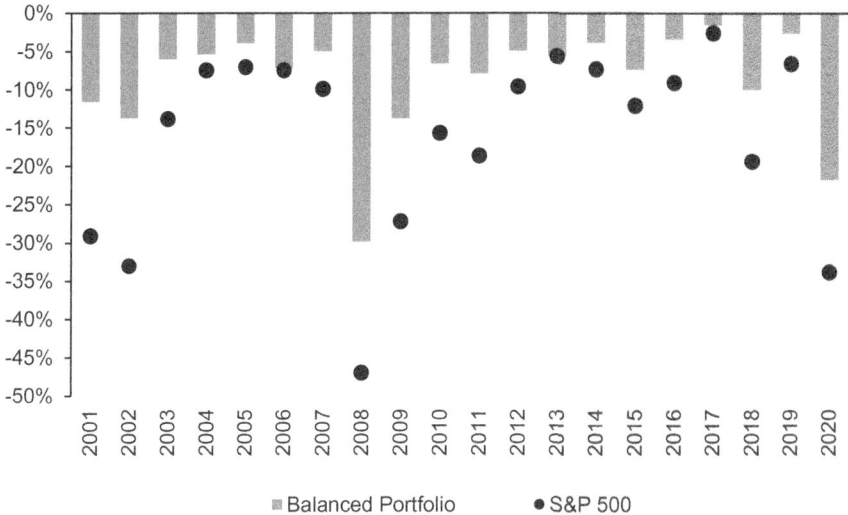

Fig. 6.3 Maximum drawdowns of a balanced portfolio and the S&P 500 Index

portfolio is a combination of equities, bonds and gold, represented by the S&P 500 Index, ICE BofA US Corporate Index and gold spot price respectively. The ICE BofA US Corporate Index data are retrieved from the data library of the Federal Reserve Bank of St. Louis. The portfolio is rebalanced annually and assigns the weightings of 50%, 35% and 15% respectively to the three asset classes. The results show that the balanced portfolio consistently has a lower maximum drawdown than the S&P 500 Index across the 20 individual years. It recorded a maximum decline of 29.9% in 2008, while the broad equity market index endured a substantial maximum loss of 47.0%. This reflects the advantage of diversification in downside protection. For the purpose of capital protection, conservative investors generally diversify across defensive and growth assets to achieve a balanced portfolio composition.

6.4 Upside Capture

Diversification is a practical approach to achieving reasonable returns without excessive investment risk. It is a simple and effective strategy to capture upside performance while providing downside protection. Diversification in equity investing is supported by the fact that the distribution of cumulative stock returns is very skewed. Most stocks fail to deliver positive excess returns against the market over the long term. The overall market return is primarily explained by a small percentage of stocks. A paper published by the leading

Journal of Financial Economics analyses the performance of stocks in the CRSP (Centre for Research in Security Prices) database [4]. The database covers all common stocks listed on the NYSE, Amex and Nasdaq exchanges. The research found that the best-performing 4% of stocks fully explain the excess return of the entire US equity market against 1-month Treasury bills from 1926 to 2016. The lifetime performance of the other 96% stocks collectively only matches the return on 1-month Treasury bills. The results indicate that it is practically challenging to outperform the market through stock selection. Diversification allows equity portfolios to increase the chance of capturing superior stocks.

Common asset classes perform differently as the economic and market conditions change across the business cycle. The idea of tactical asset allocation is intuitively appealing. However, it is almost impossible to reliably predict the future performance of asset classes. Historically, tactical allocation strategies overall have produced disappointing results. Maintaining diversified and consistent exposure to different asset classes is a more feasible option to capture upside performance than active asset rotation. Table 6.1 displays the annual returns of eight asset classes between 2011 and 2020. Equities are represented by the S&P 500, MSCI World ex USA, MSCI Emerging Markets and MSCI World Small Cap indices. Corporate bonds are the ICE BofA US Corporate Index. The alternative investments of real estate, hedge funds and gold are respectively based on the NCREIF Property Index, HFRI Fund Weighted Composite Index and gold spot price. The results show that the asset classes rotated to take the leading position in the performance table. Their positions in the ranking table are fairly random and unpredictable. Dynamic asset allocation will have great difficulty in reliably capturing strong returns of the asset classes. The diversification approach allows investors to effectively capture upside performance through balanced exposure. Suppose a portfolio simply applies equal weighting to the eight asset classes and receives annual rebalancing. It would generate a reasonable annualised return of 7.3% over the 10 years. The portfolio outperformed developed markets (excluding US) equities (5.7%), corporate bonds (5.6%), hedge funds (4.2%), emerging markets equities (4.0%) and gold (2.9%).

6.5 Risk-Adjusted Return

The enormous investment universe supports investors to form portfolios with diverse risk and return profiles. Investors can combine assets with low or negative correlations to significantly reduce portfolio volatility. The reduction in

6 Portfolio Diversification   75

Table 6.1 Annual returns of eight asset classes (2011–2020)

2011	2012	2013	2014	2015	2016	2017	2018	2019	2020
RE 14.3%	EM 18.6%	SC 32.9%	US 13.7%	RE 13.3%	SC 13.3%	EM 37.8%	RE 6.7%	US 31.5%	GD 25.0%
GD 10.0%	SC 18.1%	US 32.4%	RE 11.8%	US 1.4%	US 12.0%	DM 24.8%	GD -1.5%	SC 26.8%	EM 18.7%
BD 7.5%	DM 17.0%	DM 21.6%	BD 7.5%	SC 0.1%	EM 11.6%	SC 23.2%	BD -2.2%	DM 23.2%	US 18.4%
US 2.1%	US 16.0%	RE 11.0%	HF 3.0%	BD -0.6%	GD 8.5%	US 21.8%	US -4.4%	EM 18.9%	SC 16.5%
HF -5.2%	RE 10.5%	HF 9.1%	SC 2.3%	HF -1.1%	RE 8.0%	GD 13.1%	HF -4.8%	GD 18.3%	HF 11.7%
SC -8.7%	BD 10.4%	BD -1.5%	GD -1.8%	DM -2.6%	BD 6.0%	HF 8.6%	SC -13.5%	BD 14.2%	BD 9.8%
DM -11.8%	GD 7.1%	EM -2.3%	EM -1.8%	GD -10.4%	HF 5.5%	RE 7.0%	DM -13.6%	HF 10.5%	DM 8.1%
EM -18.2%	HF 6.4%	GD -28.0%	DM -3.9%	EM -14.6%	DM 3.3%	BD 6.5%	EM -14.2%	RE 6.4%	RE 1.6%

US: S&P 500 Index. DM: MSCI World ex USA Index. EM: MSCI Emerging Markets Index. SC: MSCI World Small Cap Index.
BD: ICE BofA US Corporate Index. RE: NCREIF Property Index. HF: HFRI Fund Weighted Composite Index. GD: Gold Spot Price.

volatility risk through diversification is an option to enhance risk-adjusted returns. In Section 6.3, the balanced portfolio is constructed with equities, bonds and gold. They are represented by the S&P 500 Index, ICE BofA US Corporate Index and gold spot price respectively. The portfolio is rebalanced annually and allocates the weightings of 50%, 35% and 15% to the three asset classes. It had an annual volatility of 10.3% during the 20 years to 2020, significantly lower than 17.3% for the S&P 500 Index. This shows the ability of diversification to reduce portfolio volatility. Diversification also provides the core benefits of mitigating downside risk and capturing upside performance. Portfolios can really exploit the diversification benefits without necessarily compromising on investment returns. The balanced portfolio realised an annualised return of 7.9% from 2001 to 2020, marginally exceeding 7.5% provided by the S&P 500 Index. It achieved a much higher Efficiency ratio (0.77) than the broad equity market index (0.43).

Investors with low risk tolerance typically limit exposure to equities. Assume a defensive portfolio is constructed by equally weighting the S&P 500 Index, ICE BofA US Corporate Index and gold spot price. It has a starting value of 100 and applies annual rebalancing. Figure 6.4 exhibits the performance of the portfolio and the rebased S&P 500 Index (total return) over the 20 years to 2020. The portfolio realised an average return of 8.5% per annum. This represents an annualised excess return of 1.0% against the S&P 500 Index. The portfolio delivered the excess return with significantly

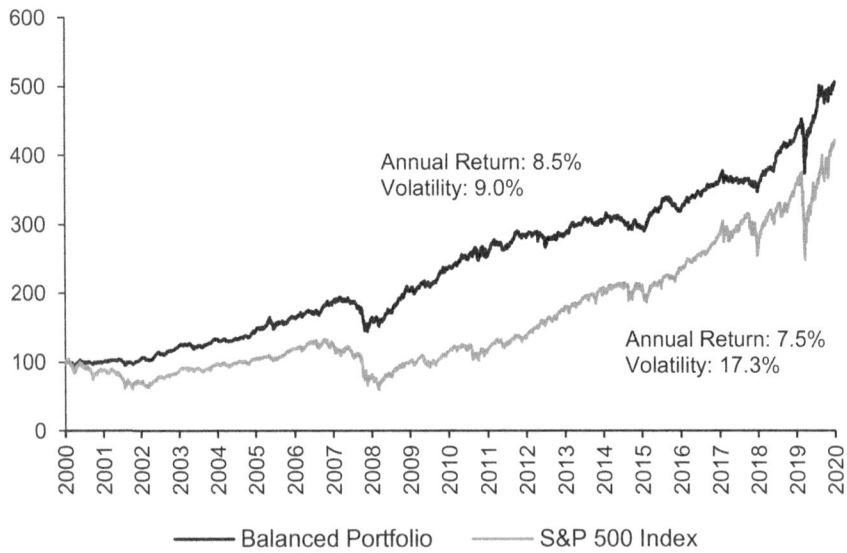

Fig. 6.4 Performance of a balanced portfolio and the S&P 500 Index (rebased)

lower volatility (9.0%) than the equity index (17.3%). Suppose the risk-free rate is based on the yield on 3-month Treasury bills. The average risk-free rate was 1.4% during the 20 years. The defensive portfolio achieved a Sharpe ratio of 0.79, materially higher than 0.35 for the S&P 500 Index. The results demonstrate that diversification across different asset classes can potentially help portfolios improve risk-adjusted returns.

References

1. Markowitz, H., *Portfolio Selection.* Journal of Finance, 1952. **7**(1): p. 77–91.
2. Fisher, L. and Lorie, J.H., *Some Studies of Variability of Returns on Investments in Common Stocks.* Journal of Business, 1970. **43**(2): p. 99–134.
3. Tang, G.Y.N., *How Efficient Is Naive Portfolio Diversification? An Educational Note.* Omega, 2004. **32**(2): p. 155–160.
4. Bessembinder, H., *Do Stocks Outperform Treasury Bills?* Journal of Financial Economics, 2018. **129**(3): p. 440–457.

7

Loss Control

7.1 Disposition Effect

The disposition effect is a common behavioural bias in investing. It is the tendency of investors to frequently realise small gains while continuing to hold losing positions [1]. The disposition effect is related to the concept of loss aversion that investors prefer avoiding losses to acquiring equivalent gains. A research paper published by the Journal of Finance in 1998 provides empirical evidence that investors are unwilling to realise losses [2]. The study analyses the trading records of 10,000 accounts at a large brokerage firm. The results show that investors demonstrate a strong bias towards realising winners rather than losers. The profitable stocks sold actually produced an average excess return of 3.4% in the following year against the losing stocks retained in the accounts. This supports the observation that stocks often continue to move in the direction of an established price trend. The disposition effect is essentially contrary to the momentum effect in the market. It causes investors to miss great return opportunities and retain losing positions. This behavioural bias partially explains the fact that many individual investors fail to achieve reasonable returns even in rising markets.

A primary determinant of investment success is the ability to capture upside returns and limit capital losses. It is essential that investors avoid the disposition effect and act quickly when the original investment case is broken. Table 7.1 provides a simple example to illustrate the potential impact of the disposition effect on investment outcomes. The portfolio is composed of ten investments with equal weighting. Assume eight investments deliver strong

Table 7.1 The impact of the disposition effect on investment results

Investment	Return	Actual Return		
		Scenario 1	Scenario 2	Scenario 3
1	15%	15%	15%	10%
2	20%	20%	20%	10%
3	25%	25%	25%	10%
4	30%	30%	30%	10%
5	35%	35%	35%	10%
6	40%	40%	40%	10%
7	45%	45%	45%	10%
8	50%	50%	50%	10%
9	-40%	-40%	-20%	-40%
10	-70%	-70%	-20%	-70%
	Average:	15%	22%	-3%

returns and the other two suffer large losses. The default scenario is that the portfolio adopts the buy-and-hold approach and receives a return of 15%. In the second scenario, the portfolio follows the momentum strategy and realises an enhanced return of 22%. It retains winning investments and strictly limits losses to −20% before losing positions likely deteriorate further. In the third scenario, the portfolio produces a negative return of −3% as a result of the disposition effect. It always realises small gains of 10% and continues to keep losing investments. The failure to capture strong returns and control losses leads to poor investment results.

Investors are reluctant to realise losses because they expect losing positions to recover eventually. Unfortunately, many investments suffer permanent losses with limited recovery. From 1983 to 2006, 39.0% of stocks in the Russell 3000 Index produced negative lifetime returns and 18.5% lost more than 75% of their market value [3]. A study of J.P. Morgan clearly demonstrates the downside risk of failing stocks [4]. The research examines the performance of about 13,000 stocks in the Russell 3000 Index between 1980 and 2014. It found around 40% of the stocks suffered a permanent catastrophic loss from their peak value. The catastrophic loss is defined as a price decline of 70% or more from the peak value with little recovery afterwards and an eventual loss of 60% or more. The research also reveals that over 320 stocks were removed from the S&P 500 Index during the 35 years because of business distress reasons. Considering the prevalence of unprofitable investments in the market, a disciplined approach is essential to manage losing positions. Investors are advised to leave companies with deteriorating fundamentals to protect capital from further losses. It is practically impossible

Table 7.2 A sample of stocks with downward price trends

Company	Country	Monthly Return (2018)						Total
		Jul	Aug	Sep	Oct	Nov	Dec	
SENVION	Germany	-14%	-11%	-14%	-17%	-27%	-40%	-76%
SLM SOLUTIONS	Germany	-24%	-3%	-13%	-27%	-17%	-29%	-72%
GAM	Switzerland	-27%	-25%	-7%	-16%	-10%	-27%	-72%
THOMAS COOK	UK	-11%	-13%	-31%	-22%	-33%	2%	-71%
U-BLOX	Switzerland	-7%	-21%	-4%	-10%	-26%	-16%	-60%
RENEWI	UK	-10%	-10%	-9%	-10%	-21%	-19%	-58%
GIMA	Italy	-5%	-7%	-13%	-21%	-17%	-8%	-54%
GEOX	Italy	-6%	-3%	-2%	-26%	-19%	-9%	-52%
LE BELIER	France	-13%	-10%	-18%	-11%	-6%	-5%	-48%
METRO BANK	UK	-1%	-13%	7%	-25%	-5%	-19%	-48%

that all investments become profitable. Investments should be managed as a portfolio rather than individual assets.

Table 7.2 presents a sample of stocks that endured poor performance during the six months to December 2018. Investors would suffer heavy capital losses if they failed to leave the losing stocks with discipline. The market apparently lost confidence in these stocks. Thomas Cook and Metro Bank caused further disastrous damages to investors in 2019. Thomas Cook entered compulsory liquidation after its failure to secure rescue funding. Metro Bank shares crashed 87.8% in 2019 following a major accounting error and profit warnings. The cases demonstrate the importance of cutting losses quickly to preserve capital. The legendary investor Peter Lynch advises that: *There's no shame in losing money on a stock. Everybody does it. What is shameful is to hold on to a stock, or, worse, to buy more of it, when the fundamentals are deteriorating* [5].

7.2 Breakeven Return

Successful investing requires the ability to protect capital against extreme losses. Holding onto failing investments with limited visibility of recovery is not a proper investment strategy. Risky assets such as equities expose investors to significant downside risk. Investors can lose substantial capital without taking a disciplined approach to managing losing positions. It is necessary that investors understand the difficulty to recover from large investment losses. Breakeven return in investing is the positive return required to fully recover from a losing position. The recovery of a 10% loss is manageable and requires a breakeven return of 11%. A 50% loss necessitates a subsequent return of 100% to restore the original value. When the loss reaches 80%, the breakeven return increases substantially to 400%. Remarkably, a dramatic 95% loss demands an extreme return of 1900% to reach the breakeven point. Figure 7.1 exhibits the relationship between investment loss and breakeven return. The return required to recover from a losing position accelerates very quickly as the loss gradually increases. If an investment loss exceeds 90%, it becomes extremely difficult to recoup the loss. The reality is that very few investments in the market can provide a dramatic return of 900%. To control capital losses, investors should seriously consider reducing the exposure to a failing investment when the loss widens to 20%.

The results clearly demonstrate the importance of limiting losses in investing. But many investors cling to losing investments in the hope that they will recover ultimately. They often underestimate the returns required to recoup heavy investment losses. The failure to cut losses quickly can cause severe damage to investment capital. Numerous investments suffer permanent disastrous losses with limited recovery afterwards. For example, the share price of the Royal Bank of Scotland (RBS) suffered a dramatic decline of 98.3% from the peak value during the global financial crisis in 2008. Many investors failed to leave the embattled bank quickly and lost substantial capital. The market was worried that RBS could not survive without a government bailout. Since rescued by the British government, RBS reported 10 years of consecutive annual losses. Its share price continued to struggle and

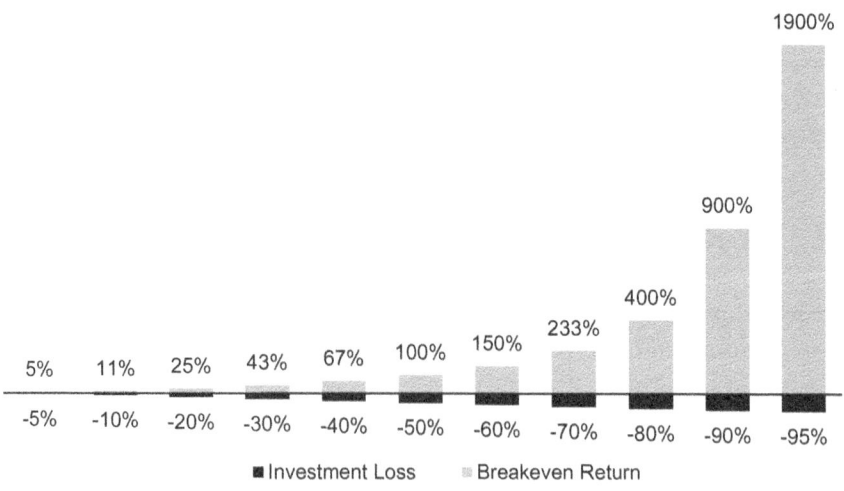

Fig. 7.1 The relationship between investment loss and breakeven return

reached a new historical low on 21 September 2020. The case supports the view that losing investments should be managed with discipline to preserve capital.

7.3 Profit Warning

Public companies are required to report regularly on financial results and business outlook. Profit warning is an announcement made by a public company that its forward earnings will be materially below market expectations. It is usually issued before the formal release of earnings results. This allows investors and analysts to adjust expectations ahead of the official earnings announcement. Profit warnings are unexpected company events that cause painful experiences to investors. The share price of a company often falls sharply following its warning on profits. For example, Capita shares tumbled 47.5% on 31 January 2018 after the outsourcing company announced a profit warning and radical business change. Shares in Ted Baker plunged 40% on 3 October 2019 as the clothing retailer warned that full-year profits would be disappointing due to tough trading conditions. Figure 7.2 exhibits the share prices of the two companies between 2011 and 2020. Both stocks suffered a maximum decline of over 95% from their peak value following a series of profit warnings.

Business performance of firms is susceptible to many external factors, such as market competition and consumer preferences. It is difficult for companies

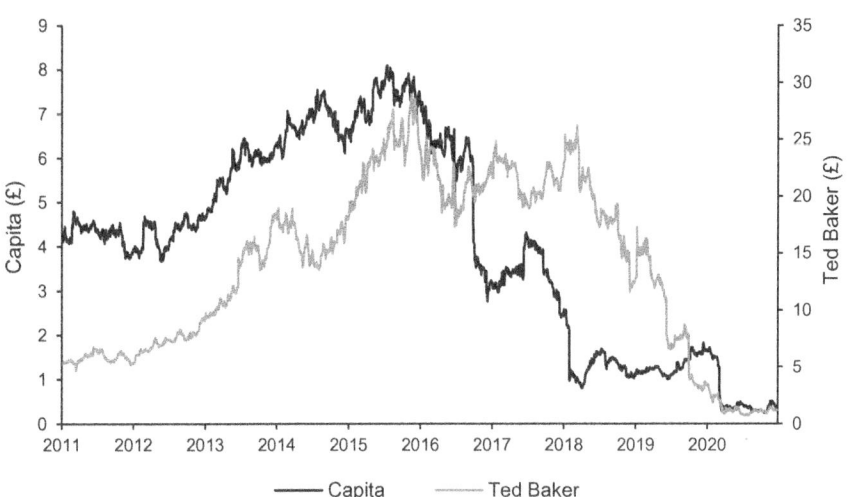

Fig. 7.2 Historical share prices of Capita and Ted Baker (2011–2020)

to consistently maintain or increase earnings over time. Many profit warnings are issued each year across different sectors. EY started the analysis of UK profit warnings in 1999. Its research provides valuable insights into profit warnings in the UK. More than 2,000 UK companies issued profit warnings during the 20 years to 2018 [6]. Profit warning happened to all FTSE sectors, with support services, software & computer services and general retailers recording the highest numbers. On average, 15% of public companies in the UK issued profit warnings each year between 1999 and 2018. Profit warning becomes a more common phenomenon in difficult years. The global coronavirus pandemic prompted a surge in profit warnings. The percentage of UK companies releasing profit warnings reached a record high of 35% in 2020 [7].

A profit warning provides investors with an opportunity to revise earnings forecasts. It is essential that investors understand its causes and implications before taking decisive actions. Many investors simply ignore profit warnings and continue to hold shares in troubled companies. They even believe profit warnings create an ideal buying opportunity as share prices decline. However, profit warnings are rarely an isolated company event. The earnings challenge disclosed in the first warning often leads to more profit warnings and radical business change. Tesco issued five profit warnings in 2014 and lost nearly half of its market value. Following its accounting scandal and dismal earnings results, the embattled retailer was forced to undertake a radical strategic business review to restore investor confidence. The continuing difficult trading conditions in the UK grocery market pose a serious challenge for Tesco to rebuild its business and return to the path of steady growth. Numerous troubled companies in a challenging business environment never recover after profit warnings. The collapse of Thomas Cook, Carillion and Debenhams clearly demonstrates the risk of investing in companies with struggling business and a weak financial position. Carpetright shares suffered an extreme loss of about 90% in 2018 after a string of profit warnings. The flooring retailer was eventually acquired by its largest shareholder to avoid the collapse into administration.

The investment in companies with profit warnings requires a prudent approach. It is necessary to understand if a profit warning reflects a temporary earnings issue or fundamental business challenges. In general, investors are advised to avoid companies with severe profit warnings to mitigate downside risk. A severe profit warning is often followed by a strategic business review and restructuring program. But many companies struggle to rebuild their failing business and issue more profit warnings before ultimate collapse. The case of HMV demonstrates the difficulty of reviving a failed company with a broken business model. The music and film retailer provided a series of severe profit warnings before its collapse in 2013. The retailer entered administration again in 2018 as it succumbed to the relentless rise of digital media. During the 20 years to 2018, 20% of UK public companies that issued three or more profit warnings became delisted within a year after the last warning [6]. This shows the great risk of investing in companies with distressed business. It is advisable that investors reduce exposure to troubled companies to protect capital against potential extreme losses.

7.4 Broker Research

Broker research serves as a valuable source of information to support investment decisions. Equity analysts at brokerage firms and investment banks produce research reports on public companies. They provide earnings estimates and typically issue a target price and investment recommendation. The consensus estimates of research analysts represent the market views on a stock. Broker research is widely followed by the investment community. A change in analyst views on a stock can significantly affect its share price and trading volume. However, investors need to adopt a cautious stance towards analyst ratings. It often happens that some equity analysts still maintain buy ratings on companies that are on the brink of collapse. Many investors continue to hold failing investments on the basis of favourable analyst ratings. They fail to consider potential biases in analyst research. For example, academic studies found equity analysts tend to provide optimistic earnings forecasts for companies with low predictability [8]. They generally recommend stocks with favourable characteristics, such as high growth and positive momentum [9].

Investment success requires the ability to protect capital against extreme losses. The failure to leave companies with deteriorating fundamentals and cut losses quickly often leads to poor investment results. Investors are encouraged to make independent investment decisions rather than overly rely on broker research. Many studies provide strong evidence that analyst ratings are often unduly positive. Analysts frequently assign buy ratings to companies while seldom issuing sell ratings. A Stockopedia study examines analyst ratings of stocks listed on the London Stock Exchange in 2016 [10]. The results show that 77% of the stocks received a consensus rating of buy or strong buy, compared to only 3% with a sell rating. An analysis performed by the Bespoke Investment Group demonstrates the skewed distribution of analyst recommendations towards the buy rating [11]. The constituents of the S&P 500 Index collectively received more than 12,000 analyst ratings in February 2015. The buy rating occupied a proportion of 48.4%, significantly higher than 6.7% for the sell rating. The prevalence of the buy rating assigned to S&P 500 members is confirmed in a FactSet study [12]. The buy recommendation represented 49.5% of all ratings on stocks in the S&P 500 Index at the end of 2017. In contrast, the sell rating only carried a small weighting of 5.2%.

The bias towards the buy rating raises the question about the independence and objectivity of broker research. Research analysts at brokerage firms potentially face conflicts of interest relating to brokerage business. They may provide optimistic ratings to encourage trading activities and generate brokerage commissions [13]. A paper in Management Science provides empirical evidence that analysts at brokerage firms issue more positive stock ratings than those working at institutional investors [14]. The phenomenon of research optimism is particularly pronounced in the largecap sector as analysts may face pressure from large companies. A research conducted by S&P Global Market Intelligence examines all analyst ratings on the constituents of the Russell 3000 Index between 2003 and 2018 [15]. The aggregate results show that the largest 100 stocks had an average buy/sell ratio of 14. Excluding the top 100 stocks, the buy/sell ratio falls to a more reasonable level around 6.

7.5 Short Selling

Short selling in equity markets is a trading strategy that seeks to profit from an anticipated decline in the price of a stock. Short sellers borrow shares from a brokerage firm and sell them in the market. Subsequently, they attempt to buy the shares back at a lower price and return them to the broker to close the position. The maximum return on a short sale is 100% when the share price falls to zero. But the loss is theoretically unlimited as the share price may increase to infinity. Short selling is generally considered an important function in the financial market. It contributes to market efficiency by bringing share prices closely in line with fundamental company values. Short selling also increases market liquidity and reduces the risk of asset bubbles. Regulators generally take a positive stance on the practice of short selling. They require the disclosure of short positions to increase the transparency of market transactions. Meanwhile, short selling is regarded as one of the controversial practices in the financial industry. Many people believe short selling is unethical because it attempts to profit from the failure of companies and destroy shareholder value. They complain short selling is a primary force that drives down share prices and causes unnecessary investor panic. The collective actions of short sellers even triggered some of the worst financial market failures. During the 2008 global financial crisis, the US Securities and Exchange Commission introduced temporary bans on many short-selling activities in response to market volatility.

Short sellers typically target companies that are significantly overvalued or have serious business issues. A high short interest in a stock is a warning sign indicating deep pessimism about its future performance. In 2018, short interest reached a high level in the beleaguered UK retail sector experiencing store closures and business failures. Following a string of profit warnings across the high street, short sellers aggressively attacked Marks & Spencer, Debenhams and other retailers. In July 2018, Marks & Spencer was exposed to an exceptional short interest of almost 17% (short interest is calculated as total shares held in short positions divided by shares in issue). Morrisons was also heavily shorted against the backdrop of intense price wars among food retailers in the UK. Cineworld, Metro Bank, AA and Pearson attracted considerable short interest after their profit warnings. Short sellers are ready to capitalise on company failures and often attack distressed businesses relentlessly. Many troubled companies are heavily shorted prior to ultimate collapse. For example, Thomas Cook and Carillion appeared in the list of 10 most shorted stocks traded on the London Stock Exchange before falling into liquidation. Struggling companies are vulnerable to short selling activities. Investors should manage losing investments carefully and take decisive actions when company fundamentals deteriorate.

References

1. Shefrin, H. and Statman, M., *The Disposition to Sell Winners Too Early and Ride Losers Too Long: Theory and Evidence.* Journal of Finance, 1985. **40**(3): p. 777–790.
2. Odean, T., *Are Investors Reluctant to Realize Their Losses?* Journal of Finance, 1998. **53**(5): p. 1775–1798.
3. Wilcox, C. and Crittenden, E., *The Capitalism Distribution.* 2008, Longboard Asset Management.
4. Cembalest, M., *The Agony and the Ecstasy: The Risks and Rewards of a Concentrated Stock Position.* 2014, J.P. Morgan Asset Management.
5. Lynch, P., *Beating the Street.* 1994, Simon & Schuster.
6. Hudson, A., *What Can 20 Years of Profit Warning Data Tell Us?* 2019, EY.

7. Hudson, A., *Hidden Stresses*, in *EY-Parthenon Quarterly Analysis of UK Profit Warnings*. 2021, EY.
8. Das, S., Levine, C.B. and Sivaramakrishnan, K., *Earnings Predictability and Bias in Analysts' Earnings Forecasts*. The Accounting Review, 1998. **73**(2): p. 277–294.
9. Jegadeesh, N., et al., *Analyzing the Analysts: When Do Recommendations Add Value?* Journal of Finance, 2004. **59**(3): p. 1083–1124.
10. Croft, E., *Can You Beat the Market Using Broker Buy Recommendations?* 2016, Stockopedia.
11. *The Most Loved and Hated Stocks in the S&P 500*. 2015, Bespoke Investment Group.
12. Butters, J., *S&P 500 Companies with Lowest Percent of Buy Ratings Are Top Performers in 2018*. 2018, FactSet.
13. Cowen, A., Groysberg, B. and Healy, P., *Which Types of Analyst Firms Are More Optimistic?* Journal of Accounting and Economics, 2006. **41**(1): p. 119–146.
14. Groysberg, B., et al., *The Stock Selection and Performance of Buy-Side Analysts*. Management Science, 2013. **59**(5): p. 1062–1075.
15. Tortoriello, R., *Bridges for Sale: Finding Value in Sell-Side Estimates, Recommendations, and Target Prices*. 2019, S&P Global Market Intelligence.

8

Sustainable Investing

8.1 Sustainable Investing

Sustainable investing is an investment approach that considers environmental, social and governance (ESG) issues alongside financial factors in the investment process. This term is often used interchangeably with ESG investing and responsible investing [1–4]. The practice of sustainable investing formally started in the 1960s when socially concerned investors specifically avoided businesses perceived to have negative social effects (e.g. alcohol and gambling). Today ESG issues are increasingly recognised as critical factors that determine the success of companies. Sustainable investing has gained strong market acceptance and continues to rise in prominence. According to the research of Global Sustainable Investment Alliance (GSIA), the amount of sustainable investments reached $30.7 trillion in the five major developed markets at the start of 2018, an increase of 34% over 2 years [1]. These assets are primarily domiciled in Europe (46%) and the US (39%), followed by Japan (7%), Canada (6%) and Australia/New Zealand (2%). As sustainable investing gains momentum around the world, an increasing number of investment managers have signed up to the Principles for Responsible Investment (PRI) supported by the United Nations. Figure 8.1 shows the steady rise in the number of PRI signatories and their total assets under management. In 2006, the PRI received support from 63 signatories with the combined assets of $6.5 trillion. The number of signatories has since grown significantly to 2,372 in 2019, representing $86.3 trillion in assets under management (source: PRI).

© The Author(s), under exclusive license to Springer Nature
Switzerland AG 2022
B. Jiang, *Investment Strategies*,
https://doi.org/10.1007/978-3-030-82711-3_8

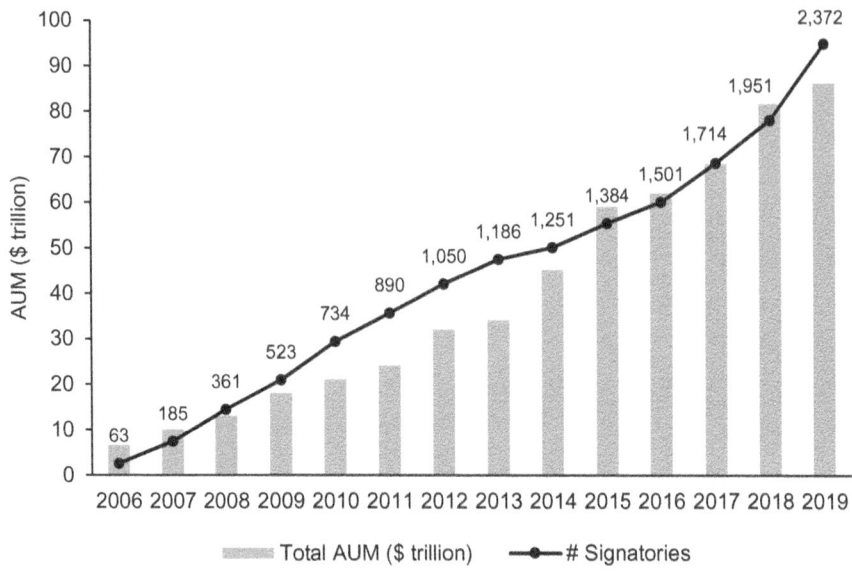

Fig. 8.1 The growth in the number of signatories to the Principles for Responsible Investment

The PRI is dedicated to promoting the principles of responsible investing and supporting its members to incorporate ESG factors into their investment practices across asset classes. The PRI developed six core principles that provide a framework for global investors to consider ESG issues. The six principles cover the adoption, implementation and promotion of ESG investing by institutional investors. The ESG guidance provided by the PRI aligns with the 17 Sustainable Development Goals established by the United Nations in 2015, including energy, climate, education and health. The acceleration in the adoption of sustainable investing during recent years is prompted by a number of factors. The force of technological change continues to disrupt industries and reshape the world. Many challenges relentlessly pose risks for investors across the globe, such as climate change, energy resources, demographic shifts and data security. Regulators have introduced numerous rules and standards to tackle environmental and social issues while enhancing corporate governance. The many ESG initiatives in the market are instrumental in helping shape the values and beliefs of investors about sustainable investing. Investors are increasingly accepting the concept of sustainable investing and adopting ESG factors in their portfolios. The case for sustainable investing becomes even more compelling when investors realise that this approach does not necessarily require the compromise on investment returns. In fact, many empirical studies provide evidence that ESG investing has great potential to enhance risk-adjusted returns. Meanwhile, the rise of ESG investing has been strongly supported by the improvement in ESG data and analytics capabilities. This allows the ESG approach to be explored in a systematic and objective manner by investors.

Sustainable investing is expected to continue its strong growth as investors take the opportunity to align investments with their values and financial objectives. Morgan Stanley conducted its third Sustainable Signals survey of individual investors in 2018 [5]. The results show that 85% of individual investors in the US are interested in sustainable investing, an increase of 10% from 2017. The survey found that 84% of respondents want the ability to tailor investments to their values. Besides, 86% of survey participants believe corporate ESG practices could potentially result in better long-term investments. Most respondents (88%) hold the view that it is possible to balance financial gains with a focus on social and environmental impact. UBS surveyed more than 5,300 investors in 10 markets on sustainable investing in 2018 [6]. In the survey, 39% of respondents indicated that they have already allocated capital to sustainable investments. The vast majority of sustainable investors (93%) in the survey support the view that investment performance is not necessarily compromised by ESG considerations. They believe that sustainable investments are capable of generating similar or better returns when compared to traditional investments, resulting from stronger business practices, better management and visionary thinking. UBS also partnered with Responsible Investor in a survey to understand the extent to which asset owners are integrating ESG into their investment process [7]. Conducted in 2019, the survey found 78% of asset owners in the study have already adopted ESG integration in the investment process. The results show that the top three reasons for the ESG integration among asset owners are: (1) the risk of ignoring ESG factors, (2) fiduciary duty, and (3) potential financial performance. A majority of survey participants agree that ESG is a relevant consideration in their process of manager search and selection. The ESG Global Survey conducted by BNP Paribas in 2019 seeks to understand the practical implications of ESG investing for asset managers and owners in the regions of Asia Pacific, Europe and North America [8]. The survey shows that a significant proportion of asset owners (75%) and managers (62%) have invested 25% or more of their assets in funds that incorporate ESG issues. The results suggest that investors adopt the ESG approach primarily for the consideration of long-term returns, reputation and investment risk. In addition, 65% of survey respondents revealed that their investment framework has already aligned with the Sustainable Development Goals of the United Nations. In 2019, State Street surveyed over 300 senior executives to gain insights into the implementation of ESG strategies in investment portfolios [9]. The survey found fiduciary duty, regulatory pressure and ESG risk mitigation are the key factors driving investors towards ESG.

The broad spectrum of sustainable investing covers a range of investment objectives and approaches. MSCI classifies the objectives of ESG investors into three categories: values, impact and integration [2, 10]. Values-based investing seeks to align investments with values and norms by specifying preferences for appropriate industries and companies. It typically uses negative screening to exclude companies with controversial businesses, such as alcohol, tobacco, gambling and weapons. This investment objective is shaped by ethical standards and unrelated to financial interests. Impact investing targets investments to generate positive social or environmental impacts alongside financial returns. Investment capital is purposefully directed to businesses with a clear social or environmental purpose. Because impact investing often prioritises towards positive social or environmental benefits, its strategies may not produce great risk-adjusted returns. The primary objective of ESG integration is to enhance risk-adjusted returns by systematically incorporating ESG factors into investment analysis and portfolio management. Institutional investors are increasingly aware of investment risks and opportunities related to ESG issues. In general, the practice of ESG investing comprises six common approaches: (1) negative screening, (2) positive screening, (3) thematic investing, (4) impact investing, (5) active ownership, and (6) ESG integration [1, 2, 11, 12]. Negative screening is the exclusion of specific industries, companies or practices from investment portfolios based on values, norms and standards. Positive screening is the selection of companies with leading sustainability practices relative to industry peers. Thematic investing focuses on trends or structural shifts that contribute to the development of sustainability. Impact investing directs capital to investments with the intention to generate measurable positive social or environmental benefits together with a financial return. Active ownership is the active corporate engagement that employs shareholder power to influence the behaviour of companies on ESG issues and policies. ESG integration is the explicit and systematic inclusion of ESG criteria into investment analysis and decisions. While these ESG approaches have distinct characteristics, they are not mutually exclusive. ESG investors can combine them practically to achieve specific sustainability objectives.

The Global Sustainable Investment Review 2018 report reveals that negative screening and ESG integration have a dominant position among sustainable investing strategies [1]. Figure 8.2 exhibits the distribution of global

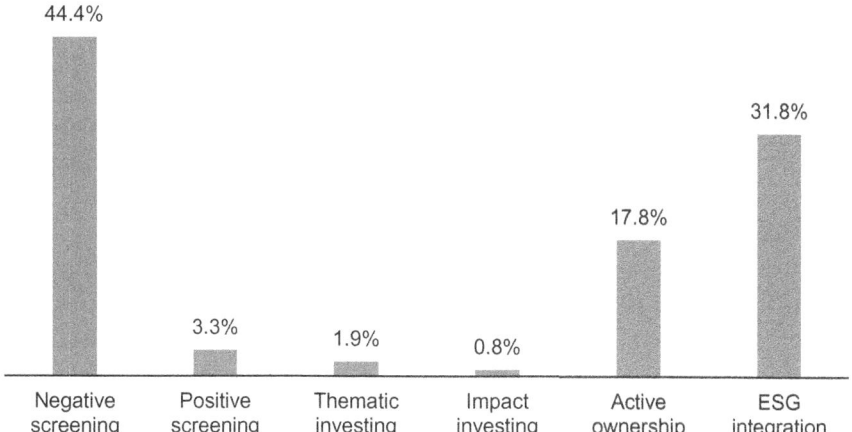

Fig. 8.2 The distribution of global sustainable investment assets by ESG approach

sustainable investment assets by ESG approach in 2018 (source: GSIA). Positive screening, thematic investing and impact investing have a negligible presence in sustainability assets. However, the three ESG approaches actually have achieved very strong growth in recent years. Their annualised growth rates reached 50.1%, 92.0% and 33.7% respectively during the 2 years to 2018. According to the report, there are significant regional differences in the adoption of ESG approaches. While negative screening is the major ESG method in Europe, ESG integration represents the leading sustainability strategy in the United States, Canada, Australia and New Zealand. In Japan, active ownership and ESG integration are the two primary approaches used in sustainable investing.

8.2 ESG Factors

Environmental, social and governance (ESG) criteria are the three central factors used to measure the sustainability impact of an investment. Investors apply ESG standards to analyse corporate behaviour, evaluate related risks and opportunities and determine the future performance of companies. Past research found that each of the three ESG pillars can affect the performance of investment portfolios [13]. The ESG term was first used in a landmark study *Who Cares Wins* launched in 2004 as a joint initiative of the United Nations Global Compact and financial institutions around the world [14]. The study believes that the effective management of environmental, social and governance issues is important for companies to operate successfully in an increasingly globalised, interconnected and competitive world. Companies that manage these issues well can increase shareholder value by reducing risks and making better investment decisions. The concerted effort to tackle ESG issues in the financial industry will result in more resilient financial markets and contribute to the sustainable development of societies. The initiative recommends that financial institutions integrate ESG factors systematically into research and investment processes. Since the launch of the initiative, ESG issues have been an increasing focus among institutional investors seeking to align their investments with the principles of sustainable investing.

The environmental factor considers issues that affect the environment, such as climate change, carbon emissions, air pollution, energy resources, waste management and water conservation. This factor is primarily concerned with the utilisation of natural resources by companies and the impact of their businesses on the environment. The ability to mitigate environmental risks and comply with related regulatory standards has important financial implications for companies. Firms that neglect environmental issues are exposed to high operational and financial risks. Historically, many environmental disasters were caused by negligence and resulted in severe financial and reputational losses for the companies involved (e.g. 2010 BP oil spill, 2015 Samarco dam collapse). They also triggered the enforcement of stricter regulations around the world to enhance environmental protection. Given the growing concern about climate change, companies are increasingly recognising the need to disclose and reduce carbon emissions. MSCI provides carbon emissions and intensity data to help investors understand and manage carbon risk in their portfolios. The social aspect of ESG examines the relationships of a company with its various stakeholders (e.g. employees, customers). Social issues include employee relations, health and safety, gender diversity, product responsibility and data security. The effective management of social issues is essential for business sustainability and success. This is because social factors can materially affect the business development and financial performance of a company. For example, companies that fail to treat their employees fairly will be in a difficult position to secure a stable and productive workforce. Companies with serious product safety risks may face consumer protests and lawsuits which will damage corporate reputation. Supplier relationship is important for companies to access critical resources reliably. Many global companies are supported by strong supply chains that are flexible and efficient in changing markets. The governance component of ESG is the system by which a company is managed and controlled. Corporate governance is concerned with the distribution of rights and responsibilities among stakeholders. Common governance issues include shareholder rights, board composition, executive compensation, financial reporting, auditing standards and regulatory compliance. The existence of an effective governance mechanism prevents or mitigates potential conflicts of interest among different participants in the company. Strong corporate governance is critical to the long-term success of a company. Because it provides the foundation for business integrity, investor confidence and sustainable development. Conversely, poor governance practice may completely destroy shareholder value. The collapse of NMC Health can demonstrate the consequence of poor corporate governance. The investment firm Muddy Waters released a report in December 2019 that accused this former FTSE 100 company of manipulating its balance sheet to understate debt. In March 2020, NMC announced that it discovered evidence of suspected fraud, as it identified more than $2.7 billion in debt facilities never disclosed to the board. A month later, NMC fell into administration due to the insolvency caused by the fraud and accounting scandal.

ESG criteria provide valuable insights into potential sustainability risks of companies. They are increasingly recognised as important factors for company valuation, risk management and regulatory compliance. Investors can actively evaluate the ESG risks of companies and integrate them into financial analysis and investment decisions. Alternatively, investors can rely on ESG ratings provided by financial data companies such as Refinitiv and Bloomberg. ESG rating systems are designed to measure the ESG performance of companies in a transparent and objective way. To calculate ESG scores, Refinitiv captures and selects about 200 company-level measures from reported data in the public domain [15]. These measures are grouped into 10 categories across the three ESG pillars. The environmental factor is defined by the three categories of resource use, emissions and innovation. The social factor is represented by workforce, human rights, community and product responsibility. The governance aspect is captured by measures relating to management, shareholders and CSR strategy. The aggregation of individual ESG scores across the 10 categories results in the overall ESG rating of a company. As a leading provider of market indices and portfolio tools, MSCI is among the largest ESG rating agencies in the world. MSCI assesses ESG risks through 37 key ESG issues divided into 10 themes [16]. For example, the environmental pillar covers the four themes of climate change, natural resources, pollution & waste, and environmental opportunities. Individual scores of the key ESG issues are combined by weighted average to form the composite ESG score. The composite score is further normalised by industry and converted to a rating between AAA and CCC. The ESG rating effectively provides an objective assessment of the overall ESG performance of a company relative to its industry peers. MSCI has extended its ESG rating system to investment funds by aggregating ESG characteristics of portfolio holdings. Morningstar also provides ESG fund ratings to help investors understand and compare ESG risks of portfolios [17]. The sustainability rating for a portfolio is calculated by combining ESG ratings of underlying companies supplied by Sustainalytics. In April 2020, Morningstar announced its decision to acquire Sustainalytics in a move to enhance its capabilities in the ESG space.

8.3 ESG Integration

ESG integration is the practice of systematically incorporating material environmental, social and governance issues into investment processes to enhance risk-adjusted returns. It seeks to assess risks and opportunities related to ESG issues in an effort to construct more resilient investment portfolios. Along with negative screening, ESG integration is a primary investment approach used in sustainable investing across many asset classes and strategies. It has been increasingly adopted by institutional investors in investment analysis and portfolio management. During the 2 years to 2018, ESG integration in the developed markets experienced a strong growth of 69% [1]. The rise of ESG integration is supported by the increasing evidence that it is positively related to investment performance. This practice essentially allows investors to identify additional sources of risk and return provided by ESG information. The examination of ESG exposures and sustainability performance can help investors make more informed investment decisions.

ESG integration is a complex process that involves the evaluation of risks and opportunities associated with environmental, social and governance issues. While negative screening simply excludes controversial businesses, ESG integration needs to formally incorporate sustainability information into full investment analysis. The CFA Institute launched a study in collaboration with the Principles for Responsible Investment to provide a practical guidance on ESG integration for analysts and investors. The joint effort resulted in the publication *Guidance and Case Studies for ESG Integration: Equities and Fixed Income* in 2018 [18]. This report provides insightful information concerning ESG integration techniques and practices around the world. The case studies contained in the report can help investment practitioners understand best practices in ESG integration and develop their own approach to including ESG information in investment processes. The report presents an ESG integration framework that illustrates the application of ESG investment techniques. The framework is composed of three levels: research, security and portfolio. The research level covers the collection and qualitative analysis of ESG information. The security level assesses the impact of ESG factors and make relevant adjustments to forecasts and valuations for companies. The portfolio level considers ESG risks of individual securities and adjusts their weightings in the portfolio to achieve desired ESG exposures.

ESG integration is often implemented as a qualitative approach to support investment decisions. With the proliferation of ESG data, it has become increasingly common for ESG factors to be integrated into quantitative models. Abundant ESG indices are available in the market designed to gain enhanced exposure to positive ESG factors. For example, the MSCI ACWI ESG Leaders Index provides exposure to companies with high ESG ratings relative to their sector peers. An MSCI research paper compares the risk and return characteristics of this ESG index against the broad market benchmark MSCI ACWI Index [19]. The research findings suggest that the integration of ESG criteria into passive strategies can improve risk-adjusted returns. ESG integration can also be applied to factor strategies to enhance ESG exposure or potential investment performance. An MSCI study examines the effects of ESG integration on the risk characteristics and performance of factor portfolios [20]. The results show that the inclusion of ESG criteria does not significantly change portfolio exposure to target factors (e.g. value, volatility), while the ESG profile can be greatly improved. This indicates that ESG measures can be successfully integrated into traditional factor strategies without affecting their ability to generate abnormal returns. The study also found ESG score is positively correlated with the factors of size, quality and low volatility.

Considering its many unique characteristics, investors may wonder if ESG should be treated as an independent factor that possibly delivers long-term outperformance. According to the Invesco Global Factor Investing Study in 2019 [21], there is divided opinion among institutional investors regarding the potential role of ESG as a systematic risk factor. According to the views of 132 institutional investors in the study, only 28% of them consider ESG an independent investment factor, while 40% believe ESG is a combination of multiple style factors. The remaining 32% of institutional respondents actually think ESG is a variation of the quality factor. This view is supported by the fact that the positive link between ESG and quality has been identified by 70% of survey respondents who have performed factor analysis for their ESG portfolios. Besides, 53% of survey participants found ESG portfolios usually have negative exposure to the value factor. Despite the disagreement about the role of ESG as an independent risk factor, most institutional investors (84%) in the study have incorporated ESG into their investment process.

8.4 Investment Benefits

The active adoption of sustainable investing requires a clear understanding of its value proposition. Subject to investment objectives, sustainable investing in practice can be implemented through different approaches. While negative screening seeks to exclude companies with controversial activities due to ethical considerations, ESG integration is primarily concerned with investment performance. Because of significant variations in the investment objective, it is difficult to generalise about the value of sustainable investing. The consensus is that sustainability issues are important to the long-term interests of companies and society. ESG investing provides investors with a good opportunity to align personal values with financial objectives. Institutional investors are increasingly incorporating ESG standards into their investment process. With the rising awareness of sustainability issues, ESG investing is expected to continue its growth in prominence. For investors focusing on investment returns, ESG integration is the most relevant approach to sustainable investing. The analysis of ESG information can provide valuable insights on risk and opportunities that are not captured in traditional financial analysis. It allows investors to gain a deeper understanding of the risk profile and long-term prospects of a company. Companies with strong ESG criteria are often more capable of providing sustainable revenue streams and stable earnings through responsible risk management practices. A research conducted by Bank of America Merrill Lynch ranked companies into 5 groups by ESG score to compare their earnings volatility over the subsequent 5 years [22]. The results show that companies in the best ESG group realised the lowest volatility in earnings, while those in the worst ESG group experienced the highest volatility. The advantage of risk reduction is clear for companies with strong governance practices. For example, a Barclays study found bonds with high governance scores are less likely to experience credit rating downgrades than their peers with weak governance ratings [4]. At the portfolio level, investment funds targeting companies with sound ESG practices tend to feature more positive volatility and downside risk characteristics. In a 2019 study, Morgan Stanley compares the volatility risk between sustainable and traditional funds [23]. The analysis of over 10,000 mutual funds in the Morningstar database shows that sustainable funds overall achieved lower price volatility than their traditional peers consistently across the 15 years to 2018.

Alongside the dramatic rise of sustainable investing, a plethora of studies have been conducted to investigate the financial effects of ESG factors. Past research only provides mixed results concerning the relationship between ESG criteria and financial performance. The inconclusive results can be explained by the fact that many ESG practices are not directed at generating compelling financial results. Nevertheless, insightful evidence can be obtained from results produced by the meta-analysis method. This statistical method combines results from multiple studies to draw more convincing conclusions. A joint research between University of Oxford and Arabesque in 2015 employs a meta-analysis of over 200 studies to examine the effects of corporate sustainability practices [24]. The research findings suggest that sound sustainability standards and practices can materially reduce the cost of capital and enhance both operational and financial performance for companies. The study demonstrates that responsibility and profitability are not incompatible but actually rather complementary. A research paper published in 2015 by the Journal of Sustainable Finance & Investment aggregates the findings of about 2,200 individual studies to assess the financial effects of ESG standards [25]. The combined results show that a large majority of studies support a positive relationship between sustainability and financial performance at the company level. For investment portfolios, the relationship between ESG score and performance is rather weak. The positive relationship is only supported by 15.5% of studies, while most studies (73.5%) report neutral or mixed results. A Morningstar research paper provides a reasonable explanation for the observed weak relationship between ESG and investment performance [26]. This study argues that the aggregation of ESG portfolios with different objectives may fail to capture the performance contribution of ESG factors. The reality is that ESG investments are often driven by values and norms rather than financial incentives. While ESG integration has great potential to improve returns, some sustainable investing approaches (e.g. negative screening) may negatively affect performance. Therefore, the positive return effect is possibly offset by the negative effect in a mixed sample, resulting in statistically insignificant results. The general conclusion is that sustainable investing overall does not hurt investment returns [27].

The complexity of sustainability issues will likely cause confusion in the analysis of ESG factors. The variations in the objective and approach of ESG strategies can explain the failure of previous studies to reach consensus on the performance of sustainable investing. Numerous ESG indices in the market are designed with different sustainability objectives and methodologies. For example, the S&P 500 ESG Index selects securities with good ESG scores, while it also applies negative screening to exclude companies with controversial business activities (e.g. tobacco and weapons). For the 10 years to April 2020, it delivered an annualised gross total return of 12.0% (source: index factsheet). This is marginally higher than 11.7% provided by its benchmark S&P 500 Index during the same period. The MSCI KLD 400 Social Index comprises 400 US securities with outstanding ESG ratings and excludes companies whose products cause negative social or environmental impacts. MSCI provides a very wide range of ESG indices associated with common approaches to sustainable investing: (1) ESG integration, (2) values/screening, and (3) impact investing. The existence of numerous sustainability indices in the market poses a real challenge to select representative benchmarks for assessing the return effects of ESG factors. Clearly, a market index used to evaluate ESG performance must specifically target companies with strong ESG scores. MSCI ESG Leaders indices select companies with high ESG ratings and are suitable for assessing the return potential of ESG strategies. The MSCI ACWI ESG Leaders Index posted an average annual return of 8.0% during the 10 years to April 2020 (source: index factsheet). This represents a marginal outperformance of 0.5% per year relative to the benchmark MSCI ACWI Index. In comparison, the MSCI Emerging Markets ESG Leaders Index outperformed the MSCI Emerging Markets Index by an average of 3.4% per annum over the same period. The significant return premium may suggest that ESG strategies have great potential to enhance investment returns in emerging markets where ESG practices are relatively weak.

References

1. 2018 *Global Sustainable Investment Review*. 2019, Global Sustainable Investment Alliance.
2. *Introducing ESG Investing*. 2018, MSCI ESG Research.
3. *Decoding ESG: A Guide to Responsible Investing*. 2019, Aegon Asset Management.
4. Desclée, A., et al., *Sustainable Investing and Bond Returns*. 2016, Barclays.
5. *Sustainable Signals: Individual Investor Interest Driven by Impact, Conviction and Choice*. 2019, Morgan Stanley.
6. *UBS Investor Watch: Return on Values*. 2018, UBS.
7. Fritsch, D., *ESG: Do You or Don't You?* 2019, Responsible Investor.
8. *The ESG Global Survey*. 2019, BNP Paribas.

9. *Into the Mainstream: ESG at the Tipping Point.* 2019, State Street Global Advisors.
10. *The MSCI Principles of Sustainable Investing.* 2019, MSCI.
11. *Understanding Sustainable Investment and ESG Terms.* 2020, Schroders.
12. *Environmental, Social, and Governance Issues in Investing: A Guide for Investment Professionals.* 2015, CFA Institute.
13. Hitchens, R., McCullagh, S. and Parks, C., *Finding Alpha in ESG.* 2015, Credit Suisse.
14. *Who Cares Wins: Connecting Financial Markets to a Changing World.* 2004, United Nations.
15. *Environmental, Social and Governance (ESG) Scores from Refinitiv.* 2020, Refinitiv.
16. *MSCI ESG Ratings Methodology: Executive Summary.* 2019, MSCI ESG Research.
17. *Morningstar Sustainability Rating: Methodology.* 2019, Morningstar.
18. *Guidance and Case Studies for ESG Integration: Equities and Fixed Income.* 2018, CFA Institute.
19. Giese, G., et al., *Foundations of ESG Investing: Integrating ESG into Passive Institutional Portfolios.* 2018, MSCI.
20. Melas, D., Nagy, Z. and Kulkarni, P., *Factor Investing and ESG Integration.* 2016, MSCI.
21. *Invesco Global Factor Investing Study.* 2019, Invesco.
22. Subramanian, S., et al., *ESG Part II: A Deeper Dive.* 2017, Bank of America Merrill Lynch.
23. *Sustainable Reality: Analysing Risk and Returns of Sustainable Funds.* 2019, Morgan Stanley.
24. Clark, G.L., Feiner, A. and Viehs, M., *From the Stockholder to the Stakeholder: How Sustainability Can Drive Financial Outperformance.* 2015, University of Oxford.
25. Friede, G., Busch, T. and Bassen, A., *ESG and Financial Performance: Aggregated Evidence from More Than 2000 Empirical Studies.* Journal of Sustainable Finance & Investment, 2015. **5**(4): p. 210–233.
26. Hale, J., *Sustainable Investing Research Suggests No Performance Penalty.* 2016, Morningstar.
27. *Does Socially Responsible Investing Hurt Investment Returns?* 2019, RBC Global Asset Management.

9

Size Effect

9.1 Size Effect

The size effect is a phenomenon in investing that smaller companies tend to outperform those with larger market capitalisations in the long term. The size premium was identified by Rolf Banz and formally presented in his research paper *The Relationship between Return and Market Value of Common Stocks*. Published in 1981 by the Journal of Financial Economics, the research found empirical evidence that smaller companies on average achieved significantly higher risk-adjusted returns than their larger peers over a 40-year period to 1975. Despite the identification of the size effect, the paper does not provide a theoretical foundation to explain this market anomaly. The paper concludes that it is unclear if size is essentially a factor or just a proxy for some unknown factors. However, the evidence of the size premium raises a serious question about the validity of the classic capital asset pricing model (CAPM). The CAPM specifies that the expected return of a security is determined by its sensitivity (i.e. beta) to the market return. The size effect indicates that the CAPM is misspecified in that size represents a second source of return beyond the systematic risk. This means that both beta and size are required to understand the expected return of a security. Besides, the size premium poses a real fundamental challenge to the efficient market hypothesis (EMH). The EMH states that prices reflect all available information and it is impossible to consistently beat the market. But the size effect documented in the research paper demonstrates that it is possible to earn excess returns by holding a diversified portfolio of smaller companies. Since the initial discovery, the smallcap effect has been examined by numerous academic studies. A research paper published by the Journal of Banking & Finance in 2011 reviews 30 years of research on the size effect [1]. The evidence of the size effect exists widely in the US and many international equity markets, such as Australia [2], Japan [3], Europe and emerging markets. In 1993, the Nobel laureate Eugene Fama and his research partner Kenneth French formally established size as a risk factor in their famous 3-factor asset pricing model [4]. This model extends the CAPM framework by adding the size and value factors to explain equity returns.

Following decades of research on the size effect, the investment community has been intrigued by the great return potential of smaller companies. Smallcap now represents a distinctive asset class that receives wide recognition among institutional investors. In 1992, Morningstar introduced its popular stylebox to help individual and professional investors understand the investment positioning of a mutual fund. The stylebox comprises the two dimensions of size and investment style, where size is divided into largecap, midcap and smallcap. In January 2001, MSCI as a global leader of market indices formally launched a series of smallcap indices (e.g. MSCI World Small Cap Index). The global universe of smaller companies provides investors with an enormous opportunity set to explore investment ideas. According to the methodology of MSCI global market indices, the smallcap segment covers about 14% of the investable equity universe by market value (free-float adjusted) [5]. The universe of smallcap stocks is significantly larger in number than the largecap universe. As of 31 March 2020, the MSCI ACWI Small Cap Index comprised 5,929 constituents across 23 developed countries and 26 emerging markets, while the MSCI ACWI Large Cap Index contained only 1,519 constituents. The sheer size of the smallcap universe is directly observable in the US market. As a broad smallcap benchmark, the Russell 2000 Index holds substantially more constituents than the S&P 500 Index. The vast smallcap universe allows investors to explore companies with compelling growth prospects and attractive valuations.

Smaller companies offer the potential benefits of strong growth, portfolio diversification and long-term outperformance. While generally accepted as a distinctive asset class, smallcap has been significantly underweighted in institutional investment portfolios. According to the S&P Global Ownership database, smallcap stocks only represented about 6% of equity assets among institutional investors in 2018 [6]. This may be due to the relatively low analyst coverage of smaller companies in the investment universe. Besides, smallcap stocks are often perceived to have higher risk than their larger counterparts in terms of volatility, liquidity and transparency. The market efficiency for smallcap stocks is considered relatively low as information is not readily available. Many market participants simply exclude smallcap companies in their portfolios to avoid the trouble of assessing smallcap risks. Another reason for the underinvestment in smallcap stocks is the reservation about the size effect. Despite the proven long-term outperformance, smallcap stocks underperformed the market materially over the period between 1984 and 1998. Figure 9.1 compares the historical performance of a smallcap portfolio against the S&P 500 Index. The smallcap portfolio is sourced from the data library maintained by Professor Kenneth French at Dartmouth College. This value-weighted smallcap portfolio is constructed annually and represents the bottom 30% of US stocks ranked by market capitalisation. From 1930 to 2019, the smallcap portfolio delivered an annualised return of 12.2%, materially higher than 9.4% produced by the S&P 500 Index.

Smallcap stocks successfully outperformed their larger peers (represented by the S&P 500 Index) for all the time periods in Fig. 9.1, except the 20 years to 1999. They recorded a negative relative return of 4.1% per annum over this 20-year period. The underperformance may be driven by the herding behaviour of investors seeking to exploit the size premium since its discovery in 1981. This raised the valuation levels of smallcap stocks and reduced their long-term return potential. Another convincing explanation for the serious underperformance relates to the innovation and technological advances in the 1990s. Most large technology companies saw their share prices increase substantially in this period and ultimately move beyond levels unjustified by company fundamentals. The severely inflated share prices suffered free fall

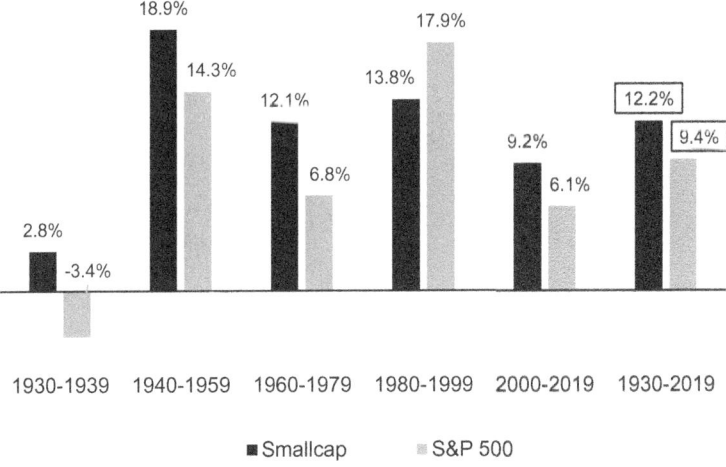

Fig. 9.1 Historical performance of smallcap and the S&P 500 Index

when the dot-com bubble eventually burst. This shows the potential impact of disruptive technological forces on the relative performance of smallcap stocks. Whereas systematic return drivers are able to generate positive excess returns in the long term, their behaviour is very susceptible to market forces and conditions. Risk factors like size may consistently produce positive or negative relative returns over an extended period of time. For example, the smallcap portfolio outperformed the S&P 500 Index consecutively over the 9 individual years to 1983, recording a cumulative performance of 1100% against 273% provided by the largecap benchmark. Conversely, it continually trailed the S&P 500 Index in annual return through the 5 years to 1998, resulting in a total underperformance of 124%.

The material underperformance of smallcap over the 15 years to 1998 prompted concerns about the existence of the size premium. During this period, large companies benefited substantially from positive shocks of profitability and produced much stronger returns than smallcap stocks. The paper *Resurrecting the Size Effect* published by the Review of Financial Studies in 2019 found the size effect was still very robust from the early 1980s, after adjusting for the price impact of profitability shocks [7]. While the size effect was continually under heavy scrutiny, the outperformance of smallcap stocks returned strongly at the turn of the century. Figure 9.2 displays the cumulative relative performance of smallcap against largecap from 1927 to 2019. The relative performance is based on geometric difference to allow compounding. Smallcap and largecap are respectively represented by two annually rebalanced

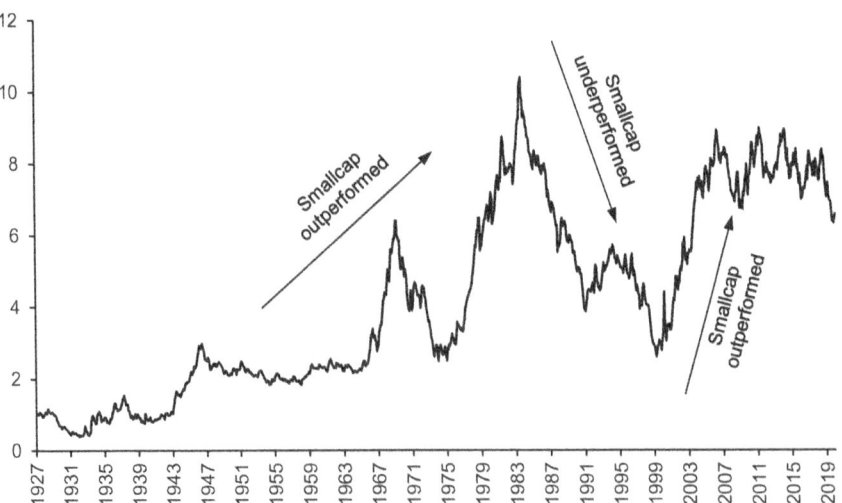

Fig. 9.2 Cumulative relative performance of smallcap against largecap

portfolios containing the bottom 30% and top 10% of US stocks ranked by market capitalisation in the data library of Professor Kenneth French. An upward (downward) curve indicates that smallcap outperformed (underperformed) relative to largecap. Smallcap delivered phenomenal outperformance over a relatively short period of 9 years to 1983. Subsequently, it experienced two lengthy periods of underperformance until 1998 and relinquished the entire excess return accumulated through the previous remarkable 9 years. The following 6-year period witnessed the strong recovery in the relative performance of smallcap stocks. They delivered a cumulative return of 157.7% during this period, compared to −5.7% provided by the largecap portfolio. From 1999 to 2019, smallcap generated an annualised return of 10.2%, representing a return premium of 4.2% per annum against largecap.

Historically, smaller companies overall delivered superior returns over the 90 years to 2019. The smallcap portfolio converted $1 in 1930 to $31,686 at the end of 2019. In comparison, the $1 invested in the S&P 500 Index would increase to only $3,381 through the same period. Given the proven historical performance, smallcap stocks should deserve serious attention from investors. The scale of the smallcap universe suggests that there are abundant opportunities to explore in this size segment. However, investors often avoid smaller companies due to negative perceptions about their risks and trading costs. Smallcap stocks are generally more volatile than established largecap names. Based on the standard deviation of annual returns between 1980 and 2019, the smallcap portfolio has a higher volatility level than the S&P 500 Index (21.6% vs 16.5%). But the smallcap portfolio actually never resulted in a loss over any rolling 10-year period between 1930 and 2019. This indicates that the holding period is an influential factor to consider when investing in smallcap stocks. For the 5-year holding period, the smallcap portfolio outperformed the S&P 500 Index with a frequency of 57% over the 90 years to 2019. If the holding period is extended to 10 years, the frequency would increase reasonably to 67%. When the holding period rises to 20 years, the smallcap portfolio outperformed the broad market benchmark with a frequency of about 80%. This demonstrates the advantage of adopting a long-term perspective when investing in the smallcap segment with relatively high price volatility. Smallcap stocks typically suffer material losses during recessions or market crashes. But they tend to recover quickly with substantial returns afterwards. According to a research paper by T. Rowe Price, US smallcap stocks historically returned an average of about 50% in the subsequent year following previous recessions or major market events [8].

9.2 Definition of Smallcap

Smallcap represents the lower tier of publicly listed companies by market capitalisation. There is no consensus in the market regarding the range of market value for the definition of smallcap stocks. Market participants have the freedom to classify stocks by company size. For example, smallcap can be defined as companies with a market capitalisation between $100 million and $2 billion. In general, smallcap occupies the size segment between microcap and midcap. Leading index providers have their own methodology to construct size indices. MSCI defines largecap as the top 70% of the investable universe by market value (free-float adjusted), with midcap and smallcap respectively providing the next 15% and 14% market coverage [5]. For each size segment, MSCI indices make necessary adjustments to the defined range and index constituents so that a target market is properly covered. S&P global equity indices utilise a similar methodology for the classification of stocks by size [9]. Companies in a specific market are first ranked by market capitalisation in descending order. Float-adjusted market value is then accumulated to 70% and 85% respectively to identify the size boundaries of largecap and midcap. The smallcap category represents the bottom 15% of the investable universe by market value. FTSE employs a comparable set of cut-off values to define size segments. The largest 68% of companies in a market are assigned to the largecap section, with the next 18% and 12% respectively represented by the midcap and smallcap categories [10]. STOXX has developed a wide range of smallcap indices, either containing a fixed or variable number of constituents. For example, the STOXX Europe Small 200 Index is composed of 200 companies to provide a representation of smallcap stocks in Europe [11]. The STOXX Europe TMI Small Index comprises a variable number of components to cover the smallcap section of the European equity universe. It also uses the above ranking method to select stocks for index construction.

Smallcap indices may have very different size characteristics arising from the variations in the definition of smallcap. Table 9.1 compares four European smallcap indices concerning the market values of their constituents. The data are sourced from index factsheets (as of 31 March 2020). The results show that the number of constituents varies considerably across the four indices. The S&P Europe Smallcap Index contained the largest number of 1,070 stocks, while the STOXX Europe Small 200 Index comprised a fixed number of only 200 components. Besides, there are significant differences in the range of market capitalisation. For both FTSE and STOXX indices, the market value of the largest constituent was below €5 billion. In contrast, the

Table 9.1 Constituent sizes of four European smallcap indices (31 March 2020)

Index	Number of constituents	Market Cap (€ million)		
		Smallest	Largest	Median
MSCI Europe Smallcap	964	21	7,087	566
S&P Europe Smallcap	1,070	5	13,335	787
FTSE Developed Europe Smallcap	695	14	4,262	584
STOXX Europe Small 200	200	600	4,400	2,100

largest component of the S&P index reached a market value of over €13 billion. This disproportionately large constituent may face elimination from the smallcap index at the next rebalancing point. For the STOXX index, the median market value of its constituents was significantly larger than that of the other three indices. This is because it limits the constituent number to only 200, rather than extending the selection list to add even smaller companies.

9.3 Characteristics of Smaller Companies

Smallcap as a distinctive asset class has many unique characteristics. The smallcap universe represents a large opportunity set that offers great return potential. Many smaller firms operate in a niche market with a sustainable competitive advantage. These firms maintain strategic positions in the market and often become a takeover target. Smallcap investing allows investors to gain exposure to companies that are managed by entrepreneurs with material insider ownership. The management team of a smallcap company likely has sizeable ownership interests in the business. High insider ownership enhances investor confidence that the management will focus on long-term value creation for shareholders due to the alignment of financial interests. Because of greater corporate flexibility, smaller companies are arguably more capable of achieving efficient capital allocation than their larger peers.

Smaller companies overall have more attractive growth prospects than larger firms as a result of the size advantage. Practically, it becomes more challenging for a company to maintain strong growth as the business scale increases. Established large companies eventually have limited growth opportunities when their business matures. Smaller companies, however, have sufficient room to grow in an improving economy. They are more capable of sustaining growth by capturing new market opportunities and adapting to changing trends. Since growth is a key driver of long-term performance, it is essential for investors to identify quality companies with good growth potential. There is significant dispersion in company quality across the immense smallcap universe. While some smaller companies have experienced phenomenal growth, a substantial number of firms in the smallcap sector actually never make any profits. At the end of 2018, about 45% of companies in the Russell 2000 Index produced negative earnings, compared to only 10% in the S&P 500 Index [12]. The high business failure rate in the smallcap segment suggests that disciplined research and diversification are necessary in the active management of smallcap stocks.

Smaller companies typically have a narrower business scope and involve less complex analysis than their larger counterparts. The smallcap sector is considered to have a lower level of market efficiency than the largecap sector. Many investors completely avoid smallcap stocks because of negative perceptions about their investment risks. Compared to largecap stocks, smaller companies are generally associated with higher levels of liquidity and volatility risk. MSCI conducted a study in 2016 to compare the liquidity of smallcap stocks against their largecap peers [13]. Assume $1 billion capital needs to be invested with a 20% of daily trading volume. It will take less than 1 day to form a portfolio that exactly replicates the MSCI USA Index. In comparison, it will take about 3 days to create a passive portfolio that tracks the MSCI USA Small Cap Index. When this capital is allocated to replicate the MSCI USA Small + Micro Cap Index, the trading period will be significantly stretched to 20 days. This shows the relevance of liquidity risk when investing in smaller companies. Low liquidity usually results in high trading costs (e.g. bid-ask spread). This can be mitigated by reducing transaction frequency and avoiding stocks with thin trading volume. The sheer size of the smallcap universe offers many promising investment ideas without the compromise on liquidity. According to an Invesco study, there were over 3,000 largecap stocks globally that had an average daily trading volume of above $5 million in September 2018 [14]. Although smallcap stocks generally have lower liquidity, the total number still exceeded 2,000 as a result of the large smallcap universe.

Some investors are reluctant to explore the smallcap space for the reason that they believe large companies generally have stronger governance and disclosure practices. Many small companies have limited information transparency as they do not disclose material information in a timely and frequent manner. This provides a strong rationale for investors to follow the principle of quality investing when selecting smallcap companies. Quality investing in the smallcap sector is also supported by the fact that smaller companies generally have lower profitability and higher leverage than their largecap counterparts [15]. Meanwhile, a lower level of transparency creates many mispriced smallcap stocks for diligent investors to explore. Investors with a disciplined research approach can systematically harvest the smallcap premium in the immense smallcap universe with weak market efficiency. The prevalence of mispriced smallcap securities is also caused by the relatively low research and media coverage in the smallcap sector. Many studies provide evidence that largecap stocks typically have greater analyst coverage than smallcap firms. For example, a research conducted by Aberdeen Standard Investments found that nearly 50% of companies in the MSCI ACWI Small Cap Index were covered by 7 or fewer analysts in December 2018 [15]. This only happened to about 5% of companies in the global large/midcap benchmark MSCI ACWI Index. Besides, only 28% of companies in the smallcap index were covered by more than 12 analysts, compared to 90% for the MSCI ACWI Index. The under-researched smallcap sector provides ample opportunities for investors to exploit. According to a UBS research paper, European stocks with low research coverage on average outperformed those with high coverage by 15% over the 9-year period to 2011 [16].

Large firms with strong resources often compete in the global market, while small companies tend to be more domestically focused. In 2010, foreign sales represented 49% of total revenue for large/midcap companies in the world [17]. Global smallcap companies overall relied less on foreign sales, with only 32% of revenue derived from foreign countries. In general, smaller companies have a more focused range of business activities than their larger peers. The smallcap and largecap sectors in a market can have very different industry compositions. This can be examined by comparing industry weights of broad smallcap and largecap market indices. For example, health care (18.0%) and consumer staples (17.8%) were the two largest sectors in the MSCI Europe Large Cap Index at the end of March 2020. Together with utilities, these three defensive sectors had a combined weight of over 40% in the largecap index. In comparison, they only occupied a total weight of about 20% in the MSCI Europe Small Cap Index. This smallcap index was heavily exposed to the industrials (20.7%) and financials (13.6%) sectors (source: index factsheets).

9.4 Fama–French 3-Factor Model

The Fama–French 3-factor model is an asset pricing model developed by the Nobel Prize winner Eugene Fama and his research partner Kenneth French. It was first presented in their research paper *Common Risk Factors in the Returns on Stocks and Bonds* published in 1993 by the Journal of Financial Economics [4]. In asset pricing and portfolio management, the 3-factor model has been extensively applied to explain equity returns due to its theoretical strength and practical performance. It is a significant extension of the traditional capital asset pricing model (CAPM). The CAPM has received heavy criticism from both academics and practitioners primarily because of its many unrealistic and even invalid assumptions [18]. It is overly simplified in that beta serves as the only variable in the model to explain return variations. The 3-factor model enhances the CAPM by adding the size and value factors. It describes the expected return of an equity portfolio as:

$$R = R_f + \beta(R_m - R_f) + b_s \times SMB + b_v \times HML + \alpha$$

Here, R is the expected portfolio return, R_f is the risk-free rate, R_m is the expected market return, and β is the sensitivity of portfolio return to the market risk premium $R_m - R_f$. These are the basic elements of the classic CAPM. The 3-factor model includes two additional factors: SMB (small minus big) and HML (high minus low). These two variables respectively measure the factor returns of size and value. The two parameters b_s and b_v represent the portfolio exposure to the size and value factors. The variable α is the excess return generated by the portfolio that cannot be explained by the model. If α is estimated to be statistically insignificant from zero, then this means the model can perfectly explain variations in portfolio returns.

To measure the factor returns of size and value, the research constructed value-weighted portfolios formed on the basis of market value and the book-to-market ratio. In June of each year from 1963 to 1991, all stocks listed on NYSE were ranked by market capitalisation and the median value was selected to divide the universe of NYSE, AMEX and NASDAQ stocks into two groups: small (S) and big (B). Similarly, stocks were sorted by the book-to-market ratio and divided into three groups: high (H), medium (M) and low (L). The three groups essentially represent the value, neutral and growth styles. At the intersection of the two ranking variables, a total of six portfolios could be formed: S/H, S/M, S/L, B/H, B/M and B/L. For example, the S/H portfolio consists of smaller companies with the value style, while the B/L portfolio comprises larger companies with growth characteristics. The return of the size factor SMB is then calculated as the difference between the average return of the three small portfolios and the average return of the three big portfolios:

$$SMB = 1/3 \times (S/H + S/M + S/L) - 1/3 \times (B/H + B/M + B/L)$$

Similarly, the return of the value factor HML is calculated as the difference between the average return of the two value portfolios and the average return of the two growth portfolios:

$$HML = 1/2 \times (S/H + B/H) - 1/2 \times (S/L + B/L)$$

The research created another 25 portfolios to test the performance of the model. Portfolio construction followed the same principle described above. Stocks were ranked by market value to form 5 size groups and then sorted independently by the book-to-market ratio to create 5 groups with different valuation levels. The interaction of the two ranking variables resulted in 25 portfolios. For each portfolio, its monthly returns from 1963 to 1991 were used as the dependent variable in the time-series regression to test the model. The results show that the 3-factor model captures a significant amount of variations in portfolio returns. The model explains over 90% of the variance in portfolio return for 21 portfolios. For the other 4 portfolios, the lowest R^2 is still very significant at 0.83. Besides, most intercepts of the 25 regressions are very close to 0 (only three differ from 0 by more than 0.2% per month). This demonstrates the strength of the model to explain portfolio returns. The results also prove that size is an essential factor to help explain return variations. The t-statistic for the regression coefficient of SMB remains very significant across almost all portfolios.

The return premium of the size factor is represented by SMB in the model. For the period of 28 years to 1991, the average return of SMB was estimated to be 0.27% per month (i.e. 3.2% per year). A significant contribution of the 3-factor model is that it formally establishes size as a key factor in asset pricing and portfolio management. Fama and French performed further tests for the 3-factor model in their paper *Multifactor Explanations of Asset Pricing Anomalies* published by the Journal of Finance in 1996 [19]. The research findings suggest that the model is capable of explaining several asset pricing anomalies in finance. In 2015, Fama and French extended the 3-factor model by adding the profitability and investment factors [20]. This enhanced model was found to reasonably improve the performance of the original model. Nevertheless, the 3-factor model will undoubtedly continue to serve as a fundamental framework in empirical research on asset pricing.

9.5 Return Premium

The size premium has been extensively studied and acknowledged in academic research since its identification in 1981. It is well documented that smallcap stocks have the tendency to outperform their larger peers in the long term. Smallcap now represents a distinctive asset class to support the construction of diversified portfolios. MSCI has formally launched a series of smallcap indices since 2001 to systematically capture the size premium. MSCI classifies size as a pro-cyclical factor that tends to outperform the market during periods of economic expansion. According to the simulated results, the MSCI World Equal Weighted Index generated an annualised return of over 11% through the 40-year period to 2017 [21]. The equal weighting method allows the index to effectively achieve a positive bias towards smaller companies by increasing their weightings in the index. The historical relative performance of MSCI smallcap indices provides further insight into the size effect. The global smallcap benchmark MSCI ACWI Small Cap Index delivered an annualised gross total return of 9.2% from 2001 to 2019, compared to 6.5% for the MSCI ACWI IMI Index (source: index factsheets). The size factor has performed reasonably well in the US market. The MSCI USA Small Cap Index outperformed the MSCI USA Index by about 2.9% per annum during the 19-year period. In 2016, MSCI published a research paper in response to the claim that the size premium never exists given the material underperformance of smallcap stocks over the 15 years to 1998 [22]. The research sorted the universe of about 4,000 US stocks into 10 portfolios by market capitalisation. The portfolios applied equal weighting to stocks and were rebalanced monthly. The results show that the annualised return from 1998 to 2015 increases steadily across the 10 portfolios as the size declines. The portfolio of the smallest companies produced an annualised return of 28.5%, significantly exceeding 7.7% provided by that containing the largest companies.

The size factor recorded substantial outperformance in the five decades to the early 1980s when its return premium was discovered. Subsequently, smallcap stocks failed to beat the market for the extended period of 15 years to 1998. This raises a serious question regarding the existence of the size premium. The argument is that factors must deliver long-term outperformance in order to be qualified as a systematic return driver. Considering the cyclical nature of factor returns, it is advisable to examine the size performance over a sufficiently long period of time. The size portfolios in the data library of Professor Kenneth French can provide valuable insight into the size premium. These portfolios are created by ranking US stocks in the descending order of market capitalisation and assigning them into relevant size groups. The portfolio containing the bottom 30% smallest companies produced an annualised return of 12.2% over the 90-year period to 2019. This represents an excess return of 2.8% per year compared to the S&P 500 Index over the long period. In the UK, the Numis Smaller Companies Index (NSCI) is a leading smallcap benchmark that comprises the bottom 10% of the UK equity market. The NSCI was developed by Professor Elroy Dimson and Professor Paul Marsh at London Business School. It was first published in 1987 and backtested to extend its history to 1955. For the period from 1955 to 2019, the NSCI (ex. investment companies) returned an average of 15.0% per year, outperforming both midcap (13.7%) and largecap (11.7%) stocks in the UK [23]. At the lowest end of the size spectrum, microcap stocks delivered the best annualised return of 17.4% during the 65-year period. These significant differences in performance clearly demonstrate the return premium of the size factor. Beyond the US and UK markets, the size premium has been found to exist in many other countries, such as Australia, Japan and Germany. A research paper published in 2011 by the Journal of Banking & Finance provides a comprehensive review of the size effect [1]. The substantial empirical evidence compiled in this study shows that the size premium is truly a global phenomenon. This is supported by the research findings of a Journal of Portfolio Management paper published in 2017 [24]. The research found that smaller companies generated attractive outperformance over a long period of time for most of the 23 countries examined in the study.

The smallcap universe contains numerous firms with varying levels of company quality. Many smaller companies struggle to make profits and deliver decent returns for their investors. Clifford Asness (a founder of AQR Capital Management) co-authored a research paper that demonstrates the strength of quality in enhancing the size premium [25]. Published in the leading Journal of Financial Economics, the research found the size premium becomes more robust and stable over time when the effect of company quality is controlled. This result is consistent across the 30 industries and 24 countries covered in the study. The research ranked US stocks to form 5 groups according to market capitalisation and company quality respectively. The intersection of the two factors resulted in 25 portfolios whose value-weighted returns were calculated monthly. Table 9.2 displays the average monthly excess returns of the 25 portfolios (1: largest, 5: smallest; 1: junk, 5: quality) over the period from July 1957 to December 2012. The 1-month US Treasury rate served as the benchmark to calculate monthly excess returns. The results clearly show the strong return premiums of the size and quality factors.

Table 9.2 The performance of 25 portfolios formed on size and quality

Quality (1: low, 5: high)	Size (1: large, 5: small)					
	1	2	3	4	5	5 - 1
1	0.12%	0.40%	0.44%	0.42%	0.35%	0.23%
2	0.37%	0.56%	0.68%	0.73%	0.84%	0.47%
3	0.34%	0.59%	0.74%	0.77%	0.87%	0.53%
4	0.47%	0.77%	0.76%	0.86%	0.89%	0.42%
5	0.53%	0.78%	0.83%	0.89%	0.97%	0.44%
5 - 1	0.41%	0.38%	0.39%	0.47%	0.62%	

Source: Journal of Financial Economics

Across the quality spectrum, the portfolio of the smallest stocks consistently outperformed that containing the largest stocks. For each size segment, the portfolio comprising the highest-quality companies always performed better than that formed of the lowest-quality companies. The first portfolio with the largest and lowest-quality stocks provided the lowest average excess return. It only outperformed the 1-month Treasury bill by an average of 0.12% per month during the sample period. In comparison, the last portfolio containing the smallest and highest-quality stocks achieved the best result of 0.97%. This represents a substantial excess return of 0.85% per month against the first portfolio.

References

1. van Dijk, M.A., *Is Size Dead? A Review of the Size Effect in Equity Returns.* Journal of Banking & Finance, 2011. **35**(12): p. 3263–3274.
2. Brown, P., et al., *Stock Return Seasonalities and the Tax-Loss Selling Hypothesis: Analysis of the Arguments and Australian Evidence.* Journal of Financial Economics, 1983. **12**(1): p. 105–127.
3. Chan, L.K.C., Hamao, Y. and Lakonishok, J., *Fundamentals and Stock Returns in Japan.* Journal of Finance, 1991. **46**(5): p. 1739–1764.
4. Fama, E.F. and French, K.R., *Common Risk Factors in the Returns on Stocks and Bonds.* Journal of Financial Economics, 1993. **33**(1): p. 3–56.
5. *MSCI Global Investable Market Indexes Methodology.* 2020, MSCI.
6. Ning, V., *International Small Cap Investing: Unlocking Alpha Opportunities in an Underutilized Asset Class.* 2019, S&P Global Market Intelligence.
7. Hou, K. and van Dijk, M.A., *Resurrecting the Size Effect: Firm Size, Profitability Shocks, and Expected Stock Returns.* Review of Financial Studies, 2019. **32**(7): p. 2850–2889.

8. *The Case for Small- and Mid-Cap Equities*. 2010, T. Rowe Price.
9. *S&P Global BMI, S&P/IFCI Methodology*. 2020, S&P Dow Jones Indices.
10. *FTSE Global Equity Index Series: Ground Rules*. 2020, FTSE Russell.
11. *STOXX Index Methodology Guide*. 2020, STOXX.
12. Mack, M., *The Case for Small Cap, Quality and Value*. 2019, Pacer.
13. Subramanian, R.A., *How to Think Bigger about Small Cap Investing*. 2016, MSCI.
14. *Small Caps… Big Opportunity: Invesco Global Smaller Companies Strategy*. 2019, Invesco.
15. Nimmo, H., *Smaller Companies: Big Opportunity?* 2019, Aberdeen Standard Investments.
16. *Think Big, Act Small: Taking Advantage of Smaller Company Investing*. 2012, UBS.
17. Bender, J., et al., *Small Caps—No Small Oversight*. 2012, MSCI.
18. Fama, E.F. and French, K.R., *The Capital Asset Pricing Model: Theory and Evidence*. Journal of Economic Perspectives, 2004. **18**(3): p. 25–46.
19. Fama, E.F. and French, K.R., *Multifactor Explanations of Asset Pricing Anomalies*. Journal of Finance, 1996. **51**(1): p. 55–84.
20. Fama, E.F. and French, K.R., *A Five-Factor Asset Pricing Model*. Journal of Financial Economics, 2015. **116**(1): p. 1–22.
21. *Factor Focus: Size*. 2018, MSCI.
22. Oberoi, R., et al., *One Size Does Not Fit All: Understanding Factor Investing*. 2016, MSCI.
23. Dimson, E., Marsh, P. and Staunton, M., *Credit Suisse Global Investment Returns Yearbook 2020 (Summary Edition)*. 2020, Credit Suisse.
24. Dimson, E., Marsh, P. and Staunton, M., *Factor-Based Investing: The Long-Term Evidence*. Journal of Portfolio Management, 2017. **43**(5): p. 15–37.
25. Asness, C., et al., *Size Matters, If You Control Your Junk*. Journal of Financial Economics, 2018. **129**(3): p. 479–509.

10

Quality Investing

10.1 Quality Investing

Quality investing is an investment approach that seeks to identify companies with superior quality characteristics according to defined fundamental criteria. This strategy targets companies that have strong competitive advantages and the potential to grow sustainably. Historically, companies with stable growth, quality earnings and a strong financial position have delivered attractive excess returns. Quality investing can trace its origins back to the time when Benjamin Graham published his two seminal investment books. In the book *The Intelligent Investor*, Benjamin Graham advises that investors should consider quality criteria in the selection of stocks, such as earnings growth, earnings stability and financial condition [1]. The legendary investor Philip Fisher believes in holding a concentrated portfolio of outstanding companies with great growth prospects. He offers 15 points to select quality companies in his book *Common Stocks and Uncommon Profits* [2]. The list includes growth potential, profit margin, competitive advantage, financial strength, management quality as well as business outlook. The approach of quality investing is adopted by many famous investors, including Peter Lynch and Charlie Munger. In the book *Beating the Street* [3], Peter Lynch advises that investors should not hold onto a stock when the fundamentals are deteriorating.

The consideration of quality issues in corporate strategy has resulted in many business analysis models. The BCG matrix employs the two dimensions of growth and market share to support companies in strategic decisions.

The framework of competitive advantage developed by Michael Porter helps companies understand their core competency and maintain a strategic position in the market. Quality investing aims to understand primary drivers of business performance and achieve superior investment returns. As a key concept in traditional fundamental analysis, quality is not formally recognised as an independent style factor and return driver until the 1990s. This may be attributed to the challenges in forming a reliable and objective definition for this broad risk factor. Quality is a multidimensional concept that covers a wide range of company aspects. It has been measured subjectively with various financial metrics in the academic literature and investment community. The quality factor is commonly captured by measures relating to profitability, earnings quality and financial strength, while it often contains the component of growth. Traditionally, growth investing is viewed as the natural complement to value strategies. However, growth as a common investment style fails to gain recognition as a systematic return driver in factor investing. This is because growth has not proved its ability to generate a significant long-term return premium. Historically, the MSCI World Growth Index produced an annualised return of 10.0% over the 45 years to 2019, marginally lower than 10.9% returned by the MSCI World Index (source: index factsheets). In comparison, the MSCI World Quality Index delivered an annualised excess return of about 1.5% against the broad market index during the 40 years to 2017 [4]. Quality is arguably a better complement to value investing than growth strategies given its proven return premium.

Quality was formally identified as a driver of investment returns in the 1990s. A paper published by the Accounting Review in 1996 found that investing in stocks with good earnings quality is rewarded with abnormal returns [5]. Earnings quality as a component of the quality factor has been measured with various proxies in the academic literature, such as earnings persistence, abnormal accruals and earnings smoothness [6]. Academic studies also provide evidence that profitability as a quality indicator is a strong predictor of future returns. Historically, profitable companies have produced significantly higher returns than their unprofitable peers [7]. The profitability factor has been added to the classic Fama–French 3-factor model to enhance its explanatory power [8]. A research in the Review of Financial Studies presents a q-factor model comprising market, size, investment and profitability factors [9]. This model proves to have good performance in explaining return anomalies. The Piotroski F-score is presented in a paper published by the Journal of Accounting Research in 2000 [10]. The score is a function of nice metrics relating to profitability, financial leverage/liquidity and operating efficiency. The study found this accounting-based quality strategy could produce superior returns.

Quality investing has attracted significant investor interest since the 2008 financial crisis. Leading index providers have launched a series of quality indices to track the performance of the quality factor. MSCI published its first quality indices in 2012 to capture the outperformance of companies with high-quality scores. These quality companies have the characteristics of high return on equity, stable earnings growth and low financial leverage. In 2014, S&P Dow Jones Indices launched the S&P 500 Quality Index to track the returns of high-quality stocks in the S&P 500 Index. Subsequently, many passive funds designed to replicate the performance of quality indices have been introduced to the market (e.g. Invesco S&P 500 Quality ETF). Some investment funds even combine long and short positions in the portfolio to increase the exposure to the quality factor (e.g. Direxion S&P 500 High minus Low Quality ETF).

Quality is classified as a defensive style factor in that quality strategies typically outperform in falling markets. Quality companies are resilient and well positioned to withstand difficult market conditions due to their business quality and financial strength. Compared to the low-volatility factor, quality delivers smoother returns across the business cycle. It provides reasonable downside protection during times of economic downturn, while retaining meaningful upside participation when the economy is in the expansion mode. Table 10.1 compares the annual returns of the MSCI World Quality Index

Table 10.1 Annual performance of the quality factor

Year	Quality	Minimum Volatility	MSCI World
2008	-33.5%	-29.2%	-40.3%
2009	33.5%	17.2%	30.8%
2010	11.4%	12.8%	12.3%
2011	4.4%	8.0%	-5.0%
2012	13.7%	8.9%	16.5%
2013	27.7%	19.4%	27.4%
2014	9.0%	12.1%	5.5%
2015	4.3%	5.8%	-0.3%
2016	5.1%	8.2%	8.2%
2017	26.6%	18.0%	23.1%
2018	-5.1%	-1.4%	-8.2%
2019	36.7%	24.0%	28.4%

Source: MSCI

and its two peer indices over the 12 years to 2019 (source: index factsheets). During this period, it posted an annualised return of 9.4%, exceeding 7.7% and 6.1% respectively returned by the MSCI World Minimum Volatility and MSCI World indices. The results show that both quality and minimum-volatility indices outperformed when the market was in negative territory (2008, 2011, 2015 and 2018). This reflects the defensive attribute of the quality and low-volatility factors during market downturns. However, the minimum-volatility index trailed the market materially in the five years with strong market performance (2009, 2012, 2013, 2017 and 2019). In contrast, the quality index delivered comparable or even much higher returns against the market during the five years. This demonstrates the ability of the quality factor to capture upside performance in rising markets.

Quality companies generally have high profitability, stable earnings growth and a strong financial profile. Given these compelling characteristics, quality companies are typically associated with premium valuations. For example, the MSCI World Quality Index had a high P/B ratio of 5.9 on 31 March 2020, compared to only 2.0 for the MSCI World Index. The Gordon growth model can be used to explain the premium valuations of quality companies. According to the model, the intrinsic value of a company can be estimated as:

$$V = \frac{D_1}{r - g}$$

where D_1 is the dividend next year, r is the required rate of return and g is the constant dividend growth rate. If the stock is fairly valued, the market price P is equal to the intrinsic value:

$$P = V = \frac{D_1}{r - g}$$

Divide both sides of the equation by the book value B:

$$\frac{P}{B} = \frac{\frac{D_1}{r-g}}{B} = \frac{\frac{D_1}{B}}{r-g} = \frac{\frac{D_1}{E_1} \times \frac{E_1}{B}}{r-g} = \frac{\text{Payout} \times ROE}{r - g}$$

where E_1 is the earnings (per share) next year, D_1/E_1 is the dividend payout ratio, and E_1/B is the return on equity (ROE). The formula exhibits that the P/B ratio is a function of four variables: payout ratio, ROE, required rate of return and growth rate. Quality companies generally feature high profitability (ROE) and growth, while having a relatively low required rate of return due to strong financial position. Quality companies often have a high payout ratio because of stable earnings. All these attributes contribute to high valuations of quality companies.

10.2 Characteristics of Quality Companies

Quality investing aims to identify companies with attractive quality characteristics. It requires quality investors to clearly understand the fundamental strength of companies. Quality companies have many positive characteristics that support them to maintain a competitive position in the market. Disciplined investors commonly employ a clearly defined set of criteria to identify quality companies. Quality checklist can help investors evaluate company quality in a systematic and objective way. It can contain both quantitative and qualitative criteria relating to fundamental quality. Quantitative measures can be applied to objectively assess quantifiable quality criteria, such as profitability, earnings variability, sales growth and financial strength. Qualitative measures used to analyse company quality are subjective in nature, including the evaluation of industry trends, growth prospects, business model, management quality and intangible assets. Quantitative and qualitative measures can be combined through a weighting scheme to form a quality rating system. The system can help investors effectively identify companies with strong quality characteristics. This section presents a selection of criteria that can be adapted to develop a quality rating system in company analysis. The criteria listed below represent the common attributes of quality companies. Whereas quality companies should have a high composite quality score, they are not expected to consistently perform well across all the measures.

1. **Industry Attractiveness**
   - High growth potential
   - Good profitability
   - Low sensitivity to business cycle
   - High barriers to entry
   - Low intensity of rivalry among competitors
   - Low bargaining power of customers
   - Low bargaining power of suppliers
   - Low threat of substitute products/services

2. **Competitive Advantage**
   - A market-leading position

- Growing market share
- Sustainable competitive advantage
- Strong pricing power
- Strong brand equity
- Highly cash generative
- Capital light

3. **Sales**
    - Strong growth prospects
    - Low growth volatility
    - Low customer concentration
    - Significant recurring revenue stream
    - Good order visibility

4. **Earnings**
    - High return on equity
    - High operating margin
    - Stable/growing profit margin
    - Stable earnings growth
    - Strong cash conversion

5. **Financial Strength**
    - Conservative and efficient capital structure
    - Ability to generate strong cash flows
    - Low financial leverage
    - Strong cash position
    - High interest coverage
    - High current ratio

6. **Business Operations**
    - Consistent operating performance
    - Company expenses under control
    - Stable and productive workforce
    - Stable and efficient supply chains
    - Excellent distribution channels
    - Good track record of innovation excellence
    - Low operational risk

7. **Management**
    - Competent and experienced management team
    - Commitment to creating shareholder value

- Open and transparent communications with investors
- Effective board structure
- Strong corporate governance
- High insider ownership

10.3 Quality Measures

Quality investing pursues companies that have the ability to deliver strong and sustainable returns. Quality companies have many positive characteristics and great potential to maintain enduring competitive advantages in the market. Since company quality contains various elements, it is practically difficult to develop a generic quality measure. This complex risk factor has been measured with many different metrics in the academic literature. The investment sector also has no consensus on the composition of the quality factor. Global index providers rely on their own methods to define company quality and construct quality indices. For example, the MSCI World Quality Index employs three fundamental variables to identify companies with strong quality characteristics: high return on equity, stable earnings growth and low financial leverage. The S&P 500 Quality Index measures company quality with the three metrics of return on equity, accruals ratio and financial leverage. FTSE Russell and STOXX employ more than three metrics to calculate quality scores. To identify quality indicators, index providers conduct a comprehensive review of variables that are empirically linked to the quality factor in academic research. The selected variables are subject to further analysis to ensure that they are valid and effective to capture the quality factor.

Quality is generally viewed as a concept with multiple dimensions, despite significant variations in its measurement. Table 10.2 presents a sample of quality measures used in the investment community. The composition of quality varies considerably across the measures, reflecting the inherent complexity of this style factor. Nevertheless, the results confirm that quality is commonly captured by three company aspects: profitability, earnings quality and financial strength. Profitability is a key indicator of company quality and business performance. It is generally measured by margin and return ratios, such as operating margin, net profit margin, return on equity and return on assets. Earnings quality is frequently represented by earnings variability and accruals ratio. Earnings variability can be calculated as the standard deviation of earnings growth rates. The accruals ratio indicates the extent to which earnings are effectively converted to cash flow. Financial strength is a core quality

Table 10.2 A sample of quality measures used in the investment sector

Source	Quality	Measure
MSCI	MSCI World Quality Index	1. return on equity 2. earnings variability 3. financial leverage
S&P Dow Jones	S&P 500 Quality Index	1. return on equity 2. accruals ratio 3. financial leverage
FTSE Russell	FTSE Quality Factor	1. return on assets 2. change in asset turnover 3. accruals 4. leverage (operating CF / total debt)
STOXX	iSTOXX Europe Quality Factor Index	1. operating income to equity 2. cash to current liabilities 3. net external financing 4. coverage 5. accruals quality
Fidelity	Fidelity US Quality Factor Index	1. free cash flow margin 2. return on invested capital 3. free cash flow stability
JP Morgan	JP Morgan US Quality Factor Index	Ten metrics over 3 themes: 1. profitability 2. solvency & risk 3. earnings quality
WisdomTree	Global Quality Dividend Growth ETF	1. long-term earnings growth 2. 3-year average ROE 3. 3-year average ROA
Northern Trust	Northern Trust Quality Score	Multiple dimensions in 3 categories: 1. profitability 2. cash flow 3. management efficiency

indicator that is often measured by financial leverage. Common measures of financial leverage include debt/equity, debt/assets and debt/EBITDA.

Quality measures defined with distinct metrics can produce very different factor returns. A study of Northern Trust compares the performance of its proprietary quality model and six alternative quality measures[11]. It constructed advanced factor mimicking portfolios to represent the performance of the quality measures. The research found the Northern Trust Quality Score model performed much better than the other quality measures from 1985 to 2012. The variations in the performance of quality measures can also be illustrated by the historical returns of the MSCI USA Quality and S&P 500 Quality indices. The two indices are designed to capture the performance of stocks in the US market that have strong quality characteristics. The MSCI index generated an annualised return of 10.3% over the 5 years to 31 March 2020, compared to 5.9% for the S&P index (source: index factsheets). The material variation in return is partially explained by the fact that the quality factor is measured differently between the two indices. Meanwhile, they have delivered more comparable returns over a longer time period. For example, the annualised returns provided by the two indices were 13.0% and 11.0% respectively during the 10 years to 31 March 2020. As of this date, the two quality indices actually had a strong overlap in sector distribution and leading constituents. Both indices had the largest positions in the information technology, health care and consumer staples sectors. For the list of top 10 constituents by weight, they shared 9 names: Apple, Johnson & Johnson, Visa, Mastercard, Procter & Gamble, Intel, Merck, PepsiCo and Cisco Systems. Microsoft occupied the leading position of 6.0% in the MSCI index, while Pfizer appeared in the top 10 list of the S&P index.

10.4 Return Premium

Companies with compelling quality characteristics have historically delivered attractive excess returns. Quality has been formally accepted as a common style factor in factor investing. The return premium of the quality factor is well documented in the academic literature. The Piotroski F-score is a popular quality measure introduced in a research paper published in 2000 [10]. The research identified a fairly monotonic positive relationship between the F-score and subsequent 1-year return following portfolio formation. The results show that an investment strategy that buys the portfolio of stocks with high F-scores and sells the portfolio with low scores would have generated an average annual return of 23% between 1976 and 1996. As a core component of quality, profitability has been empirically validated as an important factor to explain variations in stock returns [8]. A paper published by the Journal of Financial Economics in 2013 examines the effect of gross profitability on stock performance [7]. The research provides strong evidence that profitable companies significantly outperform their unprofitable peers. Specifically, the quintile of companies with the highest gross profitability earned an average excess return of 0.31% per month against that containing the most unprofitable companies from July 1963 to December 2010. The return premium of the gross profitability factor cannot be explained by the classic Fama and French 3-factor model. Operating profitability can also provide evidence of

Table 10.3 Performance of portfolios formed on profitability and size

Size (1: small, 5: large)	Operating Profitability (1: low, 5: high)				
	1	2	3	4	5
1	8.4%	14.7%	13.7%	14.3%	12.1%
2	9.4%	12.5%	13.5%	12.9%	14.5%
3	9.1%	12.5%	12.9%	12.7%	14.3%
4	9.6%	11.8%	12.3%	12.5%	13.3%
5	7.1%	8.6%	10.0%	10.3%	11.0%
All	7.6%	9.4%	10.6%	10.9%	11.5%

the quality premium. Table 10.3 compares the annualised returns of 25 value-weighted portfolios formed on size and operating profitability from 1964 to 2019. Monthly returns of these portfolios are available in the data library of Professor Kenneth French at Dartmouth College. The results demonstrate that the portfolio of stocks with the highest operating profitability consistently outperforms that comprising the lowest-profitability stocks across the size spectrum. For example, the largecap portfolio with the highest profitability delivered an annualised excess return of 3.9% against the largecap portfolio with the lowest profitability.

The quality minus junk (QMJ) factor constructed by AQR Capital Management replicates the performance of an investment strategy that buys high-quality stocks and sells low-quality ones. For the US equity market, the QMJ factor generated an average monthly return of 0.37% from 1958 to 2019. This quality factor has been found to deliver significant risk-adjusted returns across 24 developed countries [12]. It provides a strong confirmation that the quality factor has the ability to produce sustainable return premiums in different markets. A Schroders paper demonstrates that quality companies outperform the market in the long term [13]. The study sorted global stocks into quintile portfolios on the basis of quality score. The portfolios were rebalanced monthly with their returns tracked from 1988 to June 2015. The research found the portfolio of highest-quality companies delivered an annualised excess return of 4.0% against the market. The excess return declines steadily as the quality level falls across the portfolios. The portfolio containing the lowest-quality companies underperformed the market substantially by an average of about 4.5% per year during the period.

Northern Trust manages a proprietary model for the measurement of company quality. It published a research paper in 2013 to examine the characteristics of the quality factor [11]. The paper provides empirical evidence that the quality factor consistently delivers excess returns across the United States, developed (excluding US) and emerging markets. The research applied the Northern Trust Quality Score model to the constituents of the Russell 3000, MSCI World ex US and MSCI Emerging Markets indices. Based on quality score, companies in each index were ranked and assigned to equal-weighted quintile portfolios. All portfolios were rebalanced on a monthly basis, with their returns tracked over time. Table 10.4 compares the performance of the portfolios in the three investment universes. The data in the table are contributed by the author of the original paper Michael Hunstad. The results are very impressive in that there is a monotonic positive relationship between portfolio performance and quality level across the three markets. For example, the quintile portfolio of US companies with the highest-quality scores generated an average annual return of 16.5% from 1979 to 2019. As the quality level falls across the quintiles, the portfolio return declines gradually to only 7.9% for the quintile with the lowest-quality companies. The risk-adjusted return measured by the Sharpe ratio exhibits a similar pattern. The Sharpe ratio decreases steadily as the quality level falls across the quintile portfolios.

Leading index providers have launched a range of quality indices to capture the quality premium. The MSCI World Quality Index generated an annualised return of 11.4% from June 1994 to December 2019, significantly exceeding 7.8% returned by the MSCI World Index (source: index factsheets). An MSCI study examines the frequency of the quality index outperforming its parent index during the period of about 40 years to March 2014 [14]. The quality index was found to outperform with a frequency of 75% based on 10-year rolling period. The frequency increases to 99% if the rolling window is extended to 20 years. This demonstrates the ability of the quality factor to generate excess returns over an extended period of time. A

Table 10.4 Global evidence of the quality factor premium

Quality (1: high, 5: low)	United States 1979 ~ 2019		Developed ex US 1996 ~ 2019		Emerging Markets 1996 ~ 2019	
	Return	Sharpe	Return	Sharpe	Return	Sharpe
1	16.5%	1.07	9.2%	0.61	11.8%	0.56
2	15.7%	0.97	8.4%	0.52	10.1%	0.48
3	14.2%	0.85	7.3%	0.45	8.7%	0.39
4	12.5%	0.70	7.2%	0.42	8.5%	0.36
5	7.9%	0.38	4.5%	0.24	5.8%	0.21

Source: Northern Trust

research paper of FTSE Russell compares the performance of stocks with different quality scores [15]. It sorted the constituents of the FTSE Developed Index into quintile portfolios based on quality score. The portfolios were rebalanced annually with their returns calculated from September 2000 to March 2014. The results show that the highest-quality portfolio achieved an average excess return of 5.1% per annum compared to the lowest-quality portfolio, while exhibiting a much lower level of volatility.

S&P Dow Jones Indices conducted a study to investigate the performance of the quality factor in different markets [16]. The research reviews the performance of S&P quality indices in major regions, such as Europe, US, developed markets and emerging countries. It found that all the quality indices outperformed their respective benchmarks with generally lower levels of volatility and maximum drawdown over the 14 years to 2013. The strongest relative return was delivered by the S&P 500 Quality Index, which outperformed the S&P 500 Index by an average of 5.4% annually during this period. The research also constructed portfolios with different quality levels across the US, developed (excluding US) and emerging markets. Constituents of regional S&P indices were sorted into quintiles according to quality score. The portfolios were rebalanced monthly with their returns tracked from November 1994 to December 2013. The results confirm the pattern of portfolio return identified by the Northern Trust study [11]. For each of the three markets, the annualised portfolio return consistently decreases as the quality level falls across the portfolios. The excess return delivered by the quality factor was substantial in the emerging markets. The top quintile of highest-quality stocks dramatically outperformed the bottom quintile by an average of 13.0% annually. In the US markets, the top quintile delivered a smaller but still significant annualised excess return of about 5.0% against the bottom quintile during the period.

References

1. Graham, B., *The Intelligent Investor*. 1973, HarperCollins.
2. Fisher, P.A., *Common Stocks and Uncommon Profits*. 1996, Wiley.
3. Lynch, P., *Beating the Street*. 1994, Simon & Schuster.
4. *Factor Focus: Quality*. 2018, MSCI.
5. Sloan, R.G., *Do Stock Prices Fully Reflect Information in Accruals and Cash Flows about Future Earnings?* The Accounting Review, 1996. **71**(3): p. 289–315.
6. Dechow, P., Ge, W. and Schrand, C., *Understanding Earnings Quality: A Review of the Proxies, Their Determinants and Their Consequences*. Journal of Accounting and Economics, 2010. **50**(2): p. 344–401.

7. Novy-Marx, R., *The Other Side of Value: The Gross Profitability Premium.* Journal of Financial Economics, 2013. **108**(1): p. 1–28.
8. Fama, E.F. and French, K.R., *A Five-Factor Asset Pricing Model.* Journal of Financial Economics, 2015. **116**(1): p. 1–22.
9. Hou, K., Xue, C. and Zhang, L., *Digesting Anomalies: An Investment Approach.* Review of Financial Studies, 2015. **28**(3): p. 650–705.
10. Piotroski, J.D., *Value Investing: The Use of Historical Financial Statement Information to Separate Winners from Losers.* Journal of Accounting Research, 2000. **38**: p. 1–41.
11. Hunstad, M., *What Is Quality?* 2013, Northern Trust.
12. Asness, C.S., Frazzini, A. and Pedersen, L.H., *Quality Minus Junk.* Review of Accounting Studies, 2019. **24**(1): p. 34–112.
13. *The Benefits of Quality Investing.* 2017, Schroders.
14. Alighanbari, M., Subramanian, R.A. and Kulkarni, P., *Factor Indexes in Perspective: Insights from 40 Years of Data.* 2014, MSCI.
15. *Factor Exposure Indexes: Quality Factor.* 2014, FTSE Russell.
16. Ung, D., Luk, P. and Kang, X., *Quality: A Distinct Equity Factor?* 2014, S&P Dow Jones Indices.

11

Momentum Investing

11.1 Momentum Investing

Momentum investing is an investment strategy that seeks to profit from price trends in the market. This strategy purchases securities with strong performance and sells those on a downward price trend. The success of momentum investing is supported by the phenomenon that share price often continues to move in the direction of an established trend. The pioneering academic work on momentum investing is a research paper published by the Journal of Finance in 1993 [1]. The paper found strategies that buy stock winners and sell losers can generate significant positive returns. Following this seminal work, numerous studies have provided evidence that investing in stocks exhibiting strong momentum characteristics could achieve superior returns. The momentum effect has been identified in many different asset classes, such as equities, bonds and commodities. Figure 11.1 illustrates the upward and downward price momentums of London Stock Exchange and BT between 2016 and 2019. The share price of London Stock Exchange climbed steadily during the period, driven by strong financial results and takeover speculation. In contrast, the telecom giant BT saw its shares continually decline in value since January 2016, primarily caused by weak earnings. After the accounting scandal at its Italian unit, BT failed to improve financial performance and restore investor confidence.

The proven performance of momentum investing has confounded both the academic and investment communities. In a paper published by the Journal of Finance in 2008 [2], Fama and French describe momentum as a

© The Author(s), under exclusive license to Springer Nature Switzerland AG 2022
B. Jiang, *Investment Strategies*,
https://doi.org/10.1007/978-3-030-82711-3_11

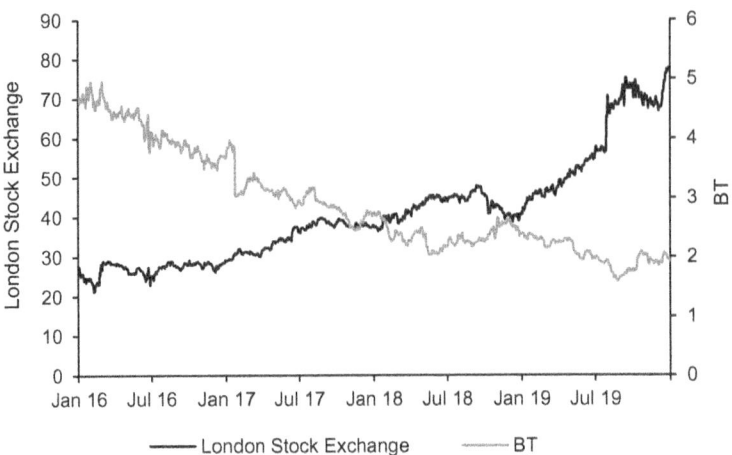

Fig. 11.1 An illustration of upward and downward price momentums

premier anomaly in investing. The momentum effect profoundly challenges the efficient market theory that share prices reflect all available information. The momentum anomaly indicates that shares can be inefficiently priced and remain mispriced for an extended period of time. Many academic studies have attempted to explain this market anomaly. The momentum anomaly is mainly attributed to behavioural biases in investing. When new information is released to the market, investors often underreact and fail to quickly update target prices. The share price only adjusts gradually as the market takes time to digest the new information. Besides, the momentum effect is partially driven by the overreaction behaviour of investors. It is observed that investors are often overconfident in winners while being unduly pessimistic about losers. Investors frequently follow the crowd in making investment decisions without independent judgement. The herd behaviour causes price trends to persist in the short term. Price momentum helps explain the fact that bull and bear markets can continue while deviating from fundamental value. A typical example is the dot-com bubble where momentum drove the share prices of technology companies to exceptional levels.

Momentum investing as a technical investment approach has many unique characteristics. This strategy is contrary to the disposition effect that investors tend to sell winners too early and cling to losing positions [3]. It suggests that investors should follow trends and ignore price levels. This counter-intuitive principle might cause confusion to investors pursuing other strategies. For example, value investors are fundamentally concerned with intrinsic value, while quality investors target companies with attractive quality characteristics. Momentum investing requires frequent monitoring of market conditions and price movements. It involves regular trading to capitalise on existing price trends. Investors need to consider the impact of trading costs when designing momentum strategies. An efficient momentum strategy should avoid overreaction to market noise with frequent trading, while gaining sufficient exposure to the momentum factor. As a technical strategy, momentum investing is insensitive to fundamentals and valuations. This indicates that momentum can be combined with other strategies to improve investment performance. Fundamental analysis can help momentum investors identify securities that are ready to experience a reversal in price trend. Some investors employ a combination of price momentum and earnings strength to capture the momentum effect. This is because forward earnings growth is a fundamental driver of price momentum. The positive link between the two variables is formally confirmed in a study conducted by AXA [4]. Momentum as a systematic return driver can be combined with other style factors to form the core of investment portfolios in strategic allocation. Historically, momentum has exhibited a low or negative correlation with the value factor. The two factors are frequently combined in multifactor strategies to reduce portfolio volatility and increase risk-adjusted returns. A study of S&P Global integrates momentum with value in a model featuring a dynamic risk-weighting scheme [5]. The model is designed to capture the upside of momentum while limiting capital loss through the value effect. The model was found to consistently outperform both momentum and value strategies across the six regions covered in the study. The performance of the momentum factor is cyclical in nature and sensitive to market conditions. The momentum effect is typically strong in rising markets with favourable economic conditions. But it is vulnerable to market volatility, since the momentum strategy relies on price trends. This weakness can be mitigated when momentum is implemented in conjunction with other strategies.

The momentum factor has proven its ability to generate excess returns in the long term. During the 40 years to 2017, the MSCI World Momentum Index produced an annualised excess return of more than 3% relative to the MSCI World Index [6]. According to MSCI World factor indices, momentum was the leading performer among common style factors from 2001 to 2017. Figure 11.2 shows the annual returns of the MSCI World Momentum Index and its parent index over the 10 years to 2019. The momentum index delivered an average annual return of 13.5% during the period, exceeding the benchmark index by 3.4% per year. The momentum factor typically performs well in rising markets. The momentum index delivered strong returns in the years with favourable market conditions. For

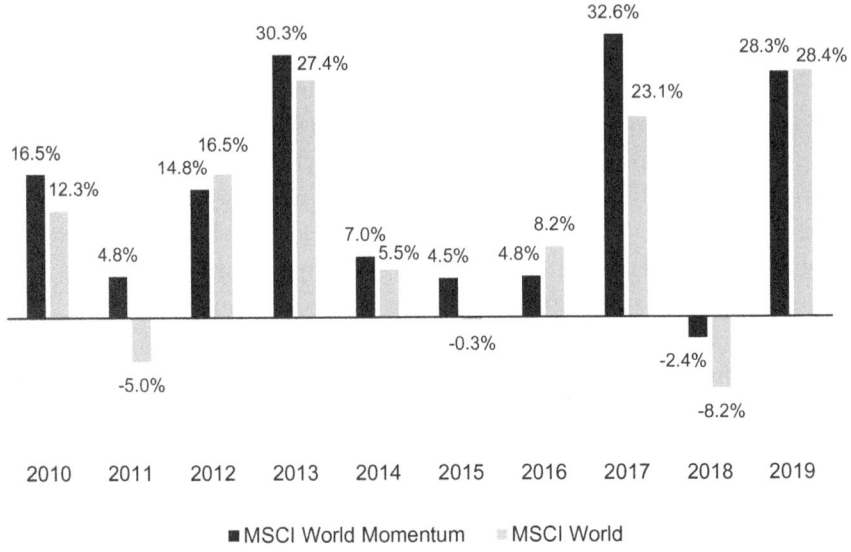

Fig. 11.2 Annual performance of the momentum factor

example, it achieved an exceptional return of 32.6% in 2017, compared to 23.1% for the MSCI World Index.

11.2 Momentum Measures

A basic element in momentum investing is the time frame used to evaluate a price trend. The strength of momentum is generally measured as the price change over a defined time period. A short-term momentum often uses one month as the time window to calculate price change. A medium-term momentum is typically measured over a period of 6 or 12 months. A long-term momentum usually has a time frame of 3 or more years. Empirical tests show that time window is an essential factor that affects the performance of momentum strategies. The data library of Professor Kenneth French at Dartmouth College contains portfolios formed on stock return. These portfolios can be used to illustrate the relevance of time window in developing momentum strategies. They are constructed monthly by sorting US stocks into decile portfolios based on their performance in the last 1-month, 1-year or 5-year period. Table 11.1 compares the performance of the top and bottom decile portfolios across the three time windows. The results are based on monthly portfolio returns from 1931 to 2019. There is a clear pattern of performance reversal for both short-term and long-term momentums. The

Table 11.1 The relevance of time window in momentum investing (1931–2019)

	Short-Term		Medium-Term		Long-Term	
	Loser	Winner	Loser	Winner	Loser	Winner
Annualised Return	14.5%	3.7%	0.1%	16.7%	13.1%	8.9%
Standard Deviation	28.8%	23.5%	33.5%	21.9%	30.2%	21.6%
Efficiency Ratio	0.50	0.16	0.00	0.76	0.44	0.41
Max Drawdown	-81.7%	-87.1%	-94.7%	-59.6%	-71.2%	-72.9%

portfolio with worst-performing stocks delivered a significant excess return against that containing best-performing stocks. The short-term reversal effect is particularly strong, as the loser portfolio outperformed the winner portfolio by more than 10.0% per annum. In contrast, the two medium-term momentum portfolios demonstrate a clear pattern of performance continuation. The winner portfolio generated an exceptional annualised return of 16.7%, while the loser portfolio almost earned no return. In fact, this winner portfolio achieved a significantly higher risk-adjusted return and lower maximum drawdown than the other five portfolios over the 89-year period. The dramatic differences in the results explain the reason that momentum is usually measured over a medium-term time frame. According to the research of FTSE Russell [7], momentum portfolios in the academic literature are typically constructed with the time window of 6, 9 or 12 months and rebalanced every 6 or 12 months. In addition, the most recent month is usually excluded from the calculation to avoid the short-term reversal effect.

Leading index providers employ similar methodologies to construct momentum indices. For S&P Dow Jones Indices, its momentum indices calculate the momentum value of a security as the 12-month price change in local currency [8]. The most recent month is excluded from the calculation to eliminate the reversal effect. The momentum value is divided by price volatility to obtain the risk-adjusted value. The adjusted momentum values are transformed to standard z-scores. The z-scores are capped at ± 3 to control the impact of extreme values and further converted to momentum scores. Securities are ranked in descending order by momentum score into five groups. The top quintile of securities with the highest momentum scores is selected for index construction. Security weights in the index are determined by the product of market capitalisation and momentum score, subject to security and sector constraints.

MSCI momentum indices calculate the momentum value of a security by combining its recent 6-month and 12-month returns [9]. The returns are first calculated in local currency and adjusted by the local risk-free rate R_f:

$$\text{6-month momentum: } P_{T-1}/P_{T-7} - 1 - R_f$$
$$\text{12-month momentum: } P_{T-1}/P_{T-13} - 1 - R_f$$

where P_{T-1}, P_{T-7} and P_{T-13} are the local prices 1, 7 and 13 months before the rebalancing date (the most recent month is excluded). If the 12-month price return is not available, the momentum value is simply based on 6-month momentum. If the 6-month return is also missing, then the momentum value is not calculated and the security is not eligible to be included in the momentum index. The price momentums are adjusted by volatility and transformed to z-scores. The two z-scores are combined with equal weighting to arrive at the composite score:

$$0.5 \times (\text{6-month z-score} + \text{12-month z-score})$$

The composite scores are further standardised to z-scores (capped at ± 3) and converted to momentum scores based on the formula below. Securities are ranked and selected for index inclusion according to momentum score. Securities in an MSCI momentum index are weighted by the product of their momentum score and weight in the parent index. The resulting weights are normalised to be 100% in total.

$$\text{Momentum Score} = \begin{cases} 1+z & z \geq 0 \\ 1/(1-z) & z < 0 \end{cases}$$

Momentum indices are designed to capture the performance of securities with strong price strength. They tend to have a higher valuation level than relevant broad market indices. For example, the S&P 500 Momentum Index had a forward P/E ratio of 28.4 on 30 November 2020, compared to 22.9 for the S&P 500 Index (source: index factsheets). The P/B ratio also exhibited the premium valuation of the momentum index (6.2) against its parent index (3.5). Similarly, the MSCI Europe Momentum Index had a considerably higher forward P/E ratio (26.0) than the MSCI Europe Index (17.2). Their P/B ratios were materially different at 4.0 and 1.9 respectively. The results reflect the fact that momentum indices are generally insensitive to valuations and fundamentals. They are technical strategies with a specific focus on price strength. As of 30 November 2020, the information technology sector had a dominant position of 39.0% in the S&P 500 Momentum Index. Remarkably, the six broad sectors of financials, industrials, materials, utilities, consumer staples and real estate only had a combined weighting of 15.9%. The energy sector even had no representation in the momentum index. In comparison, the S&P 500 Index as a broad market benchmark had a much lower level of sector concentration. It selects and weights stocks according to market value, thus providing a more representative picture of sector distribution.

11.3 Momentum Quality

The momentum anomaly is primarily explained by behavioural biases in investing. Investors often overreact to negative news and underreact to positive information. The herd behaviour is rampant in the market where investors follow the crowd to trade and lose their own judgement in investment decisions. Momentum investing seeks to profit from the continuation of established price trends. Momentum quality is an essential factor to consider when evaluating price trends. Figure 11.3 illustrates four potential patterns of share price movements. In panel A, share price follows a strong upward trend, while panel B exhibits a clear downward price trend. The momentum quality for these two trends is very high as price moves gradually in a clear direction. The two price patterns reflect the fact that investors

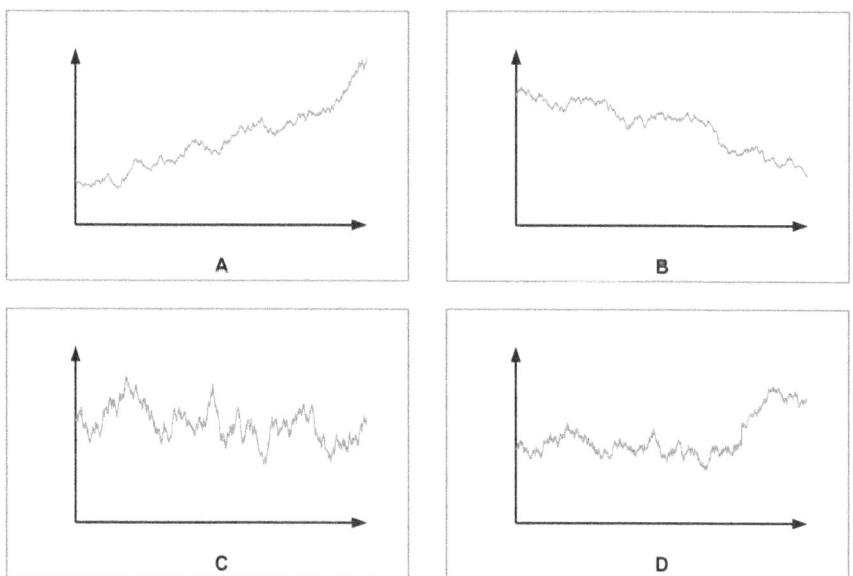

Fig. 11.3 Four patterns of share price movements

are usually inattentive to information arriving continuously in small amounts. Share prices only adjust gradually as investors slowly respond to new information. In comparison, share price in panel C moves in a rather random manner. In the absence of a clear pattern, momentum quality for the price movements in panel C is considered very low. In panel D, price moves randomly until a late stage when investors react strongly to available information. Although the magnitude of price change is significant, the pattern of price movements in panel D is still viewed as low quality. This is because available information has already been quickly embedded into the share price. After the discrete and material change, share price reverts to the pattern of random movements. The pattern cannot give momentum investors a strong conviction that a clear price trend has been established.

A paper published by the Review of Financial Studies quantifies momentum quality and examines its significance in momentum investing [10]. The research provides empirical evidence that trend quality can enhance the momentum effect. It found that the 6-month excess return generated by a momentum portfolio increases monotonically as the momentum quality improves across the portfolios. In the paper, momentum quality is measured by information discreteness (ID) that captures the relative frequency of small signals:

$$ID = \operatorname{sgn}(r) \times (\%neg - \%pos)$$

Here, r is the cumulative return over the formation period and sgn is the simple sign function. The expression sgn (r) is equal to 1 if r is positive and -1 if negative. The $\%neg$ and $\%pos$ are respectively the percentage of days with negative and positive returns during the period. A large positive ID value indicates discrete information, while a very negative ID means continuous information (i.e. high-quality momentum). The smallest possible value of ID is -1 when $\%neg = 1$ (perfect downtrend) or $\%pos = 1$ (perfect uptrend). The largest positive value of ID happens when all days have positive (negative) returns, except one day that causes the cumulative return to be negative (positive). This indicates that the largest possible ID value is close to 1.

The patterns of price movements in Fig. 11.3 are associated with different ID values. For the price trend in panel A, the sign function sgn (r) is equal to 1 given the positive cumulative return. The expression $\%neg - \%pos$ is very negative because most days have positive returns. Conversely, sgn (r) is -1 and $\%neg - \%pos$ is very positive for the trend in panel B. Therefore, the two price trends in panels A and B have very negative ID values as a result of good momentum quality. The ID value of the pattern in panel C is close to

Table 11.2 The strength of momentum quality in enhancing returns

	Momentum Quality			S&P 500
	High	Low	Standard	
Annualised Return	17.1%	13.0%	15.6%	10.0%
Standard Deviation	23.5%	25.2%	23.6%	19.1%
Sharpe Ratio	0.65	0.48	0.59	0.41

Source: Quantitative Momentum

zero, because price movements are virtually random. The sgn (r) is equal to 1 and $\%neg - \%pos$ is slightly negative in panel D, resulting in a marginally negative ID value. Despite the strong cumulative return, the pattern of price movements in panel D is only assigned a neutral momentum quality score.

The effect of momentum quality on investment performance is examined in the book Quantitative Momentum [11]. Table 11.2 compares the performance of three momentum portfolios and the S&P 500 Index. The portfolios are constructed with value-weighted US stocks and rebalanced quarterly from 1927 to 2014. The standard momentum portfolio is composed of stocks with the highest 12-month returns. It is further divided into two portfolios based on momentum quality measured by the ID: high-quality momentum (HQM) and low-quality momentum (LQM). All the three momentum portfolios outperformed the S&P 500 Index over the 88-year period. In particular, the HQM portfolio realised an exceptional annualised return of 17.1%, exceeding the broad market index by 7.1% per annum. Besides, it generated a significant annualised excess return of 4.1% relative to the LQM portfolio. This demonstrates the potential of momentum quality to enhance the investment returns of momentum portfolios.

Figure 11.4 illustrates momentum quality with the share prices of Whitbread, Next, Marks & Spencer and Metro Bank. Momentum quality emphasises gradual and consistent price movements in response to the arrival of new information in small amounts. Share price often continues to move in the direction of an established trend. Whitbread shares climbed steadily from £15.64 at the end of 2011 to the peak price of £54.40 on 27 April 2015, reflecting a cumulative price return of 247.8%. Subsequently, Whitbread experienced a reversal in the price trend, with its share price declining gradually until early March 2016. Next had a similar pattern of share price movements during the 7 years to January 2017. Marks & Spencer and Metro Bank exhibited a clear pattern of downward price movements. The two stocks have consistently remained in the list of most shorted stocks on the London Stock Exchange. Marks & Spencer suffered poor share performance primarily

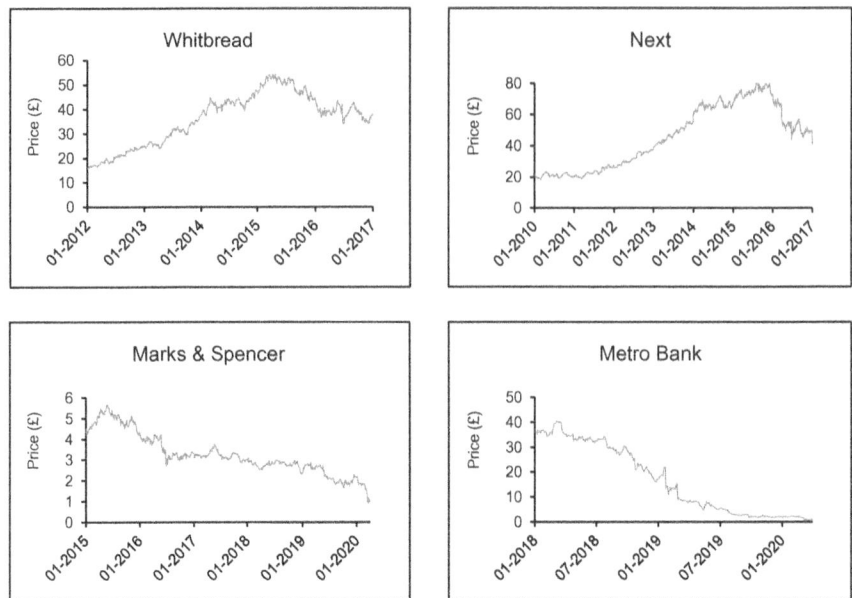

Fig. 11.4 An illustration of momentum quality with real share prices

because of industry challenges. After reaching a peak of £5.66 on 27 May 2015, its share price continually drifted lower to only £0.92 on 23 March 2020. The shares of Metro Bank suffered a disastrous loss of 97% through the 2 years to 31 March 2020. This was caused by a combination of profit warnings and accounting error. The share price collapsed by almost 40% on 23 January 2019 when Metro Bank disclosed that it miscalculated the risk weighting of commercial loans. These cases clearly show the relevance of trend quality in momentum investing. Investment strategies designed to exploit the momentum effect should consider both price strength and trend quality.

11.4 Return Premium

Momentum has been widely accepted as a performance factor driving investment returns. Historically, momentum strategies have posted attractive returns across a range of asset classes. The momentum effect was formally identified by the research paper *Returns to Buying Winners and Selling Losers* published in 1993 [1]. The research formed relative strength portfolios in two steps: (1) rank stocks into 10 deciles according to past performance and (2) buy the top decile of winner stocks and sell the bottom decile of loser stocks. It constructed a total of 32 portfolios by varying the period of past performance (3, 6, 9 or 12 months), the time lag to form portfolios (0 or 1 week) and the holding period (3, 6, 9 or 12 months). The research found all the portfolios generated positive returns over the period between 1965 and 1989. The most successful portfolio produced a significant average return of 1.49% per month. The research findings strongly support the existence of the momentum premium.

The paper *Momentum Strategies* published by the Journal of Finance in 1996 provides further evidence of the momentum effect [12]. The study constructed equal-weighted portfolios with US stocks from 1977 to 1993. At the beginning of each month, stocks were ranked and assigned to decile portfolios based on past 6-month return. Portfolio returns in the next 6 months, first, second and third years following portfolio formation were tracked over the entire period. Table 11.3 presents the performance of the 10 portfolios across the four holding periods. The momentum effect is very pronounced for the holding periods of 6 months and 1 year, as the portfolio return increases monotonically with the past 6-month performance. However, the momentum effect apparently disappears when the holding period is extended to the second and third years.

A study in the Journal of Finance examines the impact of macroeconomic risk on the momentum effect around the world [13]. The research findings suggest that the momentum premium is significant and unaffected by macroeconomic variables such as GDP growth. This study formed momentum portfolios by first ranking stocks into quintile groups according to past 6-month return. Subsequently, the momentum strategy buys the winner quintile and sells the loser quintile, with the resulting portfolio held for 6 months. The results show that all the relative strength portfolios produced positive returns across the Africa, America (excluding the US), Asia, Europe and US markets. Specifically, the average monthly returns for

Table 11.3 Performance of portfolios formed on past 6-month return

Return	1	2	3	4	5	6	7	8	9	10
Past 6m	-30.8%	-12.6%	-5.5%	0.0%	5.0%	9.9%	15.3%	21.9%	31.9%	69.6%
Next 6m	6.1%	8.6%	9.3%	9.6%	10.2%	10.4%	10.5%	11.1%	12.0%	14.9%
Year 1	14.3%	18.5%	19.8%	20.8%	21.4%	22.2%	22.3%	23.5%	24.8%	29.7%
Year 2	20.5%	20.1%	20.5%	20.6%	20.8%	20.8%	20.4%	20.8%	20.7%	19.9%
Year 3	19.4%	19.6%	19.7%	19.6%	19.9%	20.2%	20.5%	20.1%	20.8%	20.6%

Source: Journal of Finance

these 5 markets were 1.63%, 0.78%, 0.32%, 0.77% and 0.59% respectively. The research also confirms that the momentum effect reverses when the holding period is extended beyond one year. Fama and French examine the momentum anomaly in their paper *Dissecting Anomalies* published in 2008 [2]. Stocks were sorted into quintile portfolios on the basis of past 12-month return. The strategy of buying the winner quintile and selling the loser quintile delivered an average return of 0.74% per month from July 1963 to December 2005.

A paper in the Journal of Portfolio Management provides empirical evidence of factor premiums [14]. To investigate the momentum effect, the research assigns stocks into winner and loser portfolios according to past 6-month return. For the US market, the winner portfolio delivered an annualised return of 17.5% from 1926 to 2016, compared to only 9.5% for the loser portfolio. The momentum effect is also very significant in the UK market. The winner portfolio produced an average annual return of 14.1% from 1900 to 2016, dramatically exceeding 3.6% returned by the loser portfolio. A research in the Financial Analysts Journal extended the analysis of the momentum effect to the period before 1900 [15]. It confirms the existence of the momentum premium based on a data sample covering over 200 years. The winner portfolio of stocks with the best 12-month returns was found to outperform the loser portfolio by an average of 0.4% per month from 1801 to 2012.

The momentum portfolios in the data library of Professor Kenneth French can provide further insight into the momentum effect. The portfolios are constructed monthly by sorting US stocks into deciles based on past 12-month return. Figure 11.5 exhibits the annualised returns of the 10 portfolios

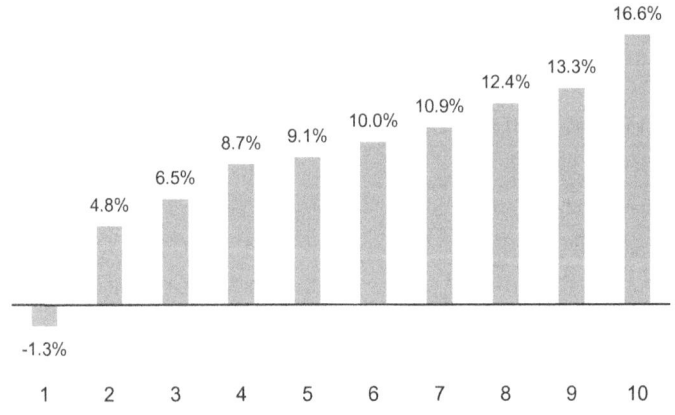

Fig. 11.5 Annualised returns of portfolios formed on momentum (1927–2019)

from 1927 to 2019. The results demonstrate a monotonic relationship between portfolio return and past 12-month performance. The portfolio of stocks with the best 12-month returns delivered a substantial annualised return of 16.6%. In contrast, the portfolio of the worst-performing stocks provided a negative average return of −1.3% per annum. The dramatic difference proves the significant momentum effect in investing.

Academic studies have found the existence of the momentum effect in many different asset classes. For example, a Journal of Finance paper found consistent evidence of momentum premium across equities, bonds, currencies and commodities [16]. Momentum has been firmly established as a common style factor, supported by the pervasive evidence of its return premium. However, the momentum effect is still treated with scepticism by some investors. Momentum strategies are often questioned about their ability to generate excess returns after trading costs are factored in. This is because momentum portfolios require regular rebalancing in order to capture the momentum effect. A paper in the Journal of Portfolio Management clarifies ten myths about momentum investing [17]. It argues that momentum return can easily survive transaction costs in the case of moderate portfolio turnover. This argument may be supported by the strong historical performance of the momentum factor represented by the MSCI World Momentum Index. During the 40 years to 2017, it generated an annualised excess return of over 3% against the MSCI World Index [6].

References

1. Jegadeesh, N. and Titman, S., *Returns to Buying Winners and Selling Losers: Implications for Stock Market Efficiency.* Journal of Finance, 1993. **48**(1): p. 65–91.
2. Fama, E.F. and French, K.R., *Dissecting Anomalies.* Journal of Finance, 2008. **63**(4): p. 1653–1678.
3. Shefrin, H. and Statman, M., *The Disposition to Sell Winners Too Early and Ride Losers Too Long: Theory and Evidence.* Journal of Finance, 1985. **40**(3): p. 777–790.
4. Dean, S. and Sevilla, A., *Earnings Growth as the Fundamental Driver of the Momentum Anomaly.* 2015, AXA Investment Managers.
5. Sandberg, D.J., *Value and Momentum: Everywhere, But Not All the Time.* 2019, S&P Global Market Intelligence.
6. *Factor Focus: Momentum.* 2018, MSCI.
7. *Factor Exposure Indexes: Momentum Factor.* 2014, FTSE Russell.
8. *S&P Momentum Indices Methodology.* 2020, S&P Dow Jones Indices.
9. *MSCI Momentum Indexes Methodology.* 2017, MSCI.

10. Da, Z., Gurun, U.G. and Warachka, M., *Frog in the Pan: Continuous Information and Momentum.* Review of Financial Studies, 2014. **27**(7): p. 2171–2218.
11. Gray, W.R. and Vogel, J.R., *Quantitative Momentum: A Practitioner's Guide to Building a Momentum-Based Stock Selection System.* 2016, Wiley.
12. Chan, L.K.C., Jegadeesh, N. and Lakonishok, J., *Momentum Strategies.* Journal of Finance, 1996. **51**(5): p. 1681–1713.
13. Griffin, J.M., Ji, X. and Martin, J.S., *Momentum Investing and Business Cycle Risk: Evidence from Pole to Pole.* Journal of Finance, 2003. **58**(6): p. 2515–2547.
14. Dimson, E., Marsh, P. and Staunton, M., *Factor-Based Investing: The Long-Term Evidence.* Journal of Portfolio Management, 2017. **43**(5): p. 15–37.
15. Geczy, C.C. and Samonov, M., *Two Centuries of Price-Return Momentum.* Financial Analysts Journal, 2016. **72**(5): p. 32–56.
16. Asness, C.S., Moskowitz, T.J. and Pedersen, L.H., *Value and Momentum Everywhere.* Journal of Finance, 2013. **68**(3): p. 929–985.
17. Asness, C., et al., *Fact, Fiction, and Momentum Investing.* Journal of Portfolio Management, 2014. **40**(5): p. 75–92.

12

Value Effect

12.1 Value Investing

Value investing is an investment strategy that involves buying securities trading at a discount to their intrinsic value. This investment approach is adopted by many famous investors, such as Benjamin Graham and Warren Buffett. Through the investment vehicle of Berkshire Hathaway, Warren Buffett achieved an average annual return of 21.5% from 1965 to 2005 [1]. In comparison, the market represented by the S&P 500 Index posted an annualised total return of 10.3% during this period. Regarded as the father of value investing, Benjamin Graham defined the core investment philosophy of the value strategy in his two seminal books: *Security Analysis* and *The Intelligent Investor*. He introduced the term margin of safety as a fundamental principle of value investing. The margin of safety is simply defined as the difference between the estimated intrinsic value of a stock and its observed market price. A good margin of safety provides a cushion against possible investment mistakes and mitigates the risk of deep capital losses in market downturns. Value investors attempt to identify stocks with an attractive margin of safety and profit from the potential upside. To measure the margin of safety, the intrinsic value needs to be first estimated by fundamental analysis. Since intrinsic value is typically difficult to measure precisely, value investors often demand a significant margin of safety to compensate them for unexpected adverse outcomes and potential valuation errors. They tend to calculate intrinsic value in a conservative manner to reduce valuation risk.

Value investing assumes that the market is not efficient, resulting in many undervalued assets to be exploited. Excessive market pessimism frequently pushes stock prices down to levels not justified by fundamentals. For example, the S&P 500 Index lost 33.0% of its value over a month to 23 March 2020, caused by the fear of coronavirus outbreak. From this date, the broad market index recovered quickly and produced a dramatic total return of 70.2% when the year ended. Value investors believe that stocks can be acquired at prices below intrinsic value, because the market tends to overreact to negative news and fail to understand fundamental value. When a company loses market share or its profit margin is squeezed by rising costs, its share price is usually punished by the market. Whereas the market is right that company profits are expected to fall, it is often overly pessimistic about the earnings outlook. On the other hand, a company may experience major changes following a strategic review. The market often fails to properly interpret positive company developments and responds with falling share prices. Behavioural biases in the market create many mispriced investment opportunities for value investors to explore. Besides, the existence of undervalued assets is partially explained by the fact that valuations are subjective and cannot include all relevant information in fundamental analysis. It is practically difficult for the market to provide a perfect valuation that exactly matches the intrinsic value. In reality, stocks with low valuations are often ignored by the market as investors are frequently attracted to glamorous growth stocks. However, stocks will not trade indefinitely at prices significantly below their intrinsic value. Their prices will be corrected eventually when the market recognises their fundamental value. Value investing is intuitively appealing and well positioned as an established strategy for long-term wealth creation.

Value and growth are widely accepted as two distinct and competing investment styles. Value stocks feature attractive valuation levels as measured by common valuation metrics such as price/earnings. Compared to growth stocks, they generally have lower growth potential and more predicable revenue stream. The priority for value investors is to identify stocks with a good margin of safety. Value investors believe that the market will eventually recognise the full potential of undervalued stocks. Positive returns can be earned when the market prices of value stocks converge to their intrinsic value. In comparison, growth strategies invest in companies that are expected to have strong future growth. Growth stocks overall have a relatively high valuation level due to favourable growth prospects. Investment returns delivered by growth stocks are primarily attributed to earnings growth rather than valuation. Growth companies typically pay limited dividends, as retained earnings are reinvested to support business growth.

Investors should be mindful of value traps in the pursuit of stocks with low valuations. Value traps are companies that appear undervalued but their share prices continue to stagnate or fall. Their shares remain at low valuation levels and have limited potential to materially increase in value. Value traps are often caused by the serious deterioration in company fundamentals. For example, a company may permanently lose its ability to earn decent profits due to fierce market competition or changing consumer preferences. Structural changes in a market can severely affect the growth potential and profitability of companies. Before investing in value stocks, it is essential that investors conduct thorough research to fully understand the reasons behind attractive valuations. Value traps create an investment pitfall for investors who mainly focus on prices without carefully probing into fundamentals. A research of J.P. Morgan highlights the investment risk of value traps [2]. The research analyses the returns of companies in the Russell 3000 Index between 1980 and 2014. For the 13,000 stocks examined in the study, 40% of them suffered disastrous price declines with very limited recovery. These distressed stocks never fully recovered but actually recorded a permanent loss of 60% or more from their peak price. The results clearly show the risk of investing in severely impaired stocks and the importance of identifying value traps.

12.2 Valuation Metrics

Value investors maintain a strict valuation discipline to create a margin of safety. Many valuation metrics are readily available to help investors identify undervalued stocks. These metrics typically compare the share price of a company to its fundamental data, such as earnings, cash flow and book value. Individual valuation metrics can be combined to form a composite value indicator. The composite variable can be used to measure and compare valuation levels of stocks. It can also be applied to create models for the valuation of industries, countries and markets. This section briefly introduces a selection of basic valuation measures used in equity research.

- **Price/Earnings (P/E)**

The P/E ratio is the most common valuation metric used by investors and financial analysts. It is calculated as the share price divided by earnings per share (EPS). Earnings in the P/E ratio can be based on actual results or consensus estimates. The trailing P/E ratio typically uses EPS over the previous 12 months, while the forward P/E ratio is often based on projected

EPS in the next fiscal year. The P/E ratio is not meaningful if the earnings number is negative. Alternatively, earnings yield can be applied to value companies with negative earnings. Earnings yield is simply the inverse of the P/E ratio and expressed as a percentage.

- **Price/Book (P/B)**

The P/B ratio is a useful valuation measure when comparing companies with negative earnings. It can be calculated as market capitalisation divided by book value. Investors often exclude intangible assets when calculating the book value to get a more conservative valuation. The P/B ratio can vary significantly across industries. For example, the MSCI World Materials Index had a P/B ratio of 2.3 on 31 December 2020, compared to 8.9 for the MSCI World Information Technology Index.

- **Price/Sales (P/S)**

The P/S ratio can be calculated as share price divided by trailing 12-month sales per share. It is a useful metric to value companies with negative earnings. Since the scale of sales can vary considerably across industries, the P/S ratio is most suitable for the comparison of companies operating in the same sector. In practice, this metric is not widely applied in stock valuation. Investors are usually more concerned with the company ability to produce earnings rather than the absolute size of sales.

- **Price/Cash Flow (P/CF)**

The P/CF ratio compares the market value of a company to its cash flow. It is often calculated as market capitalisation divided by operating cash flow. Cash flow can provide a clear picture of earnings strength, because it cannot be easily manipulated through accounting methods. Low P/CF ratios are generally preferred, although this metric is sensitive to industry type.

- **EV/EBITDA**

The EV/EBITDA ratio compares the enterprise value (EV) of a company to its EBITDA. EV measures the total company value and can be simply estimated as the sum of market capitalisation and net debt. The EV/EBITDA ratio is widely applied to compare companies with different debt levels. It is also frequently used to value companies with negative earnings.

- **Dividend Yield**

Dividend yield as a traditional valuation metric is calculated as annual dividend per share divided by the current share price. Mature companies with stable business generally have a high dividend yield. Growth companies typically do not pay attractive dividends, because retained earnings are reinvested to support growth. For example, the S&P 500 Information Technology Index only had a dividend yield of 0.96% as of 31 December 2020.

Investors should exercise discretion when selecting financial ratios to value companies. There is no consensus in the investment sector regarding the optimal set of valuation measures. The value factor has been defined with various combinations of valuation metrics. For example, the MSCI World Value Index measures value with the P/B ratio, 12-month forward P/E and dividend yield. The S&P 500 Value Index defines value with the P/B, P/E and P/S ratios. The FTSE All-World Value Index employs the P/B ratio as the single metric to determine value. The Morningstar Style Box provides a graphical representation of investment style for stocks and funds. It adopts five metrics to measure value: forward P/E, P/B, P/S, P/CF and dividend yield. These valuation ratios are aggregated to form the composite value score. The value score is subtracted from the growth score to determine the overall style score. Based on the style score, a stock or investment fund is classified as value, blend or growth.

12.3 Return Premium

Value is a common investment style and widely accepted as a systematic driver of investment returns. The value effect is the observation that stocks with attractive valuations tend to outperform the market in the long term. It has been well documented in the finance literature since the 1970s. A paper published by the Journal of Finance in 1977 formally identified the value effect [3]. The research seeks to challenge the efficient market hypothesis by empirically determining the relationship between the future performance of common stocks and their valuation levels. The research formed 5 portfolios with equal size from a sample of about 500 stocks traded on the New York Stock Exchange. The portfolios were constructed based on the P/E ratio and rebalanced annually. The research findings suggest that stocks with low valuation ratios significantly outperform expensive stocks. The top quintile of stocks with the lowest P/E ratios realised an average annual return of 16.3%

over the 14 years to March 1971, compared to only 9.3% for the bottom quintile. A paper published in 1991 relates the differences in returns on Japanese stocks to the underlying behaviour of several variables, such as the P/E, P/B and P/CF ratios [4]. The research used monthly returns of stocks listed on the Tokyo Stock Exchange from 1971 to 1988. It found that all the three valuation metrics have significant power to explain variations in stock returns. The top quartile of stocks with the lowest valuations consistently outperformed the bottom quartile across the three metrics over the period. The P/B ratio resulted in an average monthly difference of 1.10% in return between the top and bottom quartiles.

Value is a core component of the famous Fama-French 3-factor model introduced in 1993 [5]. The model has been extensively applied to explain variations in stock returns. It formally confirmed the position of value as a driver of investment returns. Subsequently, an abundance of academic studies provided further evidence of the value effect. The superior returns of value strategies are clearly exhibited in a Journal of Finance paper published in 1994 [6]. The study constructed decile portfolios according to the P/B, P/CF, P/E ratios and sales growth respectively. Table 12.1 displays the average annual returns of the decile portfolios from 1968 to 1989. Portfolio return overall increases steadily as the valuation level falls across the decile portfolios. The data clearly exhibit a negative relationship between past sales growth and future return. This may be explained by the fact that stocks with strong

Table 12.1 Average annual returns of portfolios formed on valuation metrics and past sales growth

Decile (1: high, 10: low)	P/B	P/CF	P/E	Growth
1	9.3%	9.1%	11.4%	12.7%
2	12.5%	12.2%	12.6%	15.5%
3	14.6%	14.5%	14.3%	16.4%
4	15.4%	15.7%	15.2%	16.5%
5	15.8%	16.6%	16.0%	17.1%
6	16.6%	17.1%	16.7%	17.1%
7	18.4%	18.0%	18.8%	18.3%
8	18.9%	19.2%	19.1%	18.8%
9	19.6%	19.9%	19.6%	19.5%
10	19.8%	20.1%	19.0%	19.5%

Source: Journal of Finance

growth characteristics generally have high valuation levels due to favourable growth prospects.

A paper in the Financial Analysts Journal examines the long-term performance of style factors [7]. The study sorted the universe of 3,500 US stocks into quartile portfolios according to different risk factors. The value factor was measured by the trailing earnings yield. The results support the strong return premium of the value factor. During the 40 years to 2011, the portfolio with the lowest valuation achieved the highest annualised return of 16.1%, substantially exceeding 7.6% produced by the most expensive portfolio. The value effect can also be examined by the quintile portfolios formed on the book-to-market ratio in the data library of Professor Kenneth French at Dartmouth College. From 1927 to 2019, the value-weighted portfolio of US stocks with the lowest valuations outperformed that containing the most expensive stocks by an average of 3.5% per year. The value factor has delivered significant excess returns in the UK equity market. A paper in the Journal of Portfolio Management constructed value and growth portfolios according to the book-to-market ratio and tracked their returns over time [8]. The value portfolio was found to generate an annualised return of 16.0% from 1955 to 2016. This represents an annualised excess return of 5.7% relative to the growth portfolio.

Style indices provide valuable insights into the historical performance of the value factor. The MSCI World Value Index captures the returns of stocks exhibiting value characteristics across 23 developed countries. From 1975 to 2020, it produced an annualised return of 11.4%, compared to 10.5% for the MSCI World Growth Index (source: index factsheets). However, the value effect apparently disappeared in the 10 years to 2020. The value index trailed the growth index significantly by an average of 5.7% per annum during the decade. The material underperformance of value is primarily attributed to the exceptional market environment characterised by protracted low levels of growth and interest rates. In this environment, investors actively pursue stocks that can deliver significant earnings growth. The historic outperformance of growth was heavily driven by the strong returns of technology stocks. This can be illustrated by the performance of the MSCI World Information Technology Index. It recorded a substantial annualised excess return of 8.7% against the MSCI World Index over the 10 years to 2020.

Figure 12.1 examines the historical performance of value relative to growth from 1975 to 2020. The performance of the two investment styles are respectively represented by the MSCI World Value and MSCI World Growth

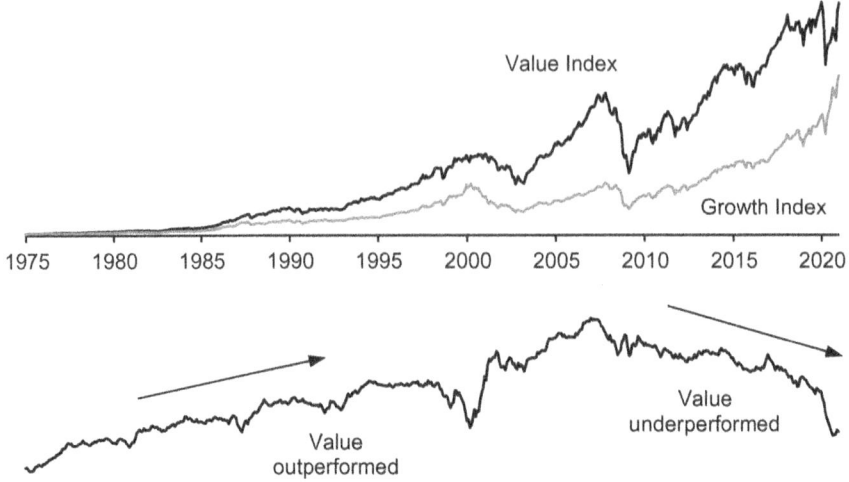

Fig. 12.1 Historical performance of value relative to growth

indices. During the entire period, value outperformed growth by an average of 0.9% annually. Value as a style factor could not consistently deliver outperformance over time. It generated substantial excess returns until 1994 and underperformed materially during the period of the dot-com bubble. Value continued to outperform from March 2000 when the bubble started to burst. The positive trend reversed in the middle of 2007, with value entering into a long period of underperformance. The relative performance of value was particularly very negative in the four years to 2020. Investors favour growth over value stocks in an environment of low growth. Excluding the last decade, value would have produced an annualised excess return of 2.7% against growth over the 36 years to 2010.

Figure 12.2 displays the monthly 10-year rolling relative returns of the MSCI World Value Index against the MSCI World Index from 1985 to 2020. The 10-year relative return of the value index largely remained in positive territory before 2014. This shows the ability of the value factor to outperform over a relatively long time horizon. Subsequently, value continually provided negative 10-year relative returns. For the entire 36-year period, value outperformed with a frequency of 76% based on the 10-year rolling returns. The results suggest that factors may underperform over an extended period of time, although they are expected to deliver long-term excess returns. The performance of style factors is cyclical in nature and sensitive to market conditions. It is practically challenging to dynamically capture factor premiums through factor rotation.

Fig. 12.2 10-year rolling relative performance of value

12.4 Return Decomposition

Earnings and valuation are core factors in equity investing that can change significantly across different stages of a business cycle. Earnings growth is a fundamental factor that drives the long-term performance of equity markets. In the short term, however, the market does not necessarily follow earnings as multiple underlying forces can move the market. Investors are particularly interested in the potential divergence of earnings and stock prices. This section presents a model that decomposes total return into several components. The model supports the position of value as a driver of investment returns. It can help investors understand the sources of return and potential driving forces behind market movements. The model can also be applied to forecast future market returns.

Assume the price of a security is P_1 and the earnings per share is E_1 at time t_1. After a period of N years, the price and earnings are P_2 and E_2 respectively at time t_2. The annualised price return r during the period can be expressed as:

$$r = \left(\frac{P_2}{P_1}\right)^{\frac{1}{N}} - 1 = \left(\frac{P_2/E_2 \times E_2}{P_1/E_1 \times E_1}\right)^{\frac{1}{N}} - 1 = \left(\frac{E_2}{E_1}\right)^{\frac{1}{N}} \times \left(\frac{P_2/E_2}{P_1/E_1}\right)^{\frac{1}{N}} - 1$$

Define:

$$e = \left(\frac{E_2}{E_1}\right)^{\frac{1}{N}} - 1 \text{ and } v = \left(\frac{P_2/E_2}{P_1/E_1}\right)^{\frac{1}{N}} - 1$$

The two variables represent the annualised earnings growth and annualised P/E change over the entire period. The price return r becomes:

$$r = (1 + e) \times (1 + v) - 1 = e + v + ev$$

Since e and v are usually small, the interaction effect ev is negligible compared to the main terms. The interaction term can be simply absorbed into the main terms to achieve a perfect return decomposition. The return formula can be simplified as:

$$r = e + v$$

This shows that the annualised price return r can be calculated as the sum of annualised earnings growth and annualised P/E change. The sources of return from an equity investment are attributed to price return and dividend yield. The total return R can be written as:

$$R = e + v + d$$

where d is the annualised dividend return. The formula shows that total return in equity investing can be decomposed into three factors: earnings growth, P/E change and dividend return. This simple model can explain the return of a stock or market index over a specific time period. Figure 12.3 shows the 8-year return decomposition of the S&P 500 Index for the 20 years

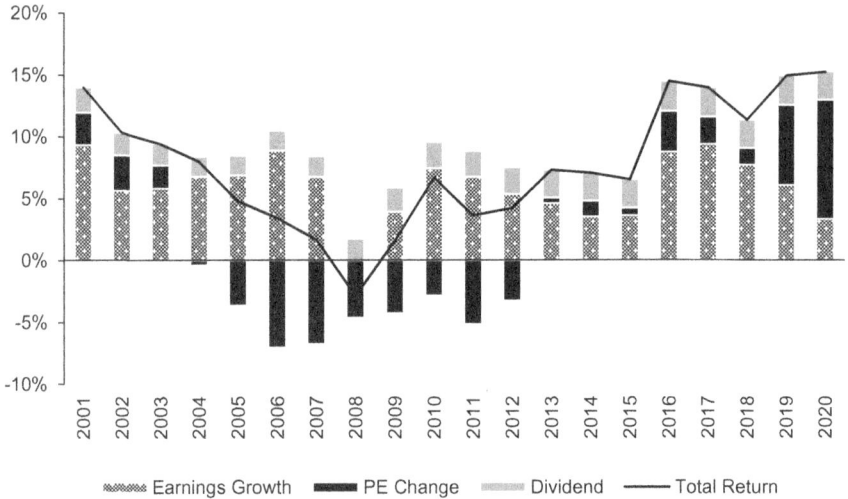

Fig. 12.3 The return decomposition of the S&P 500 Index

to 2020. The contribution to total return by earnings growth remained fairly stable and positive. However, the contribution by P/E change varied considerably across the entire period. The S&P 500 Index delivered an annualised total return of 15.2% in the 8 years to 2020. The model decomposes this return as: 3.3% (earnings growth), 9.6% (P/E change) and 2.3% (dividend return). The P/E ratio of the S&P 500 Index was 14.4 at the end of 2012 and increased to 29.9 when the year 2020 concluded. The P/E expansion contributed positively to the total return. In contrast, the P/E ratio contracted materially from 2004 to 2011, resulting in a negative annualised contribution of −5.2% to index return. The significant difference demonstrates the relevance of valuation to future returns. Assume the rule of mean reversion is applicable to the valuation level of the S&P 500 Index. When the current P/E ratio is below the long-run average, valuation will make a positive contribution to index performance as the P/E converges to the average level in the future. Otherwise, the contribution will be negative when the P/E ratio contracts towards the average level. This indicates that valuation is an essential factor that affects the future return potential of markets.

12.5 Return Forecasting

The above model can be applied to forecast future market returns. The predictive model requires that the current values of its components are accurately measured. Besides, the future values of the factors in the model must be properly estimated. A reasonable approach is to assume that all the factors gradually revert to their long-term averages over a number of years. Alternatively, future factor values can be estimated with necessary subjective judgments and assumptions. Return contributions of the factors are calculated individually and aggregated to form a return forecast. To enhance the predictive power, the model can be improved by decomposing earnings growth into sales growth and profit margin change:

$$e = \left(\frac{E_2}{E_1}\right)^{\frac{1}{N}} - 1 = \left(\frac{E_2/S_2 \times S_2}{E_1/S_1 \times S_1}\right)^{\frac{1}{N}} - 1 = \left(\frac{S_2}{S_1}\right)^{\frac{1}{N}} \times \left(\frac{E_2/S_2}{E_1/S_1}\right)^{\frac{1}{N}} - 1$$

The annualised sales growth s and profit margin change p are calculated as:

$$s = \left(\frac{S_2}{S_1}\right)^{\frac{1}{N}} - 1 \text{ and } p = \left(\frac{E_2/S_2}{E_1/S_1}\right)^{\frac{1}{N}} - 1$$

Earnings growth then becomes:

$$e = (1 + s) \times (1 + p) - 1 = s + p + sp$$

Since s and p tend to be small, the interaction term can be excluded from the formula. The annualised earnings growth is simplified as the sum of annualised sales growth and profit margin change:

$$e = s + p$$

Thus, the average annual total return R can be expressed as:

$$R = s + p + v + d$$

The formula shows that total return can be decomposed into four factors: sales growth, profit margin change, P/E change and dividend return. Figure 12.4 illustrates the application of the 4-factor model to return forecasting. This example predicts the average annual return of a broad market index in the next 8 years. Assume average annual sales growth is estimated to be 4.8% and dividend yield is considered stable at 2.5%. The current P/E ratio is 20 and profit margin is 5.0%. They are expected to revert to the long-run averages of 15 and 7.5% respectively at the end of the 8-year period. The P/E contraction leads to a negative annual contribution of −3.5% to total return, while profit margin change makes a positive contribution of 5.2%. The sum of the four individual return contributions is equal to 9.0%. Thus,

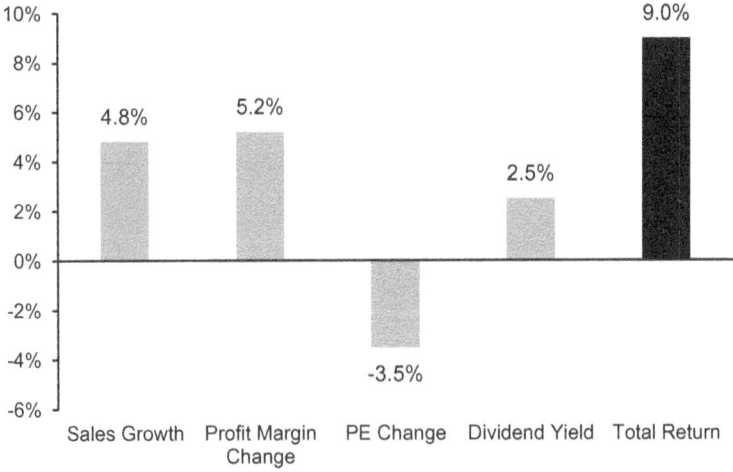

Fig. 12.4 Market return forecasting with a four-factor model

the market index is predicted to produce an average annual return of 9.0% in the next 8 years. In practice, it is difficult for the model to achieve reliable return forecasts. The model involves subjective judgements and assumptions to estimate future factor values. Besides, the market is very difficult to predict as it is subject to many unpredictable forces. Nevertheless, return decomposition allows investors to evaluate the sources of return and the future return potential of markets.

References

1. *Berkshire Hathaway 2005 Annual Report*.
2. Cembalest, M., *The Agony and the Ecstasy: The Risks and Rewards of a Concentrated Stock Position*. 2014, J.P. Morgan Asset Management.
3. Basu, S., *Investment Performance of Common Stocks in Relation to Their Price-Earnings Ratios: A Test of the Efficient Market Hypothesis*. Journal of Finance, 1977. **32**(3): p. 663–682.
4. Chan, L.K.C., Hamao, Y. and Lakonishok, J., *Fundamentals and Stock Returns in Japan*. Journal of Finance, 1991. **46**(5): p. 1739–1764.
5. Fama, E.F. and French, K.R., *Common Risk Factors in the Returns on Stocks and Bonds*. Journal of Financial Economics, 1993. **33**(1): p. 3–56.
6. Lakonishok, J., Shleifer, A. and Vishny, R.W., *Contrarian Investment, Extrapolation, and Risk*. Journal of Finance, 1994. **49**(5): p. 1541–1578.
7. Ibbotson, R.G., et al., *Liquidity as an Investment Style*. Financial Analysts Journal, 2013. **69**(3): p. 30–44.
8. Dimson, E., Marsh, P. and Staunton, M., *Factor-Based Investing: The Long-Term Evidence*. Journal of Portfolio Management, 2017. **43**(5): p. 15–37.

13

Dividend Yield

13.1 Dividend Investing

Dividends are payments made by a company to its shareholders that represent a form of profit distribution. Dividend investing is widely accepted as a simple and profitable investment strategy. It seeks to generate a steady income stream by investing in companies that issue dividends. Many famous investors such as Benjamin Graham consider dividend an important factor in stock selection. This is because dividend income is an essential source of return in equity investing. For example, dividends contributed about a third of total return provided by the S&P 500 Index from 1926 to 2018 [1]. Investors can potentially achieve both capital growth and dividend income by holding dividend stocks. For many investors, a stable and increasing dividend is a fundamental part of capital allocation strategy. Pension funds and insurance companies often maintain dividend as a key investment criterion so that they can plan their cash flows to meet future liabilities. The 2008 global financial crisis resulted in a protracted low rate environment. This prompted investors to search for investments that provide higher yields than the prevailing market interest rates. Many equity income funds have been launched to fulfil the yield demand in the market. These strategies have a primary focus on the provision of stable and growing dividends to investors.

Companies need to make strategic decisions on the use of retained earnings. Earnings can be reinvested to support business growth, distributed as dividends to shareholders or used to repurchase shares. Dividends represent a discretionary distribution of company earnings as a form of profit sharing.

On the declaration date, the issuing company releases a statement about its intension to make a dividend payment to shareholders. Shares must be owned before the ex-dividend date to be qualified for the proposed dividend. The company uses its shareholder system on the record date to identify investors entitled to the forthcoming dividend. The actual dividend payment date is typically several weeks after the record date. Some companies (e.g. Aviva) offer a dividend reinvestment plan to allow investors to directly reinvest dividends into additional shares. This dividend program enables investors to own more company shares without incurring brokerage fees. However, investors are still liable for taxes on the reinvested dividends.

Dividends are typically distributed in the form of cash payment. Companies occasionally allocate additional shares to existing shareholders as a form of compensation. This happens when companies want to preserve cash and reward shareholders with stock dividends. The additional shares can be either retained or converted to cash in the market. Dividends are normally paid at regular intervals, such as quarterly or annually. The frequency of dividend distribution varies across companies and markets, although it is often aligned with the announcement of company earnings. Outside the normal distribution schedule, companies may issue special dividends at their discretion. Special dividends are typically declared as a result of strong earnings, asset disposal or planned change of capital structure.

Companies should formulate a clear dividend policy to guide the market about future dividend payments. Dividend policy can be generally classified into three types: stable, constant and residual. Companies following a stable dividend policy link dividend payments with the forecast of future earnings. This common dividend policy often includes a target payout ratio specifying the proportion of earnings to be distributed to investors in the long term. Even during difficult years, companies with a stable dividend policy will still endeavour to achieve steady dividend payouts. Therefore, this dividend policy provides good visibility to shareholders about the future dividends. Clearly, the sustainability of stable dividends is questionable if the issuing company struggles to generate profits. Under a constant dividend policy, companies distribute a fixed percentage of earnings as dividends to investors. Because of the variability in earnings, the constant dividend policy will result in volatile dividend payouts. A primary advantage of this policy is that dividend payouts are relatively sustainable, since distributions are closely aligned with company profits. Based on the residual dividend policy, all earnings will be distributed to shareholders after capital expenditures of the current period have been financed. Given the uncertainties in business performance and spending requirements, the residual dividend policy often leads to very volatile dividend payments. Despite being intuitively appealing, this simple policy is not frequently applied by companies. Nevertheless, the residual dividend policy is considered fair and sensible by many investors, because it places business development above dividend distributions.

Companies often use dividend as an instrument to maintain investor confidence in their business prospects. Dividend is an important factor in investing that signals the fundamental strength and growth prospects of a company. Dividends are frequently used by investors to analyse company value, since they are essentially positive cash flows primarily generated from earnings. Benjamin Graham expressed his view regarding the importance of dividend in the book *Security Analysis* [2]:

The prime purpose of a business corporation is to pay dividends to its owners. A successful company is one that can pay dividends regularly and presumably increase the rate as time goes on. Since the idea of investment is closely bound up with that of dependable income, it follows that investment in common stocks would ordinarily be confined to those with a well-established dividend. It would follow also that the price paid for an investment common stock would be determined chiefly by the amount of the dividend.

Whereas dividend is an integral part of corporate strategy, companies have no legal obligation to reward investors with dividends. In Europe, only about two thirds of companies with a market capitalisation above €50 million paid dividends in 2019. Mature companies with predictable cash flows usually distribute regular dividends to maximise shareholder value. Companies with strong growth prospects often do not pay attractive dividends, as they need to reserve capital to support business growth. They will possibly initiate dividend payments when their business reaches a stage with limited growth potential. Companies with strong dividend records often attract investors pursuing stable passive income. This is because investors view consistent dividends as a positive sign of fundamental strength and management confidence in the business. To maintain investor confidence, companies typically honour the consistency of dividend payments. Otherwise, an unexpected declaration of dividend reduction or elimination may convey the message to the market that the company is facing significant challenges in its business.

Dividend income is an important source of return and can provide some downside protection against falling share prices. For example, the global energy company BP produced a negative price return of −4.9% in 2019. But the total return was actually 1.1% due to the positive contribution of dividends. Dividend strategies generally consider dividend safety and growth along with dividend yield in stock selection. Many established companies in the market provide investors with an opportunity to earn stable and rising dividend income. Despite the merits of dividend investing, individuals have the freedom to follow different investment strategies. While dividend investors generally prefer company profits to be returned in the form of dividends, growth investors favour companies that reinvest earnings to finance future growth.

13.2 Dividend Yield

Dividend yield is a financial ratio that measures the relative level of dividend income. It is normally calculated as annual dividend per share divided by the share price. Dividend yield is often considered a valuation metric that is closely related to earnings yield. It has been formally established as an independent style factor with the ability to produce long-term outperformance. Dividend yield was treated as a component of the value factor in the Barra Global Equity Model 2 (GEM2). It is positioned as an independent factor in the new Barra model (GEM3). Axioma and Northfield have also included the yield factor in their risk factor models. Dividend yield as a return driver captures the outperformance of stocks that provide attractive and sustainable dividends. During the 40 years to 2017, the simulated MSCI World High Dividend Yield Index produced an annualised return of over 12% [3]. This represents an average excess return of about 2% per annum relative to the MSCI World Index. The long-term performance of the yield factor over the 40-year period is comparable to that generated by the size and quality style factors.

Factor performance is cyclical in nature and fluctuates in changing market conditions. The yield factor falls into the defensive category together with quality and low volatility. The defensive property means that the yield factor typically outperforms during times of market downturn. The yield factor has proven its ability to generate outperformance in the long term. However, the existence of factor premiums apparently contradicts the efficient market hypothesis. Many studies have attempted to provide a theoretical explanation for the yield factor premium. An intuitive explanation is that a stable and high dividend distribution often indicates attractive valuation, strong financial position and positive earnings prospects. In fact, dividend yield can be decomposed into value and quality measures [4]:

$$\text{Dividend Yield} = \text{Book/Price} \times \text{ROE} \times \text{Payout Ratio}$$

Here, Book/Price is a valuation metric, ROE (return on equity) is a quality measure, and the Payout Ratio is the proportion of earnings paid to shareholders in dividends. The decomposition shows that dividend yield is a function of three metrics respectively related to value, quality and dividend safety. This suggests that the return premium of the dividend factor can possibly be explained by its correlations with the value and quality factors.

Dividend yield is an essential component of return from an equity investment. It is a significant contributor to the historical performance of the S&P 500 Index. During the 30 years to 2019, the S&P 500 Index generated an average price return of 7.7% per year. The annualised return will increase to 10.0% if dividends paid by index constituents are included in the calculation. This means that the average annual dividend yield was about 2.3% over the 30-year period. The contribution of dividend yield to cumulative return can be significantly amplified by the compounding effect in investing. Figure 13.1 displays the historical performance of the S&P 500 price and total return indices during the 30-year period. The indices are rebased with a starting value of 100 to facilitate comparison. Initially the price index could closely track the performance of the total return index. However, the difference in cumulative return increased steadily over time. After 30 years, the price index produced a cumulative return of 814%. This return is only about half of that delivered by the total return index (1627%). The substantial difference demonstrates the power of dividend yield in enhancing return

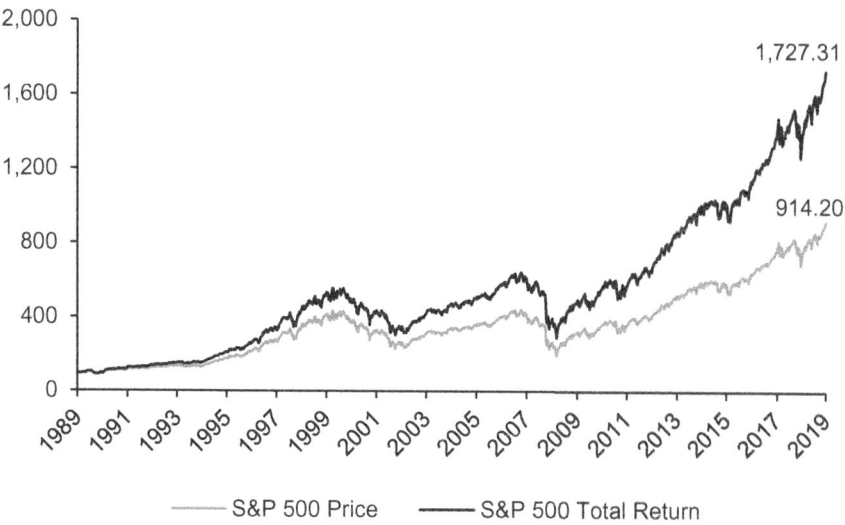

Fig. 13.1 The contribution of dividend yield to cumulative return

over an extended period of time. Note that the S&P 500 Index has a relatively low yield compared to its peer indices, such as FTSE 100 and STOXX Europe 600. As of 29 February 2020, the dividend yields of the three indices were 2.1%, 5.0% and 3.6% respectively (source: index factsheets). The return contribution of dividend yield is expected to be even more significant if the FTSE 100 Index is used in this example.

The vast equity universe allows investors to target companies with different dividend yields. Companies in the energy, utilities, financials and real estate sectors generally offer an attractive dividend yield. These sectors have relatively stable cash flows and slow growth rates. In comparison, companies in the information technology sector typically have low dividend yields. Technology companies often operate in a high-growth market. They tend to focus on reinvesting earnings into growth opportunities rather than paying dividends. The significant differences in dividend yield across sectors can be confirmed by the data in Table 13.1. The 11 sectors are represented by MSCI World sector indices. The dividend yield data are sourced from monthly index factsheets (as of 29 February 2020). The results show that the energy sector provided the highest dividend yield, followed by financials, utilities and real estate. Investors pursuing stable dividend income should allocate more capital to these sectors. As expected, the information technology sector displays a significantly lower dividend yield. Capital growth is generally the principal source of return for companies operating in this sector.

Table 13.1 The level of dividend yield by sector

Rank	Sector	Dividend Yield
1	Energy	5.9%
2	Financials	3.8%
3	Utilities	3.7%
4	Real Estate	3.6%
5	Materials	3.3%
6	Consumer Staples	3.0%
7	Industrials	2.3%
8	Health Care	2.1%
9	Consumer Discretionary	1.9%
10	Communication Services	1.9%
11	Information Technology	1.3%

Source: MSCI

13.3 Return Premium

The yield factor captures the outperformance of stocks with high and sustainable dividend yields. Academic studies identified the positive effect of dividend yield on stock returns in the 1970s. A Journal of Financial Economics paper published in 1979 found a strong positive relationship between dividend yield and expected return for stocks listed on the New York Stock Exchange [5]. A paper in the Review of Economics and Statistics quantifies the positive performance contribution of dividend yield [6]. The research shows that the risk-adjusted returns on dividend-paying stocks increased monotonically with expected dividend yield over the 41 years to 1976. Fama and French demonstrate the power of dividend yield to forecast stock returns in their paper *Dividend Yields and Expected Stock Returns* [7]. The research shows that dividend yield can explain a significant proportion of the variances in long-horizon returns. The Dogs of the Dow strategy focuses on selecting stocks with the highest dividend yields in the Dow Jones Industrial Average (DJIA) Index. It proves to be an effective strategy in generating positive excess returns. This simple dividend strategy delivered an annualised return of 9.5% over the 20 years to 2019, significantly outperforming the S&P 500 (6.1%) and DJIA (7.2%) indices.

Leading global index providers have launched a series of dividend indices to track the performance of the yield factor. MSCI published a research paper *Harvesting Equity Yield* to show the yield premium in equity investing [4]. The study found that high dividend-paying stocks outperformed the market by an average of 1.5% per year over the 88-year period to July 2015. The return premium is robust after controlling for the effects of other risk factors, such as size, value and momentum. An Invesco paper examines the ability of dividend yield and other factors to generate outperformance [8]. The study used the S&P 500 Index as the universe to select stocks for portfolio construction. For each factor, the top 20% of stocks with the highest factor scores were selected to form a portfolio for analysis. The performance of the portfolios was tracked over the 28 years to December 2019. The results show that the portfolio containing stocks with the highest dividend yields delivered an average excess return of 2.0% per annum relative to the S&P 500 Index during the period.

A WisdomTree study extended the analysis of Professor Jeremy Siegel about the long-term performance of dividend-paying stocks [9]. The research sorted the constituents of the S&P 500 Index into quintiles based on dividend yield. Portfolio returns were tracked over the period from 1958 to 2015. The top quintile with the highest yields was found to outperform the S&P

500 Index by 2.2% per annum during the period, compared to the underperformance of 0.8% for the bottom quintile. The S&P 500 High Dividend Index is designed to measure the performance of 80 high-yield companies in the S&P 500 Index. It was formally launched in 2015 and extended to 31 January 1991 through backtesting. This dividend index posted an annualised total return of 12.0% over the 29 years to January 2020, representing an average excess return of 1.7% per year against the S&P 500 Index. The S&P High Yield Dividend Aristocrats Index can also be used to examine the performance of the yield factor. It is designed to measure the returns of companies in the S&P Composite 1500 Index that have consistently raised dividends over the last 20 years. While focusing on dividend growth, this index has maintained a relatively high level of dividend yield since inception. The average dividend yields of the two indices were 3.5% and 1.8% respectively between 1999 and 2018 [10]. Combining the strength of dividend growth and yield, the S&P High Yield Dividend Aristocrats Index outperformed its parent index by an average of 4.3% per year from January 2000 to June 2019.

The data library of Professor Kenneth French at Dartmouth College provides valuable resources for the analysis of factor performance. The return premium of the yield factor can be assessed by comparing the performance of portfolios with different yield levels. For the 92 years to 2019, the portfolio comprising the top 30% US stocks with the highest dividend yields generated a strong annualised return of 11.0%. In comparison, the portfolio of the bottom 30% lowest-yielding stocks only returned an average of 9.2% per year. The portfolio composed of stocks paying no dividends performed even worse with an average annual return of 8.7%. The significant differences in performance prove the ability of the yield factor to enhance investment returns in the long term. The yield effect in the UK market is examined in a paper published by the Journal of Portfolio Management [11]. At the start of each year, the research ranked the 100 largest UK stocks by dividend yield and divided them equally into two portfolios. From 1900 to 2016, the higher-yielding portfolio delivered an annualised return of 10.8%, compared to only 7.8% for the lower-yielding portfolio.

13.4 Dividend Safety

Dividend safety is a principal concern for dividend investors seeking stable passive income. When a dividend is reduced or eliminated, the potential negative implications usually lead to the fall in share price. This causes shareholders to suffer losses in both capital and income. Companies often adopt a progressive dividend policy, pledging to maintain or increase dividend over time. However, it is reasonable to expect that companies will have to cut dividends at some point simply because dividend cannot rise indefinitely. The distribution of dividends is discretionary and generally subject to business performance. When companies face business or financial challenges, they will be in a difficult position to honour dividend commitment. Established companies with a strong balance sheet and resilient cash flows, such as Walmart and Nestlé, are more capable of maintaining dividend consistency. Figure 13.2 shows the historical dividends of Walmart and Nestlé during the 25 fiscal years to 2019. The two established names successfully maintained stable and rising dividend payments between 1995 and 2019. Walmart raised the dividend steadily from $0.085 to $2.08, an average annual growth of 14.3%. Nestlé achieved an average dividend growth of 10.2% per year during the period.

Considering the importance of dividend safety, this section presents a selection of metrics to help investors understand the sustainability of ongoing dividend streams. These metrics are frequently applied to evaluate the ability of a company to maintain its dividend payments. They can be aggregated to form a composite indicator on dividend safety. Since these metrics are measured in different units, raw scores should be converted to standard scores before they are combined.

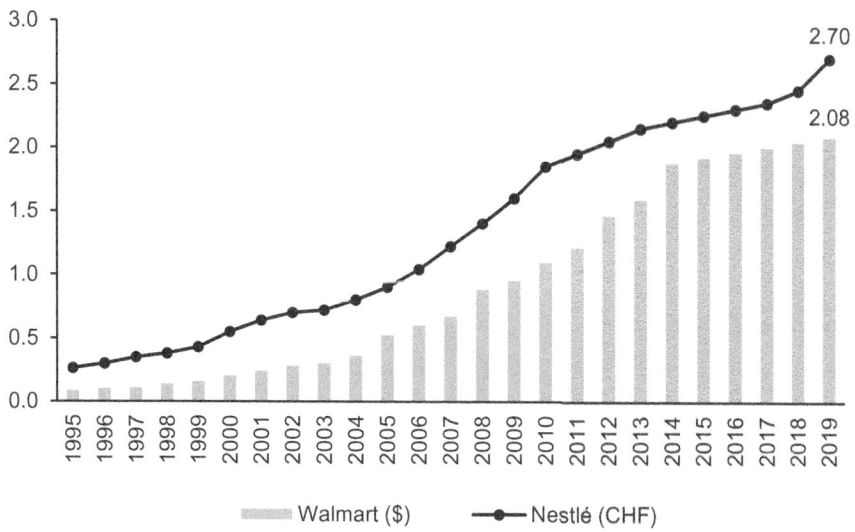

Fig. 13.2 Incremental dividend payouts of Walmart and Nestlé

- **Dividend Cover**

Dividend cover is probably the most common metric used for the assessment of dividend health. It measures the ability of a company to sustain the current dividend level based on earnings. Dividend cover is defined as the ratio of net income to the amount of dividend paid to shareholders. It indicates the number of times that the issued dividend could be covered by earnings. A dividend cover lower than 1 suggests that current dividend is not sufficiently supported by earnings. A sustainable dividend distribution normally requires the coverage ratio to be above 2.

- **FCF Cover**

FCF cover considers the impact of capital expenditure on the ability of issuing dividends. Companies with strong earnings may be unable to fulfil dividend commitment if high capital spending is required. FCF cover is expressed as free cash flow divided by total dividends. Free cash flow can be calculated as cash flow from operations minus capital expenditures. The FCF cover is usually required to be above 1.5 for companies to provide reliable dividend income.

- **Financial Leverage**

Financial leverage is a key indicator of financial strength and often defined as the ratio of total debt to equity. Companies with stable dividend distributions typically have a low leverage ratio or net cash position. Highly leveraged companies may face financial difficulties in times of economic downturn. They usually reduce or completely abandon dividend payments to service debt in difficult times. In general, a financial leverage below 50% is considered a safe level for companies to balance dividend payments with debt obligations.

- **Interest Coverage**

Interest coverage is a financial ratio that measures the ability of a company to make interest payments. It is usually calculated as operating income divided by interest expense. Before interest expense can be reasonably covered by earnings, it is difficult for companies to maintain stable dividend distributions to shareholders. A low interest coverage (e.g. below 2) is a warning sign that the company is not generating sufficient earnings to support the current dividend stream while meeting its interest obligations.

- **Earnings Variability**

Earnings variability is the volatility of reported earnings. It is calculated as the standard deviation of earnings growth rates. High earnings variability implies that it is difficult to predict future earnings. The great uncertainty in future earnings raises a serious question about the sustainability of current dividend stream. This explains the fact that dividend investors generally prefer companies with stable earnings.

- **Dividend Consistency**

The consistency of historical dividend payments is an essential factor to consider when investing in dividend stocks. It can be measured as the frequency that a company increased or maintained dividend over the last 10 years. A company with uninterrupted dividend increase is a positive sign of business quality and dividend commitment. Companies with great dividend consistency often attract income investors. This is because a strong dividend record enhances investor confidence in future dividend distributions.

- **Dividend Yield**

Dividend yield is a component of total return and offers a return premium. The yield factor captures the outperformance of companies with attractive and stable dividend yields. Investors should perform rigorous company analysis to understand if a dividend distribution is sustainable. A dividend trap occurs when a high dividend yield attracts investors to a troubled company with deteriorating fundamentals and falling share prices. Many companies can comfortably support a dividend yield of 5%. However, it is very difficult for companies to maintain a yield at the 10% level. An exceptionally high yield may send the warning signal that the dividend is unlikely to be maintained.

References

1. Chirputkar, S. and Soe, A.M., *A Fundamental Look at S&P 500 Dividend Aristocrats*. 2019, S&P Dow Jones Indices.
2. Graham, B. and Dodd, D., *Security Analysis*. 1934, McGraw-Hill.
3. *Factor Focus: Yield*. 2018, MSCI.
4. Wei, Z., Chia, C.P. and Katiyar, S., *Harvesting Equity Yield: Understanding Factor Investing*. 2015, MSCI.

5. Litzenberger, R.H. and Ramaswamy, K., *The Effect of Personal Taxes and Dividends on Capital Asset Prices: Theory and Empirical Evidence.* Journal of Financial Economics, 1979. **7**(2): p. 163–195.
6. Blume, M.E., *Stock Returns and Dividend Yields: Some More Evidence.* The Review of Economics and Statistics, 1980. **62**(4): p. 567–577.
7. Fama, E.F. and French, K.R., *Dividend Yields and Expected Stock Returns.* Journal of Financial Economics, 1988. **22**(1): p. 3–25.
8. Stoneberg, J. and Smith, B., *The Facts Behind Factor Performance.* 2020, Invesco.
9. *The Dividends of a Dividend Approach.* 2016, WisdomTree.
10. Hao, W.B. and Li, Q., *S&P High Yield Dividend Aristocrats: A Practitioner's Guide.* 2019, S&P Dow Jones Indices.
11. Dimson, E., Marsh, P. and Staunton, M., *Factor-Based Investing: The Long-Term Evidence.* Journal of Portfolio Management, 2017. **43**(5): p. 15–37.

14

Volatility Effect

14.1 Volatility Effect

Volatility is the degree of fluctuation in the price of an asset or portfolio over a period of time. It is a natural part of investing that reflects the uncertainty in price movement. The level of price volatility can vary considerably across stocks and industries. Stocks in cyclical sectors generally have more volatile price movements than those in defensive sectors. For example, Microsoft had an annual price volatility of 30.5% during the 20 years to 2019, compared to only 12.6% for Unilever. A conventional view in investing is that risk and return are closely related. Assets with greater volatility are expected to deliver higher returns than the market. However, empirical evidence shows that stocks exhibiting low-volatility characteristics actually have generated superior returns. The volatility effect is the observation that stocks with relatively low volatility tend to outperform the market in the long term. The volatility anomaly was first identified by the financial economist Robert Haugen in 1972 [1, 2]. Subsequently, it has been explored and documented in many academic studies. Despite the early identification, the volatility anomaly was not widely exploited by the market until the 2008 financial crisis. The dramatic losses caused by market crashes during the crisis made investors realise the virtue of low-volatility investing. The volatility factor has now been formally accepted as a systematic return driver and investment style.

Tactical investors often use low-volatility strategies to preserve capital and reduce risk in turbulent markets. During the last quarter of 2018, the market experienced severe volatility caused by the escalation of the trade war between the US and China. The S&P 500 Index suffered a maximum drawdown of 19.2% in this period, while the S&P 500 Low Volatility Index only fell by 11.7% from peak value. Traditionally, low-volatility strategies are designed to reduce volatility risk in portfolios. The unintended results are that they also generate excess returns over an extended period of time. This is contrary to the prevailing theory that higher returns require greater risk. From 1991 to 2019, the S&P 500 Low Volatility Index achieved an average annual return of 11.3%, exceeding 10.4% provided by the S&P 500 Index [3]. The excess return was delivered with a lower annual volatility (11%) than the broad market index (14%). The better performance in both risk and return helped the low-volatility index realise a significantly higher risk-adjusted return than its parent index.

Low volatility is classified as a defensive factor that typically generates outperformance during times of market downturn. Figure 14.1 compares the annual returns of the MSCI World Minimum Volatility Index and its benchmark between 2008 and 2019 (source: index factsheets). The results confirm the defensive nature of the volatility factor. The 2008 global crisis caused

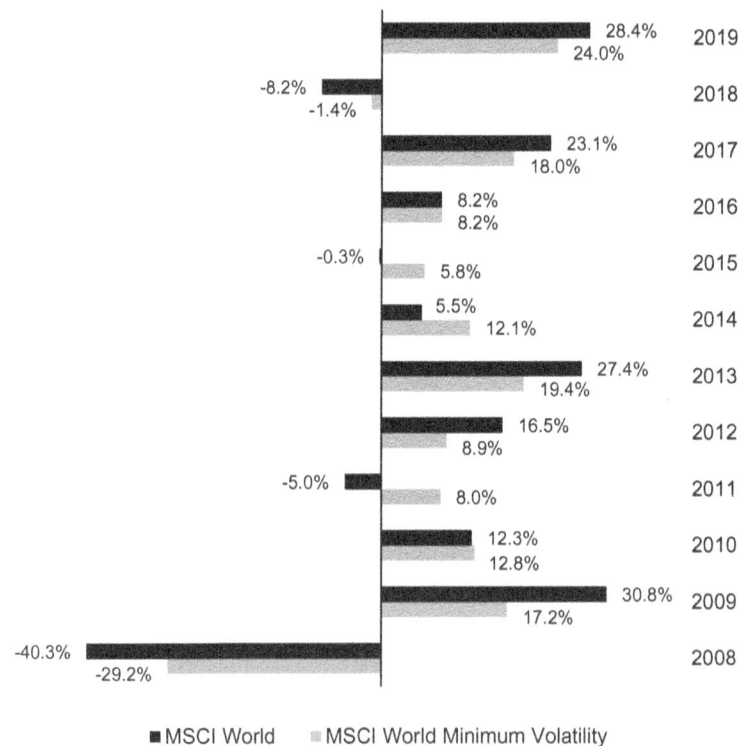

Fig. 14.1 Annual performance of the volatility factor

a dramatic impact to the financial market and profoundly shifted the risk appetite of investors to defensive strategies. The global stock market represented by the MSCI World Index suffered a substantial loss of 40.3% in 2008, compared to the decline of only 29.2% in the minimum-volatility index. The global market fell by 5.0% in 2011 when the European debt crisis intensified, while the minimum-volatility index actually produced a positive return of 8.0%. The minimum-volatility index also outperformed in other years with high market risk (e.g. 2015 and 2018). On the other hand, it underperformed the MSCI World Index in the years with strong market performance (e.g. 2009 and 2013). During the 12 years, the minimum-volatility index generated an annualised return of 7.7%, reasonably exceeding 6.1% returned by its benchmark. Besides, it had a significantly lower volatility (13.2%) than the MSCI World Index (19.3%). The results support the argument that it is possible to earn higher returns with lower risk.

The defensive characteristic of low volatility is examined in an MSCI research paper [4]. The study investigates the behaviour of the volatility factor in different market conditions. It analyses the frequency of outperformance produced by the MSCI World Minimum Volatility Index against the MSCI World Index. The results are based on 1-year rolling returns over the 27 years to 31 May 2015. The minimum-volatility index was found to outperform a negative market (i.e. negative return of the MSCI World Index) with a frequency of 89% and average excess return of 8.8%. It only underperformed by an average of 1.2% in the other 11% cases. Besides, the research examines the risk and return characteristics of the minimum-volatility index during the four bear markets that happened in the period. The results in Table 14.1 illustrate the ability of the volatility factor to protect capital in difficult times. The broad market suffered a dramatic loss of 46.3% from March 2000 to September 2002. The minimum-volatility index, however, managed to mitigate the severe damage caused by the dot-com bubble collapse. It also

Table 14.1 The performance of the volatility factor during bear markets

Bear Market	MSCI World Minimum Volatility		MSCI World	
	Return	Volatility	Return	Volatility
12/1989 - 09/1990	-20.2%	19.7%	-24.0%	21.8%
03/2000 - 09/2002	-19.8%	11.0%	-46.3%	16.5%
10/2007 - 02/2009	-43.0%	17.1%	-53.7%	21.9%
04/2011 - 09/2011	-5.1%	8.9%	-19.4%	15.9%

Source: MSCI

consistently achieved a lower volatility level than its benchmark in the four bear markets.

The efficient market hypothesis states that it is impossible to consistently beat the market. This is because all material information has been reflected in the share price. The existence of the volatility anomaly proves that the market is not efficient. The phenomenon that higher returns can be achieved with lower risk makes the volatility anomaly one of the greatest puzzles in finance. Many studies have attempted to explain this anomaly from the perspective of behavioural finance. A plausible explanation is that investors often avoid stocks with low volatility, because they are considered boring with limited upside. Conversely, investors actively pursue glamorous stocks that typically have high analyst and media coverage. This behaviour is frequently driven by the lottery effect that investors intentionally select volatile stocks in their chase for stellar returns. They tend to overvalue volatile stocks without properly understanding company fundamentals and investment risk. The excessive market demand for volatile stocks leads to stretched valuations and reduced return potential.

Investment strategies designed to target the volatility anomaly usually have overweight positions in defensive sectors, such as consumer staples, utilities and real estate. This can be confirmed by the relative sector weightings of the S&P 500 Low Volatility Index. This index measures the performance of 100 stocks with the lowest volatility in the S&P 500 Index. As of 29 February 2020, consumer staples, utilities and real estate had a combined weighting of 54.9% in the low-volatility index. In comparison, the three defensive sectors only accounted for 13.8% of portfolio value in the S&P 500 Index, considerably lower than 24.4% occupied by the information technology sector (source: index factsheets). Stocks with low-volatility characteristics are often viewed as bond proxies. This is because they generally have stable cash flows and relatively low sensitivity to market conditions. Low-volatility stocks tend to benefit from falling interest rates. But they frequently underperform when interest rates rise in an improving economic environment. A Morningstar paper provides empirical evidence that low-volatility strategies have limited upside participation during times of strong market performance [5]. Returns produced by low-volatility strategies can be decomposed into the low-volatility premium and the component due to the exposure to market risk [6]. When market returns are high, low-volatility strategies are expected to underperform the market because the low-volatility premium is relatively small compared to the strong market return.

14.2 Capital Asset Pricing Model

The capital asset pricing model (CAPM) in finance defines the relationship between expected return and risk. The model was introduced by William Sharpe and other scholars in the 1960s. The CAPM is built upon the modern portfolio theory developed by the economist Harry Markowitz. It assumes that the total risk of an asset can be divided into the systematic and specific components. Systematic risk affects all assets in the market and cannot be avoided. Specific risk is unique to an individual asset and can be diversified away. Based on this risk decomposition, the CAPM asserts that investors are not rewarded for bearing specific risk, because it can be eliminated through diversification. To enhance expected return, investors should increase the exposure to systematic risk. The CAPM is defined as:

$$R_i = R_f + \beta_i \times (R_m - R_f)$$

Here, R_i is the expected return on asset i, R_m is the expected market return, R_f is the risk-free rate, β_i is the sensitivity of asset return to the market risk premium $R_m - R_f$. The exposure to market risk β_i can be calculated as:

$$\beta_i = \rho_{i,m} \frac{\sigma_i}{\sigma_m}$$

where $\rho_{i,m}$ is the correlation between asset i and the market, σ_i and σ_m are the standard deviations of their returns. The CAPM specifies a linear relationship between the expected return of an asset and its exposure to market risk measured by beta. This means that asset return is expected to increase as the risk level rises.

The validity of the CAPM as a theoretical framework is subject to several key assumptions. The model assumes that information is freely available in the market with no transaction costs and taxes. Investors can borrow and lend an unlimited amount of capital at the risk-free rate. All investors are rational and risk-averse in the pursuit of maximum returns. Investors hold diversified portfolios and homogeneous expectations about expected returns and risks. The CAPM has been widely applied to estimate the cost of capital and evaluate investment performance. However, this model is overly simplified in that beta is the only factor to explain expected returns. The CAPM has been heavily criticised by many academic studies primarily because of its unrealistic assumptions and empirical failures. Fama and French provide a detailed review of the CAPM in their paper *The Capital Asset Pricing Model: Theory and Evidence* [7]. The research concludes that most applications of the CAPM are invalid, resulting from its problematic assumptions and failure in empirical tests. A paper in the Journal of Portfolio Management seeks to provide explanations for the volatility effect based on the CAPM assumptions [8]. The research considers the CAPM a valuable theoretical framework. However, it suggests that the model has very limited practical value due to the empirical problems and impractical assumptions.

The low-volatility effect is an anomaly in finance that challenges the validity of the CAPM framework. The CAPM asserts that asset return is expected to increase with the risk level measured by beta. However, numerous studies show that low-beta stocks actually often outperform over a long time horizon. A study of J.P. Morgan constructed a theoretical portfolio comprising long positions in low-beta stocks and short positions in high-beta stocks [6]. The portfolio was rebalanced monthly with its returns tracked from 1990 to 2011. The portfolio was found to produce an annualised return of 4.1% during the period. This demonstrates the strength of low-beta investing in delivering superior returns. A paper published by the Journal of Financial Economics also supports the fact that low-beta stocks usually outperform in the long term [9]. The research provides empirical evidence that low-beta strategies generate excess returns across different asset classes, such as equities, bonds and futures.

14.3 Return Premium

The volatility factor has been firmly established as a systematic return driver due to its proven performance. Many studies provide empirical evidence that low-volatility stocks tend to outperform their more volatile peers in the long term. A paper in the Journal of Portfolio Management examines the volatility effect across the US, developed and emerging markets [10]. The research constructs low-volatility portfolios using different methods and weighting schemes. The results show that these portfolios consistently generated excess returns across all the markets covered in the study. For example, the US portfolio created with the minimum variance method produced an annualised return of 11.4% from 1967 to 2012, exceeding the 9.8% returned by a cap-weighted benchmark index. For the global developed markets, the excess return delivered by the volatility factor was about 3.0% per annum over the 26 years to 2012. The low-volatility effect was very significant in the emerging markets between 2002 and 2012. A low-beta portfolio outperformed the market by an average of 8.9% per year during the period. Besides, all these portfolios had a lower volatility level than their benchmark. Positive excess return combined with lower risk helped the low-volatility strategies achieve much higher risk-adjusted returns than the market.

A paper published by the Financial Analysts Journal proves the long-term success of low-volatility investing [11]. It compares the performance of portfolios with different volatility levels. The research sorted US stocks into quintile portfolios based on 5-year volatility measured by standard deviation. It formed another five portfolios by ranking stocks according to trailing beta. The performance of monthly rebalanced portfolios was tracked over the period from 1968 to 2008. The results in Table 14.2 demonstrate the return premium of the volatility factor. The excess return declines steadily across the portfolios as the volatility level increases. The portfolio containing the most stable stocks realised an annualised excess return of 4.4% over the risk-free rate. In contrast, the portfolio of the most volatile stocks significantly underperformed the risk-free rate by an average of 6.8% per annum. It is a similar pattern of portfolio performance when stock volatility is measured by beta. The portfolio of the lowest-beta stocks achieved an average annual outperformance of 6.8% against that containing the highest-beta stocks.

A paper in the Journal of Portfolio Management seeks to validate the volatility effect as a challenge to the efficient markets theory [12]. The study constructed portfolios with the constituents of the FTSE World Developed Index. Stocks were ranked based on 3-year trailing volatility and assigned to equal-weighted decile portfolios. The portfolios were rebalanced monthly, with their returns tracked from 1986 to 2006. The results show that portfolio return largely decreases with the volatility level. The least volatile portfolio outperformed the risk-free rate by an average of 7.3% annually. It achieved a significantly higher Sharpe ratio of 0.72 than other portfolios, as a result of its strong outperformance and low volatility. The most volatile portfolio, however, only produced a marginal average excess return of 1.4% per year against the risk-free rate. The combination of low return and high volatility resulted in a negligible Sharpe ratio of 0.05 for this portfolio. The results

Table 14.2 Performance of portfolios with different volatility levels

Standard deviation	1	2	3	4	5
Excess return	4.4%	3.4%	2.7%	0.5%	-6.8%
Volatility	13.1%	16.7%	21.4%	27.0%	32.0%
Beta	1	2	3	4	5
Excess return	4.4%	4.5%	3.0%	1.3%	-2.4%
Volatility	12.1%	13.4%	16.3%	20.2%	27.8%

Source: Financial Analysts Journal

should really dampen the enthusiasm of investors to hold volatile stocks. They expose investors to high volatility risk while underperforming the market over time.

The long-term performance of the MSCI World Minimum Volatility Index provides valuable insight into the low-volatility premium. It produced an annualised return of 9.0% from June 1988 to January 2020 (source: index factsheet). This represents an average excess return of 1.2% per year relative to the MSCI World Index. The excess return becomes more significant when it is adjusted by volatility. The minimum-volatility index realised a Sharpe ratio of 0.54 during the period, reasonably higher than 0.36 for its benchmark index. A Robeco study analyses the long-term performance of the volatility factor from 1931 to 2009 [13]. The results show that risk-adjusted return decreases steadily across the portfolios as the volatility level rises. BMO published a paper to show potential investment opportunities associated with the low-volatility anomaly [14]. The research ranked 1,000 largest US stocks by 3-year volatility and assigned them into five portfolios. The portfolios were constructed with equal weighting and rebalanced monthly. The lowest-volatility portfolio was found to generate an annualised excess return of about 7.0% against the most volatile portfolio from 1970 to 2011.

14.4 Construction Methods

Leading index providers such as MSCI have developed a wide range of volatility indices to track the performance of the volatility factor. Abundant investment funds in the market are designed to replicate volatility indices. They provide investors with an opportunity to systematically capture the low-volatility premium. For example, iShares Minimum Volatility ETFs seek to track the returns of indices that have low-volatility characteristics. Volatility indices in the market are generally constructed with the low-volatility or minimum-variance approach [15]. The low-volatility method ranks the universe of stocks by volatility and selects those with the lowest volatility levels for portfolio construction. Constraints are often applied to ensure that selected stocks meet the basic liquidity and investability criteria. Stocks in the portfolio are weighted according to a defined weighting scheme, such as market capitalisation and volatility score. Low-volatility strategies constructed with this method include the S&P 500 Low Volatility and FTSE RAFI Developed Low Volatility indices. The low-volatility approach has the advantages of simplicity, flexibility and transparency. Because this ranking-based method simply selects stocks based on the volatility level, it may cause unintended bias towards certain sectors, countries and style factors. For example, volatility indices constructed with the low-volatility method tend to overweight defensive sectors.

The minimum-variance approach focuses on the overall portfolio rather than the selection of individual stocks. Its objective is to find the portfolio with the minimum variance, subject to defined constraints. The minimum-variance approach is essentially a constrained optimisation problem:

$$\text{Minimise: } w'\Sigma w$$

$$\text{Subject to: } \sum w_i = 1, 0 < w_i < 1 \cdots$$

where w is a vector of stock weights and Σ is a covariance matrix of stock returns. The objective is to find weights w that result in the lowest portfolio volatility. The covariance matrix can be obtained from historical stock volatilities and correlations. A fundamental factor model is often applied to achieve a stable covariance matrix and reduce the complexity of calculation. Index providers usually apply additional constraints to ensure that sector weightings and risk exposures of the volatility index do not significantly deviate from its benchmark index. For example, the S&P 500 Minimum Volatility Index imposes constraints on stock and sector weights as well as factor exposures. Sectors are allowed to have a maximum deviation of 5% from that in the S&P 500 Index. The implementation of constraints can reduce portfolio turnover at the rebalancing point and mitigate many potential problems. Although the minimum-variance approach may have potential complications, it maintains tight control over the exposure to various risk factors through constrained optimisation.

Low-volatility and minimum-variance are fundamentally different construction methods, since they respectively focus on the stock and portfolio levels. Indices created with the two approaches may have very different characteristics. Table 14.3 shows the differences between the S&P 500 Low Volatility and S&P 500 Minimum Volatility indices [16]. The risk and return data together with sector information are sourced from index factsheets (as of 29 February 2020). The two indices had comparable valuation levels and produced similar 10-year returns. Historically, they have generated excess returns relative to the S&P 500 Index. The two indices differed significantly in sector composition. The low-volatility index had large positions in the utilities and real estate sectors. In comparison, the optimisation-based index gained heavy exposure to the information technology and consumer discretionary sectors. This reflects the methodological

Table 14.3 Sample indices formed with different volatility methods

	S&P 500 Low Volatility	S&P 500 Minimum Volatility
Portfolio construction	Ranking	Optimisation
Complexity	Low	High
Constraint: stock weight	No	Yes
Constraint: sector weight	No	Yes
Constraint: factor exposure	No	Yes
Data below as of 29 February 2020		
Annual return (10Y)	13.0%	13.4%
Standard deviation (10Y)	9.8%	10.2%
Risk-adjusted return	1.3	1.3
P/E (forward)	22.5	19.0
P/B	2.8	3.4
Dividend yield	2.6%	2.1%
Top 2 sectors	Utilities Real Estate	Information Technology Consumer Discretionary

Source: S&P Dow Jones Indices

differences between the two indices. While the low-volatility index targets least volatile stocks, the minimum-volatility index is primarily concerned with the overall portfolio volatility.

References

1. Haugen, R.A. and Heins, A.J., *Risk and the Rate of Return on Financial Assets: Some Old Wine in New Bottles.* Journal of Financial and Quantitative Analysis, 1975. **10**(5): p. 775–784.
2. Haugen, R.A. and Heins, A.J., *On the Evidence Supporting the Existence of Risk Premiums in the Capital Market*, in *Wisconsin Working Paper*. 1972.
3. Chan, F.M. and Lazzara, C.J., *The Valuation of Low Volatility*. 2020, S&P Dow Jones Indices.
4. Alighanbari, M., et al., *Constructing Low Volatility Strategies: Understanding Factor Investing*. 2016, MSCI.
5. Boyadzhiev, D., et al., *Low Volatility: Searching for a Durable Edge*. 2017, Morningstar.
6. Grassi, P.E., Lastra, B. and Romahi, Y., *Low Volatility Investing*. 2012, J.P. Morgan Asset Management.
7. Fama, E.F. and French, K.R., *The Capital Asset Pricing Model: Theory and Evidence.* Journal of Economic Perspectives, 2004. **18**(3): p. 25–46.

8. Blitz, D., Falkenstein, E. and van Vliet, P., *Explanations for the Volatility Effect: An Overview Based on the CAPM Assumptions.* Journal of Portfolio Management, 2014. **40**(3): p. 61–76.
9. Frazzini, A. and Pedersen, L.H., *Betting Against Beta.* Journal of Financial Economics, 2014. **111**(1): p. 1–25.
10. Chow, T., et al., *A Study of Low-Volatility Portfolio Construction Methods.* Journal of Portfolio Management, 2014. **40**(4): p. 89–105.
11. Baker, M., Bradley, B. and Wurgler, J., *Benchmarks as Limits to Arbitrage: Understanding the Low-Volatility Anomaly.* Financial Analysts Journal, 2011. **67**(1): p. 40–54.
12. Blitz, D.C. and van Vliet, P., *The Volatility Effect.* Journal of Portfolio Management, 2007. **34**(1): p. 102–113.
13. van Vliet, P., *Low-Volatility Investing: A Long-Term Perspective.* 2012, Robeco.
14. Ramos, E. and Hans, J.C., *Finding Opportunities Through the Low-Volatility Anomaly.* 2016, BMO Global Asset Management.
15. *Low Volatility or Minimum Variance.* 2015, FTSE Russell.
16. Brzenk, P. and Soe, A.M., *Inside Low Volatility Indices.* 2017, S&P Dow Jones Indices.

15

Liquidity Premium

15.1 Asset Liquidity

Liquidity is the degree to which an asset can be quickly traded in the market without materially affecting its price. The level of liquidity can vary significantly across different asset classes. While cash is considered the standard of liquidity, many alternative investments such as real estate and private equity are rather illiquid. For example, a residential property transaction often takes several months to complete. Compared to US Treasury bills, long-term bonds issued by small companies are generally much more illiquid due to limited market interest. Public equities are traded on stock exchanges and have a relatively high liquidity level. Largecap stocks typically can be traded quickly in the market with low transaction costs. In comparison, microcap stocks are generally more difficult to trade because of low trading volume. It may take several days to complete a large buy order for a microcap stock with thin trading volume. Market condition is an influential factor that can affect asset liquidity. During times of market crash, the overall market liquidity is expected to fall as investors rush to exit their positions.

Illiquid assets expose investors to material liquidity risk and potential high transaction costs. In exceptional market conditions, illiquid assets may have to be sold at a deep discount to fair value or even cannot find any market interest. During the 2008 financial crisis, the Harvard University endowment was forced to sell some private equity investments at significant discounts to meet liquidity needs. Stocks with low liquidity generally have low trading volume and large bid-ask spread. The trading of illiquid stocks often incurs significant implicit costs in the form of bid-ask spread and market impact. The spread can easily exceed 1% for microcap stocks with thin trading volume. Illiquid assets such as real estate are typically held over a long period of time. The long holding period exposes investors to great investment risk and affects the flexibility to direct capital to other assets with higher return potential. Therefore, investors demand additional compensation for the investment in assets with low liquidity. This basically aligns with the principle of risk-return tradeoff that the potential return is expected to increase as the risk level rises. Liquidity premium represents the additional rate of return required by investors to compensate them for the risk of holding illiquid assets. It can be considered the factor to explain the difference in the required rate of return between two assets with identical characteristics except liquidity. For example, the yield spread between very illiquid bonds and those with identical properties but high liquidity can be used to quantify the effect of illiquidity on bond valuation [1]. In the finance literature, liquidity is widely accepted as an important risk factor in asset pricing. A study published by the Journal of Finance provides a theoretical framework for the valuation of liquidity in financial markets [2]. The research derives a simple upper bound on the value of marketability based on the option-pricing theory. The upper bound can be viewed as the maximum amount that an investor is willing to pay in order to achieve immediacy in liquidating a security position.

Investors should consider the overall portfolio liquidity when selecting assets with different liquidity levels. The excessive exposure to illiquid assets can become a critical problem when immediate cash needs cannot be fulfilled. A practical approach is to achieve a balanced portfolio allocation between liquid and illiquid assets. The portfolio is positioned to meet liquidity needs while retaining the ability to capture some liquidity premium. Institutional investors have the expertise and resources to properly exploit the liquidity premium. Individual investors, however, may find it difficult to achieve an optimal portfolio allocation to the liquidity factor. This is mainly because their wealth is typically concentrated in illiquid assets such as residential property. A research paper published by Management Science presents a theoretical model of optimal portfolio allocation to illiquid assets [3]. The optimal weighting of illiquid assets largely depends on the degree of illiquidity and liquidity needs. In Table 15.1, investment duration represents the liquidity level of risky assets. The second and third columns provide the optimal portfolio weighting assigned to illiquid assets, subject to the condition of consumption. If consumption is required, the allocation to illiquid assets will fall steadily as the liquidity level declines. When illiquid assets can

Table 15.1 Optimal allocation to illiquid assets

Investment duration (years)	Optimal Weighting	
	With consumption	No consumption
0	59.3%	59.3%
1/10	49.3%	54.7%
1/4	47.5%	54.4%
1/2	44.2%	53.5%
1	37.3%	52.7%
2	25.1%	52.3%
4	13.2%	52.0%
10	4.8%	51.8%

Source: Management Science

be traded 10 times per year, their optimal weighting is 49.3% at the time of portfolio rebalancing. If their liquidity level declines to only one transaction every 10 years, the optimal weighting will decrease dramatically to only 4.8%. This is because the portfolio needs to reserve enough liquid assets to meet consumption demand. As the liquidity level falls, the portfolio has to reduce the weighting of illiquid assets to achieve a balanced composition. On the other hand, the portfolio can increase the allocation to illiquid assets when there is no immediate consumption. The optimal allocation to illiquid assets remains fairly stable as the liquidity level decreases. From perfect liquidity to the 10-year holding period, the allocation to illiquid assets only declines from 59.3% to 51.8%.

Illiquid assets extend the investment opportunity set and can potentially enhance portfolio returns. Many studies provide empirical evidence that liquidity is a significant factor that affects stock returns [4]. The liquidity factor in equity investing captures excess returns delivered by stocks with low liquidity. It is included in many commercial fundamental factor models (e.g. Axioma) to help explain portfolio returns. Liquidity stands as one of the seven style factors covered by the global factor indices of FTSE Russell. However, it has received much less attention from investors than other common style factors such as quality and momentum. There are relatively few factor strategies in the market that explicitly pursue the liquidity premium. A possible reason is that institutional investors often face liquidity constraints in their asset allocation. They need to control exposure to assets with low liquidity and carefully manage liquidity risk.

15.2 Liquidity Measures

The liquidity risk factor in equity investing has been measured with different metrics. The Axioma US Fundamental Factor Model estimates stock liquidity with the metric of average daily volume over market capitalisation. The liquidity factor in the Barra US Equity Model reflects relative trading activity such as share turnover. The liquidity factor indices of FTSE Russell select stocks by their historical liquidity score based on the Amihud ratio. The Vanguard US Liquidity Factor ETF uses three metrics to measure the liquidity factor: percentage turnover, dollar turnover and Amihud illiquidity. Equity investors often use daily trading volume and bid-ask spread to estimate stock liquidity. Individual liquidity metrics can be aggregated to form a composite indicator that reflects the overall liquidity level of a stock. The composite liquidity indicator can help investors select stocks with different liquidity profiles and construct portfolios that have controlled exposure to the liquidity factor.

Stock liquidity can be measured by four metrics: share turnover, trading value, float-adjusted market value and bid-ask spread. Share turnover is defined as the average daily trading volume divided by the number of shares in issue. Trading value is the average daily value traded over a specific period of time. For both liquidity measures, the average is typically calculated over the period of 1, 3 or 6 months. Float-adjusted market value is the market capitalisation adjusted by the free float. The free-float method assumes that market capitalisation is a liquidity indicator but excludes the portion of issued shares that are restricted from trading. Bid-ask spread is simply the difference between the bid and ask prices. The four liquidity measures can be combined to form a composite liquidity indicator. Since these metrics are measured with different units, raw liquidity scores need to be standardised before they can be aggregated. For the purpose of standardisation, all raw data can be first converted to *z*-scores. After this process, *z*-scores across the four liquidity metrics are combined based on a weighting scheme. The resulting composite scores can be normalised and converted to liquidity ratings on a common scale (e.g. 1–5).

A paper in the Journal of Financial and Quantitative Analysis shows that stock liquidity matters when companies access the equity capital markets [5]. Based on a sample of over 2,000 seasoned equity offerings, the research found companies with liquid stock pay significantly lower investment banking fees than those with illiquid stock. The paper suggests that public companies can reduce the cost of raising capital by improving their stock liquidity. Nasdaq proposes potential measures to enhance the market liquidity of stocks [6].

These measures are divided into several categories, including investor awareness, share price and shareholder value. Effective ways to enhance investor awareness include investor communication, analyst coverage and index inclusion. At the share price level, stock split is a common corporate action used to improve stock liquidity. A stock split increases the number of issued shares and thereby reduces the share price. This effectively makes the shares more affordable for investors to trade in the market, thus increasing trading volume. Companies can also use different strategies to influence shareholder value, such as dividend distribution and share buyback programs.

15.3 Return Premium

The liquidity style factor has proven its ability to deliver excess returns in the long term. The research paper *Liquidity as an Investment Style* empirically confirms the existence of liquidity premium in equity investing [7]. Based on the analysis of 3,500 US stocks between 1972 and 2011, the study found that illiquid stocks delivered substantial outperformance relative to their liquid peers. During the 40-year period, the top quartile of stocks with the lowest liquidity achieved an annualised return of 14.5%, compared to 7.2% for the bottom quartile with the highest liquidity. Besides, the liquidity factor consistently produced attractive excess returns across the size spectrum. As shown in Table 15.2, the portfolio of stocks with the lowest liquidity reliably outperformed that with the highest liquidity across the four size segments. The liquidity effect is particularly strong for microcap stocks and diminishes as the market capitalisation increases. Considering the significant liquidity premium, the paper argues that liquidity should be given equal status to other common style factors, such as size, value and momentum.

Table 15.2 Size and liquidity premium

Size	Liquidity	
	Low	High
Microcap	15.4%	1.3%
Smallcap	15.3%	5.5%
Midcap	13.6%	7.9%
Largecap	11.5%	8.4%
All	14.5%	7.2%

Source: Financial Analysts Journal

The return premium of the liquidity factor is also supported by a paper published by the leading Journal of Financial Economics [8]. The study examines the liquidity premium in equities among 45 developed and emerging countries. By analysing a data sample of about 40,000 stocks over the 22-year period to 2011, the research found that the liquidity premium is very significant across countries, after controlling for the effects of risk factors and firm characteristics. The top quintile of stocks with the lowest liquidity outperformed the most liquid quintile by an average of 0.80% per month in the global markets. A research paper in the Journal of Portfolio Management provides further evidence of the liquidity premium [9]. Based on monthly data from December 1994 to February 2018, the research performed multivariate regression of stock returns against countries, industries and style factors to identify net return effects. The results confirm the return premium of the liquidity factor reported in many empirical studies.

A BlackRock study tracked the performance of a portfolio containing 1,500 largest stocks in the US [10]. The portfolio held long positions in the most illiquid stocks and short positions in the most liquid ones. It delivered a cumulative return of about 150% over the 25 years from 1988. This shows the strong performance of the liquidity factor. A Journal of Financial Economics paper investigates the empirical relation between monthly stock returns and illiquidity measures [11]. The research findings indicate that there is a significant return premium associated with illiquidity. This supports the proposition that investors demand an additional rate of return when investing in assets with low liquidity. Academic research has found the existence of liquidity premium in many different asset classes. For example, a paper in the Journal of Finance found that the liquidity premium for private equity is about 3% per annum [12].

References

1. Ericsson, J. and Renault, O., *Liquidity and Credit Risk.* Journal of Finance, 2006. **61**(5): p. 2219–2250.
2. Longstaff, F.A., *How Much Can Marketability Affect Security Values?* Journal of Finance, 1995. **50**(5): p. 1767–1774.
3. Ang, A., Papanikolaou, D. and Westerfield, M.M., *Portfolio Choice with Illiquid Assets.* Management Science, 2014. **60**(11): p. 2737–2761.
4. Keene, M.A. and Peterson, D.R., *The Importance of Liquidity as a Factor in Asset Pricing.* Journal of Financial Research, 2007. **30**(1): p. 91–109.

5. Butler, A.W., Grullon, G. and Weston, J.P., *Stock Market Liquidity and the Cost of Issuing Equity.* Journal of Financial and Quantitative Analysis, 2005. **40**(2): p. 331–348.
6. *Liquidity Enhancement.* 2019, Nasdaq.
7. Ibbotson, R.G., et al., *Liquidity as an Investment Style.* Financial Analysts Journal, 2013. **69**(3): p. 30–44.
8. Amihud, Y., et al., *The Illiquidity Premium: International Evidence.* Journal of Financial Economics, 2015. **117**(2): p. 350–368.
9. Melas, D., et al., *Integrating Factors in Market Indexes and Active Portfolios.* Journal of Portfolio Management, 2019. **45**(6): p. 1–14.
10. Riaz, K., et al., *The Liquidity Challenge: Exploring and Exploiting (Il)liquidity.* 2014, BlackRock Investment Institute.
11. Brennan, M.J. and Subrahmanyam, A., *Market Microstructure and Asset Pricing: On the Compensation for Illiquidity in Stock Returns.* Journal of Financial Economics, 1996. **41**(3): p. 441–464.
12. Franzoni, F., Nowak, E. and Phalippou, L., *Private Equity Performance and Liquidity Risk.* Journal of Finance, 2012. **67**(6): p. 2341–2373.

16

Multifactor Investing

16.1 Multifactor Investing

Factor investing is an investment approach that seeks to harvest risk premiums by targeting specific factors in an objective and transparent way. Factors are systematic drivers of return and the foundation of investment portfolios. They are frequently used to help explain differences in the returns of securities and portfolios. Academic and investment studies have identified a range of risk factors in equity investing. The previous chapters introduced seven common style factors: size, quality, momentum, value, yield, volatility and liquidity. These factors have proved the ability to enhance investment returns over time. The size factor is related to the smallcap effect that smaller companies tend to outperform their larger peers in the long term. The quality factor captures excess returns delivered by companies with superior quality characteristics. Momentum reflects the observation that share price often continues to move in the direction of an established price trend. The value effect refers to the tendency of stocks with attractive valuations to earn above-market returns over an extended period of time. The yield factor captures excess returns provided by companies with high dividend yields. The volatility effect is the phenomenon that stocks with low levels of price volatility tend to generate long-term outperformance. The liquidity premium compensates investors for holding assets with low liquidity. Figure 16.1 illustrates the positions of six factor indices in the risk and return spectrum based on their historical performance from December 1975 to February 2018. The data are sourced from an MSCI research paper that uses MSCI World

© The Author(s), under exclusive license to Springer Nature Switzerland AG 2022
B. Jiang, *Investment Strategies*,
https://doi.org/10.1007/978-3-030-82711-3_16

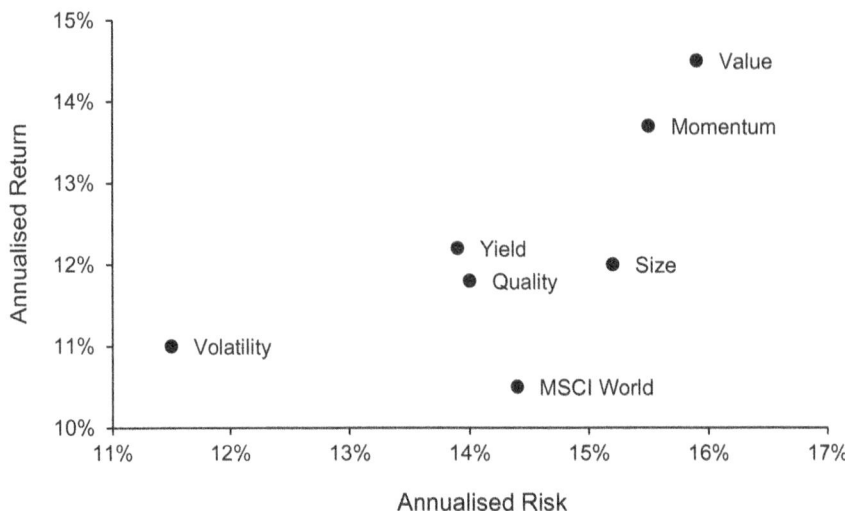

Fig. 16.1 Historical performance of style factor indices

Size: MSCI World Equal Weighted. Value: MSCI World Enhanced Value. Momentum: MSCI World Momentum. Quality: MSCI World Quality. Yield: MSCI World High Dividend Yield. Volatility: MSCI World Minimum Volatility.

style factor indices to examine factor performance [1]. For example, the size factor is represented by the MSCI World Equal Weighted Index. During the period of over 40 years, all these factor indices successfully outperformed the benchmark MSCI World Index.

A factor must meet some basic criteria to be considered fundamentally and rigorously established. It is expected to have weak correlations with other risk factors and offer unique benefits in terms of performance and diversification. The return premium of the factor should be supported by empirical evidence that it is persistent and robust over a long time period and in different markets. The factor premium can be theoretically explained and practically captured in a transparent and systematic way. The mechanism for the existence of factor premiums has been extensively studied in academic research. A factor premium exists due to one or more of the three reasons: risk compensation, behavioural biases and structural constraints. Risk compensation is based on the basic principle that investors demand higher returns to compensate them for accepting more risk. Behavioural biases reflect the fact that investors do not always act rationally and consider all available information when making investment decisions. This leads to many mispriced securities in the market to be exploited by rational investors. Structural constraints arise because of market rules, investment restrictions or any impediments placed on certain investments. The existence of structural constraints means that some markets are not efficiently priced as a result of limited access for investors. Factor investing allows investors to systematically exploit mispriced market opportunities in an efficient manner. This investment approach is positioned between active and passive management to combine their unique advantages. Factor strategies seek to provide higher risk-adjusted returns than passive investing, while achieving greater transparency and lower costs than traditional active management.

Technological advances and the success of passive investing have propelled the rise of factor investing in recent years. FTSE Russell conducted its sixth annual global survey on smart-beta strategies in 2019 [2]. The survey received responses from 178 institutional asset owners with combined assets of over \$5 trillion. The results show that 58% of institutional investors in the survey have implemented factor strategies, a sizeable increase of 10% from 2018. The many factor strategies in the market enable investors to efficiently target specific risk factors. Despite proven return premiums, common style factors exhibit significant cyclicality and volatility in performance. This is because their behaviour is strongly affected by economic and market conditions. All style factors have experienced lengthy periods of underperformance in the past. For example, the size factor underperformed the market substantially over a protracted period of time from 1984. Since the start of 2017, the value factor has recorded four consecutive years of underperformance against growth strategies, with no immediate recovery in sight. The cyclical nature of factor performance may encourage investors to dynamically change factor positions across the business cycle. The problem with factor rotation is that it is very challenging to detect turning points in the business cycle and successfully predict which factors will outperform over a short time horizon. Many studies empirically demonstrate that it is almost impossible to reliably time factors. Failing to capture strong factor returns can only result in disappointing investment performance. Multifactor strategies avoid the difficult task of factor timing and provide an alternative solution to effectively target specific factors. Multifactor investing is an investment strategy that seeks to gain diversified exposure to a number of factors identified as drivers of long-term performance. It offers a systematic approach to capturing factor premiums and reducing portfolio volatility. Due to balanced factor exposure, it is not necessary to actively predict and allocate across factors.

The emergence of multifactor strategies is a natural development in the evolution of factor investing. While the market still offers many single-factor strategies, investors have shown increasing interest in multifactor investing. This approach has consistently remained the most common form of factor investing in the last few years. The smart-beta survey of FTSE Russell in 2019 found multifactor is the preferred factor strategy among institutional investors in the study that have implemented factor investing [2]. It received the highest adoption rate of 71% in 2019, followed by the single-factor strategies of volatility (35%), value (28%), quality (23%) and size (22%). Multifactor investing has experienced strong growth in the investment sector, resulting from its compelling investment features. In 2010, there were only 43 investment funds assigned the multifactor label in the global funds database of Morningstar [3]. The number of multifactor funds increased substantially to 440 in April 2018, with $74 billion assets under management.

16.2 Cyclical Performance

The rationale for the adoption of the multifactor approach is primarily based on the fact that factor returns are cyclical and difficult to predict. Common style factors have historically experienced extended periods of underperformance. Their performance is shaped by changing economic and market conditions. This makes it rather difficult to reliably predict factor performance and dynamically change factor exposures. Therefore, the practice of factor rotation may only have limited success in earning excess returns. Compared to single-factor strategies, multifactor investing provides a more feasible solution to capture factor premiums by maintaining balanced exposure to factors. The many style factor indices provided by MSCI can be used to examine the cyclicality of factor returns. Table 16.1 presents the annual performance of six style factors respectively represented by MSCI ACWI smallcap, quality, momentum, value, high dividend yield and minimum-volatility indices. The performance of a factor is measured as the relative return of the related factor index against the broad market benchmark MSCI ACWI Index (source: index factsheets). The results demonstrate the cyclical nature of factor performance, with relative returns varying materially across the business cycle. For example, the minimum-volatility index delivered a significant excess return of 16.8% in 2008 when the market suffered heavy losses from the financial crisis. But it underperformed the benchmark index considerably by 17.4% in the following year when the market staged a strong recovery. This reflects the defensive characteristic of the low-volatility factor. For the smallcap index, its modest underperformance in 2007 and 2008 was followed by strong results in the next two years. Subsequently, its relative performance varied with changing market conditions through the business cycle. Despite trailing the market severely in 2009, the momentum index generated fairly consistent annual outperformance over the 10 years to 2019. Quality was the best performer among the six style factors for the entire

Table 16.1 Annual relative returns of style factor indices

Year	Size	Quality	Momentum	Value	Yield	Volatility
2006	-0.2%	-2.8%	1.8%	4.9%	8.2%	4.1%
2007	-5.0%	7.9%	12.6%	-4.8%	-2.4%	-4.6%
2008	-1.6%	6.0%	-3.1%	0.8%	0.9%	16.8%
2009	15.9%	1.4%	-15.6%	-2.7%	2.9%	-17.4%
2010	13.5%	-1.1%	3.1%	-2.3%	-4.6%	1.8%
2011	-4.1%	9.0%	9.3%	0.2%	7.0%	12.9%
2012	1.8%	-1.3%	1.3%	-0.4%	-1.5%	-6.0%
2013	5.7%	0.4%	4.0%	-0.2%	-4.4%	-5.8%
2014	-2.5%	4.1%	1.7%	-1.2%	-2.7%	6.9%
2015	1.2%	3.8%	4.2%	-3.7%	-2.8%	5.2%
2016	3.6%	-2.4%	-3.7%	5.0%	2.5%	-0.4%
2017	-0.3%	4.4%	9.4%	-5.5%	-4.8%	-6.0%
2018	-5.1%	2.0%	4.4%	-1.2%	2.7%	8.0%
2019	-2.1%	8.4%	0.8%	-5.8%	-2.3%	-5.5%
Average:	1.5%	2.8%	2.2%	-1.2%	-0.1%	0.7%

Source: MSCI

period from 2006 to 2019. The quality index outperformed the market by an average of 2.8% per year, while featuring relatively low volatility in returns.

The results confirm the fact that style factors cannot consistently deliver positive excess returns. The behaviour of factors is heavily influenced by market conditions, making their returns rather volatile and difficult to predict. If investors are really interested to actively target factors, it is necessary to understand their cyclical characteristics in different economic environments. MSCI classifies the six style factors into three categories: defensive, pro-cyclical and persistence [4]. The defensive category includes quality, volatility and yield factors, since they historically generated sizeable excess returns during declining market conditions. Size and value fall into the pro-cyclical category, meaning that they typically outperform the market during periods of economic recovery. The momentum factor belongs to the persistence category, as it tends to benefit from stable market conditions. The different stages of a business cycle can be used to guide investment decisions on factor rotation [5–7]. The business cycle can be divided into four distinct economic phases: recovery, expansion, slowdown and contraction. Size and value often perform better than other style factors during the recovery and expansion stages. In contrast, quality, volatility and yield tend to outperform at the slowdown and contraction stages due to their defensive characteristics. The volatility factor frequently underperforms materially in bull markets, caused by its very defensive nature. The quality factor has more consistent performance across the entire business cycle. This is because it can often capture a decent proportion of strong market performance during improving economic conditions. The momentum factor favours the expansion and slowdown phases to generate excess returns. Whereas the economic phases can be easily defined, it is practically challenging to detect economic turning points and thereby actively target factors. Investors interested in dynamic factor allocation can invest in multifactor strategies that contain the feature of factor rotation. For example, the BlackRock US Equity Factor Rotation ETF provides diversified exposure to five style factors, while tactically changing factor positions through a factor rotation model. The Invesco Russell 1000 Dynamic Multifactor ETF seeks to improve return potential by actively adjusting exposure to multiple style factors based on economic indicators and market conditions.

16.3 Investment Merits

Multifactor investing provides the key investment benefits of return enhancement, risk reduction, diversification and cost efficiency. This investment strategy targets securities with attractive characteristics across a selection of style factors. The multifactor approach essentially applies the principle of diversification to capture factor premiums. A properly diversified multifactor portfolio gains balanced exposure to factors that behave differently under changing market conditions. The underperformance of some factors in the portfolio can often be offset by the positive excess returns provided by the other factors. The strength of diversification is heavily dependent on the underlying correlations among the factors in the portfolio. Historically, common style factors adopted by multifactor strategies have exhibited fairly low or negative correlations with each other. An Invesco study calculates long-term factor correlations by using monthly excess returns of Russell 1000 style factor indexes over about 40 years to December 2019 [7]. The results show that value has a low correlation of 0.32 with the size factor, while it is negatively correlated with both quality (-0.55) and momentum (-0.45). This explains the fact that value, quality and momentum are often combined in multifactor strategies. Note that correlations among risk factors are not expected to be very stable over time, because factor performance is shaped by various unpredictable market forces.

The multifactor strategy enables investors to capture factor premiums and reduce portfolio volatility through diversified factor exposure. This means that multifactor investing can potentially help investors enhance risk-adjusted returns. A paper published by the Journal of Index Investing compares the risk and return characteristics of single- and multifactor strategies [8]. The study constructed factor portfolios and tracked their returns over the period from June 1968 to December 2016. A simple cap-weighted portfolio produced an annualised return of 10.1% during the period. This benchmark underperformed each of the five single-factor portfolios designed to target the value, momentum, profitability, investment and low-beta factors respectively. The multifactor portfolio in the study selects the top 20% stocks with the highest composite factor scores. It proved to be the best performer, providing an average excess return of 3.5% per year against the benchmark. Besides, the multifactor strategy achieved the second-lowest volatility among all portfolios (only after the low-beta strategy). The research provides strong evidence that multifactor strategies have superior risk and return characteristics.

S&P Dow Jones Indices published a research paper in 2018 to demonstrate the merits of multifactor investing [9]. In Table 16.2, the three single factors of quality, value and momentum are respectively represented by the S&P 500 Quality, S&P 500 Enhanced Value and S&P 500 Momentum indices. The QVM index is a hypothetical portfolio created by equally weighting the three style indices. Multifactor is the S&P 500 Quality, Value & Momentum Multi-Factor Index. This index is designed to measure the performance of 100 stocks in the S&P 500 Index that have the highest multi-factor scores based on the combination of quality, value and momentum factors. The research used rolling window (5, 10 and 15 years) to calculate average annual return and volatility over the period from December

Table 16.2 Performance comparison of single and multiple factor strategies

Rolling window (in years)			S&P 500	Quality	Value	Momentum	QVM	Multifactor
	5	Return:	7.36%	11.28%	9.86%	8.42%	10.26%	11.71%
		Volatility:	13.35%	12.65%	16.46%	15.03%	13.49%	12.82%
		Efficiency:	0.55	0.89	0.60	0.56	0.76	0.91
	10	Return:	5.70%	9.71%	7.98%	6.39%	8.42%	10.62%
		Volatility:	14.41%	13.45%	18.04%	16.24%	14.46%	13.58%
		Efficiency:	0.40	0.72	0.44	0.39	0.58	0.78
	15	Return:	5.96%	10.02%	8.43%	6.51%	8.72%	10.68%
		Volatility:	14.95%	13.72%	19.05%	16.84%	14.93%	13.90%
		Efficiency:	0.40	0.73	0.44	0.39	0.58	0.77

Source: S&P Dow Jones Indices

1994 to March 2018. This approach can control potential bias in the results caused by the choice of a subjective starting date. The results support the proposition that factor investing can enhance investment returns. Each of the three style factor indices consistently outperformed the S&P 500 Index across the 5-, 10- and 15-year rolling periods. For example, the average annual return over the sample period is 7.36% for the S&P 500 Index based on the 5-year rolling window. This is lower than 11.28%, 9.86% and 8.42% respectively provided by the quality, value and momentum factor indices. The two multifactor indices also achieved better performance than the broad market benchmark. The QVM index produced higher returns than the value and momentum indices, but it failed to outperform the quality index. This may be explained by the fact that the QVM index is only a simple combination of the three equally weighted style indices. In comparison, the Multifactor index containing stocks with the highest multi-factor scores could consistently outperform any other portfolio across the three rolling windows. As measured by the efficiency ratio, the Multifactor index also achieved the highest risk-adjusted returns. This demonstrates the value of multifactor investing in improving risk and return characteristics, resulting from its ability to capture strong performance and reduce volatility risk through balanced factor exposure.

Factors are expected to generate excess returns in the long term, despite the cyclical nature of their performance. This indicates that time horizon is an important element to consider when investing in single-factor strategies. The multifactor approach targets multiple drivers of return to mitigate the cyclical risk in factor investing and improve the chance of outperformance. An MSCI study examines the frequency of style factor indices outperforming the MSCI World Index over different rolling periods from November 1975 to March 2014 [10]. In Table 16.3, the six factors are respectively captured by

Table 16.3 Investment horizon and the frequency of factor outperformance

Rolling Years	Size	Yield	Momentum	Quality	Value	Volatility	Multifactor
1	62%	61%	66%	53%	69%	46%	72%
3	73%	73%	77%	59%	70%	52%	88%
5	83%	82%	91%	62%	77%	55%	92%
10	76%	98%	99%	75%	99%	65%	100%
15	85%	99%	100%	88%	100%	66%	100%
20	89%	100%	100%	99%	100%	72%	100%
25	100%	100%	100%	100%	100%	91%	100%

Source: MSCI

the MSCI World equal weighted, high dividend yield, momentum, quality, value weighted and minimum-volatility indices. The multifactor index is constructed by equally weighting the individual factor indices and rebalanced semi-annually. The research found that the probability of factor outperformance increases steadily as the investment horizon lengthens. For example, the MSCI World Momentum Index outperformed the benchmark index with a frequency of 66% based on 1-year rolling period. The frequency rises to 99% when the investment period is extended to 10 years. The results also show that the multifactor index could further improve the probability of outperforming the market. This proves the ability of multifactor investing to reduce the risk of underperformance caused by factor cyclicality.

16.4 Construction Methods

Multifactor strategies can be developed with the top-down or bottom-up approach. The top-down approach gains exposure to multiple factors by directly combining factor portfolios. For example, an investor can create a multifactor portfolio by making separate asset allocations to investment funds that target single factors. The investment in two funds respectively featuring quality and value styles effectively constructs a portfolio tilting towards the quality and value factors. Similarly, a multifactor index can be easily formed by taking a weighted average of multiple single-factor indices. The simple QVM multifactor index discussed in the previous section is created with the top-down approach. The QVM index is formed by equally weighting the S&P 500 Quality, S&P 500 Enhanced Value and S&P 500 Momentum indices. The MSCI USA Factor Mix A-Series Capped Index is also constructed based on the top-down method. This index applies equal weighting to combine the three factor indices of MSCI USA Value Weighted, MSCI USA Minimum Volatility and MSCI USA Quality. The top-down approach has the advantages of simplicity and flexibility in the choice of factors and weighting schemes. The weightings allocated to factor portfolios can be easily adjusted to reflect changing investment views. The main problem of this approach is that the composite portfolio may fail to achieve desired factor positions. The direct consequence of merging factor portfolios is the dilution of factor exposures. In some cases, factor exposures can be largely neutralised when factors with negative correlations are combined. For example, a simple combination of quality and value portfolios will possibly result in a portfolio with weak exposure to both style factors. This is because quality stocks often feature high valuations, while value stocks tend to have mediocre quality characteristics.

To address the negative dilution effect, multifactor portfolios can be constructed with the bottom-up approach. This method combines securities to efficiently gain desired factor exposures. It selects companies with the most attractive factor characteristics to form multifactor strategies. To calculate the multifactor score, individual factor exposures are standardised and aggregated according to a weighting scheme. Since the selection is subject to the interaction of multiple risk factors, securities with moderate exposures across the target factors have a good chance to be selected. Multifactor strategies often use optimisation methods to maximise desired factor exposures while controlling unintended factor tilts. The advanced bottom-up approach allows investors to target specific risk factors in an efficient and controllable way. This approach has been widely applied to construct multifactor portfolios with a focus on achieving persistent factor exposures. Leading index providers frequently adopt the bottom-up approach for the development of multifactor equity indices. For example, S&P Dow Jones Indices employs this approach to select constituents for its multifactor indices comprising the quality, value and momentum factors [11]. The process of constituent selection involves the following five steps:

1. The scores of the quality, value and momentum factors are calculated for the stocks that meet the basic eligibility criteria.
2. The scores of each factor are ranked and converted to percentile scores:

$$p_i = \frac{r_i}{N+1}$$

where r_i is the rank of stock i and N is the number of stocks.
3. The percentile scores of each factor are transformed to z-scores by using the inverse of the normal cumulative distribution function.
4. The composite z-score of stock i is calculated by averaging its three factor z-scores:

$$z_i = \left(z_i^Q + z_i^V + z_i^M\right)/3$$

5. The composite score is converted to the final multifactor score:

$$s_i = \begin{cases} 1 + z_i & z_i \geq 0 \\ \dfrac{1}{1 - z_i} & z_i < 0 \end{cases}$$

After the above steps, stocks with the highest multifactor scores are candidates for index inclusion. A buffer rule is applied to stocks already in the index to reduce portfolio turnover. Constituent weightings are determined by the product of market capitalisation and multifactor score. An optimisation procedure is applied to impose constraints on the weightings of securities, sectors and countries.

Multifactor portfolios are expected to gain robust factor exposures in order to effectively capture factor premiums. Due to the dilution effect, the top-down approach will potentially cause weak factor exposures. This means that multifactor portfolios constructed with the top-down approach may not produce expected results because of the failure to maintain persistent and strong factor exposures. Empirical studies provide strong evidence that the bottom-up approach is superior to the top-down method in enhancing return potential. In Table 16.2, the simple QVM index consistently delivered lower returns than the Multifactor index across all the investment horizons. This is attributed to the fact that the two indices are respectively created with the top-down and bottom-up approaches. An MSCI study performed a simulation to compare the risk and return characteristics of multifactor indices formed using these two approaches [1]. The multifactor index based on the top-down approach returned an average of 8.2% per annum from November 1999 to January 2018, reasonably exceeding 5.4% provided by the benchmark MSCI World Index. The multifactor index developed with the bottom-up approach further improved the annualised return to 10.7% with comparable volatility. Academic studies also present insightful information about the advantages of the bottom-up approach. A paper published by the Journal of Portfolio Management confirms that the bottom-up approach results in higher portfolio returns than its counterpart [12]. A Journal of Index Investing paper also supports the view that the bottom-up approach is the preferred option for multifactor strategies to enhance investment returns [8]. The research compares the performance of multifactor portfolios constructed with the two approaches. From June 1968 to December 2016, multifactor portfolios based on the bottom-up approach achieved an average excess return of 1.8% per year compared to that created with the top-down approach.

16.5 Factor Combinations

Multifactor strategies employ various factor combinations in an effort to outperform the market. The small set of style factors can potentially result in numerous combinations. In reality, only a limited number of factor combinations have gained wide acceptance in the investment sector. Multifactor investing needs to consider the practical value and characteristics of different factors before they can be combined. A comprehensive review of multifactor strategies reveals that quality, value and momentum are among the most common style factors used in multifactor investing. These three factors often coexist in a multifactor portfolio to provide diversification benefits, resulting from their different cyclical characteristics. Based on historical performance across the business cycle, quality, value and momentum respectively fall into the defensive, cyclical and persistence categories. The quality factor typically outperforms during the phases of economic slowdown and contraction, while value favours the recovery and expansion stages. The momentum factor usually generates excess returns during the periods of economic expansion and slowdown. A multifactor portfolio comprising the three factors is well positioned to capture factor outperformance through different phases of the economic cycle.

Volatility is another common factor used by multifactor portfolios to exploit its return premium while reducing volatility risk. Multifactor strategies sometimes do not explicitly include the volatility factor in the calculation of multifactor score, but consider its effect in the step of determining security weightings. For instance, the constituents of the WisdomTree US Multifactor Index are weighted by the combination of multifactor score and the inverse of trailing 12-month volatility [13]. The size factor is also frequently targeted by multifactor strategies to capitalise on the smallcap effect. It is often combined with the quality factor to control the exposure to unprofitable smaller companies. Dividend yield plays a central role in equity income funds aiming to produce a steady dividend income stream. The yield factor is also targeted by multifactor strategies seeking to capture its return premium. For example, FTSE Qual/Vol/Yield factor indices aggregate the quality, volatility and yield factors to track the performance of sustainable and high yielding companies, while avoiding the yield trap and reducing investment risk [14]. The liquidity factor, however, is rarely integrated with other style factors to form multifactor portfolios. This is because investment portfolios usually focus more on the management of liquidity risk than actively pursuing the liquidity premium. Table 16.4 provides a sample of 15 multifactor indices and funds to illustrate factor combinations. The results confirm the prevalence of quality,

Table 16.4 Factor combinations in multifactor investing

Source	Size	Quality	Value	Momentum	Volatility	Yield
1	×	×	×	×		
2	×	×	×	×	×	
3		×	×	×	×	
4		×			×	×
5	×	×	×	×	×	
6	×	×	×	×	×	
7		×				×
8	×	×	×	×		
9	×	×	×	×	×	
10	×	×	×	×	×	
11		×	×	×	×	
12		×	×	×		
13		×	×	×		
14		×	×	×		
15		×	×			

1: AQR TM Small Cap Multi-Style Fund. 2: BlackRock US Equity Factor Rotation ETF. 3: Franklin LibertyQ European Equity ETF. 4: FTSE Developed Europe Qual/Vol/Yield Factor Index. 5: HSBC Multi-Factor Worldwide Equity ETF. 6: iSTOXX Europe Multi-Factor Index. 7: LibertyQ Global Dividend Index. 8: MSCI ACWI Diversified Multiple-Factor Index. 9: RAFI Multi-Factor Global Index. 10: Russell 1000 Comprehensive Factor Index. 11: Russell Investments Multifactor International Equity Fund. 12: S&P 500 Quality, Value & Momentum Multi-Factor Index. 13: Vanguard US Multifactor ETF. 14: WisdomTree US Multifactor Fund. 15: Xtrackers Russell 1000 US Quality at a Reasonable Price ETF.

value and momentum styles in multifactor investing. The quality factor is particularly covered by all these multifactor portfolios. This may reflect the merits of investing in companies with compelling quality characteristics.

References

1. Kulkarni, P., Gupta, A. and Doole, S., *How Can Factors Be Combined?* 2018, MSCI.
2. *Smart Beta: 2019 Global Survey Findings from Asset Owners*. 2019, FTSE Russell.
3. Boyadzhiev, D., et al., *A Framework for Analyzing Multifactor Funds*. 2018, Morningstar.
4. *Factor Focus: Momentum*. 2018, MSCI.
5. Ang, A., *Factors: Ways to Pursue Outperformance*. 2016, BlackRock.
6. Ung, D. and Abburu, S., *Asset Performance and the Business Cycle: A US Case Study*. 2019, State Street Global Advisors.

7. de Longis, A. and Haghbin, M., *Dynamic Multifactor Strategies: A Macro Regime Approach.* 2020, Invesco.
8. Chow, T.-M., Li, F. and Shim, Y., *Smart Beta Multifactor Construction Methodology: Mixing versus Integrating.* Journal of Index Investing, 2018. **8**(4): p. 47–60.
9. Innes, A., *The Merits and Methods of Multi-factor Investing.* 2018, S&P Dow Jones Indices.
10. Alighanbari, M., Subramanian, R.A. and Kulkarni, P., *Factor Indexes in Perspective: Insights from 40 Years of Data.* 2014, MSCI.
11. *S&P Quality, Value & Momentum Multi-factor Indices Methodology.* 2019, S&P Dow Jones Indices.
12. Bender, J. and Wang, T., *Can the Whole Be More Than the Sum of the Parts? Bottom-Up Versus Top-Down Multifactor Portfolio Construction.* Journal of Portfolio Management, 2016. **42**(5): p. 39–50.
13. *WisdomTree Rules-Based Methodology: WisdomTree U.S. Multifactor Index.* 2019, WisdomTree.
14. *Methodology Overview: Qual/Vol/Yield Factor Indexes.* 2019, FTSE Russell.

Index

A

absolute return 7, 13, 24, 25, 38, 55
absolute risk 6
accruals ratio 125
active fund 33
active ownership 92, 93
aggressive investor 8
allocation effect 21, 22
alternative investment 16, 17, 54, 63, 74, 185
analyst rating 85, 86
arbitrage pricing theory (APT) 24, 25
asset class vii, ix, 2, 3, 8, 13, 15–17, 20, 21, 29, 34, 35, 37, 41, 43, 44, 49, 51, 53, 54, 60, 67, 72–77, 90, 96, 104, 109, 114, 133, 142, 145, 178, 185, 190
asset pricing model 112
asset allocation ix, 3, 7, 10, 13–15, 17, 20, 22, 41, 74, 187, 201

B

barriers to entry 123
behavioural bias 2, 79, 134, 139, 148, 194
beta 6, 24, 103, 112, 177–179
bid-ask spread 19, 110, 185, 188
board structure 125
bond ix, 4, 8, 13, 14, 16, 18, 34, 35, 37, 41–45, 47, 49–51, 67, 73, 76, 98, 133, 145, 176, 178, 185, 186
bond duration 45
bond yield 44, 47, 48
bottom-up approach 201–203
brand equity 124
breakeven return 81, 82
Brinson model 20–22, 23
broad equity market index 33, 73, 76
broker research 85, 86
business cycle vii, 31, 63, 74, 121, 123, 155, 195–198, 204
business operation 124

C

capital asset pricing model (CAPM) 103, 104, 112, 177, 178
capital gains tax 10
capital growth 1, 6, 8, 9, 29, 43, 161, 166
capital preservation 8, 43
capital structure 46, 124, 162
carbon emission 94
cash ix, 3, 8–10, 13, 14, 16, 34, 35, 37, 38, 50, 58, 124, 125, 149, 150, 161–163, 166, 169, 170, 176, 185, 186
cash conversion 124
cash generative 124
cash investment 50, 51
central bank 4, 18, 47, 58, 59, 63–65
certificate of deposit 16, 50
characteristics of gold 58
commercial paper 16, 50
commodity index 54, 65
common stock 30, 39, 74, 151, 163
competitive advantage 109, 119, 120, 123–125
compounding effect 4, 5, 165
conservative investor 7, 8, 73
constant dividend policy 162
constituent selection 202
consumer demand 64
consumer price index 3, 44, 63
continuous information 140
corporate bond 16, 41, 50, 74
corporate governance 36, 90, 95, 125
cost efficiency 198
country risk 18
coupon rate 42, 45
covariance matrix 181
credit quality 16, 44–46
credit rating 43–47, 50, 98
credit rating agency 19, 46
credit rating system 46, 47
credit rating transition 47
credit risk 19, 41, 44–47, 59
credit spread risk 44
currency risk 18, 44
current ratio 124
customer concentration 124
cyclical characteristic 197, 204
cyclical performance 196

D

declaration date 162
default risk 41, 44–47, 50
dilution effect 202, 203
direct investment 16
discrete information 140
disposition effect 79, 80, 134
distribution of stock return 38, 39
diversification ix, 9, 17, 36, 39, 43, 54, 61, 67–69, 72–74, 76, 77, 104, 110, 177, 194, 198, 204
diversification effect 60
dividend consistency 169, 171
dividend cover 170
dividend investing 161, 164
dividend policy 162
dividend reinvestment plan 162
dividend return 156–158
dividend safety 163, 165, 168, 169
dividend yield viii, ix, 10, 151, 156, 158, 163–168, 171, 193, 194, 196, 201, 204
Dow Jones Industrial Average (DJIA) 32, 167
downgrade risk 44
downside protection 19, 59, 60, 73, 121, 163
downside risk ix, 6, 9, 19, 67, 72, 76, 80, 81, 84, 98
drivers of gold price 62

Index   209

E

earnings growth 24, 119, 121, 122, 124, 125, 135, 148, 153, 155–158, 171
earnings quality 120, 125
earnings variability 123, 125, 171
earnings yield 150, 153, 164
economic downturn 1, 48, 53, 121, 170
economic outlook 43, 47, 48, 63
efficient frontier 60, 61, 69–71
efficient market hypothesis (EMH) 103, 151, 164, 176
enterprise value (EV) 150
environmental factor 94, 95
environmental risk 94
environmental, social and governance (ESG) 89–100
equity capital 29, 188
equity index 32, 77
equity investment 1, 10, 17–19, 29, 156, 165, 185
equity market 14, 31–35, 39, 55, 72, 74, 86, 104, 115, 128, 153, 155
equity risk 25, 35
ESG criteria viii, 92, 93, 95, 97–99
ESG factors 90–92, 94, 97, 99, 100
ESG integration 91–93, 96–100
ESG investing 89–92, 98
ESG issues viii, 89–92, 94–96
ESG rating 95–97, 100
exchange-traded commodity (ETC) 65
ex-dividend date 162

F

face value 42, 43, 45
factor combination 204, 205
factor cyclicality 201
factor exposure 24–26, 181, 195, 196, 198, 200–203

factor investing vii, 16, 120, 127, 193, 195, 196, 200
factor mimicking 126
factor model 24–26, 112, 113, 158, 164
factor premium vii, viii, 129, 144, 154, 164, 194–196, 198, 203
factor return vii, 24–26, 112, 114, 126, 195, 196
factor rotation vii, 154, 195–198
factor tilt 202
factor timing viii, 195
Fama-French 3-factor model 112, 120, 127, 152
FCF cover 170
financial goal 1, 2, 5, 6, 8
financial leverage 25, 120, 121, 124–126, 170
financial strength 119–121, 123–125, 170
fixed-income 8, 13, 18, 44
fixed-rate bond 41, 42
flat yield curve 47
float-adjusted market capitalisation 32
floating-rate note 41
fundamental analysis 120, 135, 147, 148
fundamental factor model 24, 26, 181, 187, 188
fundamental value 134, 148

G

Global Industry Classification Standard (GICS) 16, 30, 31, 33
Global Sustainable Investment Alliance (GSIA) 89, 93
gold 34, 53–56, 58–65, 73, 74, 76
Gordon growth model 122
government bond 16, 35, 41, 49, 50
gross profitability 127
gross return 7

growth potential 110, 119, 123, 148, 149, 163
growth stock 148
growth volatility 124

H

hedge fund 17, 54, 74
herd behaviour 134, 139
Herfindahl–Hirschman Index (HHI) 68, 69

I

impact investing 92, 93, 100
income stream 1, 7, 43, 58, 63, 161, 204
index construction 108, 137
indirect investment 16
individual investor 2, 3, 5–7, 9, 11, 15, 16, 39, 43, 50, 72, 79, 91, 186
industry attractiveness 123
industry risk 18, 46
inflation 1, 3, 4, 7, 18, 24, 34, 35, 43, 44, 48, 51, 53, 54, 59, 62, 63
inflation hedge 59
inflation-linked bond 41, 44
inflation risk 18, 44, 51
information discreteness (ID) 140, 141
insider ownership 109, 125
institutional investor 2, 7, 9, 10, 13, 16, 30, 39, 72, 86, 90, 92, 94, 96–98, 104, 186, 187, 195, 196
interaction effect 22, 156
interest coverage 124, 170
interest rate 4, 18, 24, 41–45, 47–49, 63, 153, 161, 176
interest rate risk 18, 44, 45
intrinsic value 17, 59, 122, 134, 147, 148

inverted yield curve 48
investment vii–ix, 1–10, 13, 15–20, 22, 25, 30, 32–35, 37–39, 41, 43–45, 51, 53–55, 58, 59, 61, 63, 65, 67–69, 71, 72, 74, 76, 79–85, 87, 89–100, 104, 110, 113, 115, 119–121, 125–129, 133–135, 139, 141, 142, 147–149, 151, 152, 155, 161, 164, 168, 176, 177, 180, 186–188, 193–201, 203, 204
investment constraint ix, 3, 6, 9–11
investment grade 45
investment objective ix, 2, 3, 5–7, 9, 20, 67, 92, 98
investment plan 2, 3, 5, 6, 11
investment risk ix, x, 2, 8, 17, 19, 44, 67, 72, 73, 91, 92, 110, 149, 176, 186, 204
investment style 67, 104, 120, 148, 151, 153, 173
investment vehicle ix, 16, 17, 54, 65, 147

L

largecap 16, 86, 104, 106–108, 110, 111, 115, 128, 185
leading indicator 48
leveraged buyout 13, 17
liquidity factor 186–190, 204
liquidity indicator 188
liquidity measure 188
liquidity premium viii, x, 186, 187, 189, 190, 193, 204
liquidity risk 9, 19, 44, 110, 185, 187, 188, 204
long-term momentum 136
loss aversion 79
loss control ix
lottery effect 176
low-volatility 121, 122, 173, 174, 176, 178–182
low-volatility investing 173, 179

low-volatility premium 176, 180

M

macroeconomic factor model 24
margin of safety 147–149
market condition vii, 3, 13, 15, 62, 72, 74, 121, 134, 135, 154, 164, 175, 176, 185, 195–198
market efficiency 86, 105, 110, 111
market factor 25, 26, 33
market impact 186
market liquidity 86, 185, 188
market return 16, 25, 38, 73, 103, 112, 155, 157, 158, 176, 177, 193
market risk 17, 36, 51, 67, 175–177
market risk premium 112, 177
market share 119, 124, 148
maturity date 30, 41–43
maximum drawdown (MDD) 6, 19, 36, 72, 73, 130, 137, 174
medium-term momentum 136, 137
microcap 16, 108, 115, 185, 186, 189
midcap 16, 33, 104, 108, 111, 115
minimum-variance 180, 181
minimum variance portfolio 178, 181
moderate investor 8
modern portfolio theory (MPT) 67, 69, 177
momentum anomaly 134, 139, 144
momentum effect ix, 79, 133–135, 140, 142–145
momentum factor 135, 136, 145, 197–200, 202, 204
momentum investing 133–137, 139, 140, 142, 145
momentum measure 136
momentum premium 143–145
momentum quality 139–142
momentum score 137, 138
money market 16, 17, 50

money market security 50
Morningstar Style Box 16, 151
multifactor approach vii, 196, 198, 200
multifactor index 200, 201, 203, 204
multifactor investing x, 195, 196, 198–201, 204, 205
multifactor model 24
multi-market equity index 33

N

natural resource 13, 53, 94, 95
negative screening 92, 93, 96, 98–100
net profit margin 125
net return 7, 190
nominal yield 42
normal yield curve 47
Northern Trust Quality Score 126, 129

O

operating margin 124, 125
operating profitability 127, 128
opportunity cost 3, 63
order visibility 124
ordinary share 30

P

P/E change 156–158
P/E contraction 158
P/E expansion 157
palladium 53–56
passive investing vii, 16, 33, 195
performance attribution ix, 20, 22–25
performance evaluation 20
performance reversal 136
Piotroski F-score 120, 127
platinum 53–56, 58

portfolio variance 71
positive screening 92, 93
precious metal ix, 53–57, 62, 65
preference share 30
preferred stock 30
premium valuation 122, 138
price momentum 133–135, 138
price return 2, 6, 29, 37, 60, 138, 141, 155, 156, 163, 165
price trend viii, ix, 79, 81, 133–136, 139–141, 193
price-weighting 32
pricing power 124
Principles for Responsible Investment (PRI) 89, 90, 96
private equity 17, 30, 54, 185, 190
profitability 99, 106, 111, 113, 120, 122, 123, 125, 127, 128, 149, 199
profit margin 24, 119, 124, 148, 158
profit margin change 157, 158
profit warning 81, 83–85, 87, 142
progressive dividend policy 169
public equity 30, 185
purchasing power 1, 3, 4, 18, 59, 63

Q

qualitative measure 123
quality checklist 123
quality factor viii, 25, 97, 115, 120–122, 125, 127–130, 165, 193, 198, 204, 205
quality investing ix, 110, 119–121, 123, 125
quality measure 125–127, 164, 165
quality minus junk (QMJ) 128
quality premium 128, 129
quality rating 123
quality score 121, 123, 125, 128–130
quantitative measure 123

R

real asset 17
real interest rate 62, 63
real value 3–5, 7, 18, 44, 51, 63
record date 162
regular dividend 163
reinvestment risk 44
relative return 6, 22, 24, 105, 106, 130, 154, 196, 197
relative risk 6
relative strength portfolio 142, 143
required rate of return 122, 186
required yield 42, 45
residual dividend policy 162, 163
responsible investing 89, 90
return decomposition 26, 155, 156, 159
return enhancement 198
return forecasting 157, 158
return objective 7
return on assets 125, 177
return on equity (ROE) 25, 121, 122, 125, 165
return premium vii, 35, 100, 107, 113–115, 120, 127, 128, 142, 145, 151, 153, 165, 167, 168, 171, 178, 179, 189, 190, 194, 195, 204
risk-adjusted return ix, 15, 55, 60, 61, 76, 77, 91, 92, 96, 97, 103, 128, 129, 135, 137, 167, 174, 179, 180, 195, 199, 200
risk appetite 7–9, 175
risk attitude 7
risk compensation 194
risk objective 6
risk reduction 67, 98, 198
risk tolerance ix, 3, 6–10, 15, 67, 76

S

safe-haven asset 53, 59, 62
sales growth 123, 152, 157, 158
saving 1, 4, 16

selection effect 22
share buyback 189
short interest 87
short selling 86, 87
short-term momentum 136
silver 53–56, 58
size effect ix, 103–106, 114, 115
size factor viii, 26, 112–115, 193–195, 198, 204
size premium 103, 105, 106, 114, 115
smallcap 16, 104–111, 114, 115, 196
smallcap effect viii, 104, 193, 204
smallcap index 109, 111, 196
smallcap universe 104, 107, 109–111, 115
smaller companies viii, ix, 103, 104, 107, 109–112, 114, 115, 193, 204
smart-beta 195
social factor 94, 95
special dividend 162
specific return 24
specific risk 36, 67, 68, 72, 177, 195, 202
speculative grade 16, 45
stable dividend policy 162
statistical factor model 24
stock dividend 1, 162
stock market 17, 32, 33, 36–39, 59, 63, 175
strategic asset allocation viii, 15
structural constraint 194
structured product 17
style factors 25, 26, 33, 97, 120, 121, 125, 127, 135, 145, 153, 154, 164, 181, 187, 189, 190, 193–195, 197, 198, 200, 201, 204
style index 198
Sustainable Development Goals 90, 91

sustainable investing viii, ix, 89–94, 96, 98–100
systematic risk 67, 97, 103, 177

T

tactical asset allocation 15, 74
target price 85, 134
thematic investing 92, 93
time horizon 3, 6, 7, 9, 10, 15, 19, 46, 154, 178, 195, 200
time value of money 3
top-down approach 201, 203
total return 6, 26, 34, 38, 49, 50, 55, 72, 76, 100, 114, 147, 148, 155–158, 161, 163, 165, 168, 171
total risk 67, 177
tracking error 6
traditional investment 16, 58, 91

U

upside capture 73
upside participation 121, 176
US Treasury 8, 14, 35, 37, 39, 41, 43, 44, 48–51, 115, 185
US Treasury yield curve 47, 48

V

valuation metric 148, 149, 151, 152, 164, 165
valuation ratio 151
valuation risk 147
value at risk (VaR) 6, 19
value effect viii, ix, 135, 151–153, 193
value factor viii, 26, 98, 104, 112, 113, 135, 151, 153, 154, 164, 195, 201
value indicator 149
value investing 120, 147, 148
value stock 148, 149, 154, 201

value trap 149
venture capital 13, 17
volatility viii, ix, 2, 3, 6–9, 13, 14, 19, 25, 33, 34, 43, 49, 53–56, 58–61, 67, 71, 74, 76, 77, 87, 97–99, 104, 107, 122, 130, 135, 137, 138, 164, 171, 173–176, 179–182, 193, 195–199, 201, 203, 204
volatility anomaly 173, 176
volatility effect viii, ix, 173, 178, 179, 193
volatility factor 173–175, 178–180, 196, 197, 204
volatility risk 15, 19, 43, 76, 98, 110, 174, 180, 200, 204

Y

yield curve 47, 48
yield factor viii, 164, 167, 168, 171, 193, 197, 204
yield premium 167
yield spread 44, 48, 49, 186

Z

zero-coupon 41

The manufacturer's authorised representative in the EU is Springer Nature Customer Service Centre GmbH, Europaplatz 3, 69115 Heidelberg, Germany. If you have any concerns regarding our products, please contact ProductSafety@springernature.com

Printed and bound by CPI Group (UK) Ltd, Croydon, CR0 4YY

25/03/2026

02078205-0013